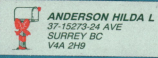

11

ITALIAN

PHRASEBOOK

#2

D1012272

Maurice Riverso

Italian phrasebook
  1st edition

Published by
  Lonely Planet Publications
  Head Office: PO Box 617, Hawthorn, Vic 3122, Australia
  Branches: 155 Filbert St, Suite 251, Oakland, CA 94607, USA
                 10a Spring Place, London NW5 3BH, UK
                 71 bis rue du Cardinal Lemoine, 75005 Paris, France

Printed by
Colorcraft Ltd, Hong Kong

Cover Illustration
  Invespagating by Penelope Richardson

Published
  January 1998

National Library of Australia Cataloguing in Publication Data

Riverso, Maurice
  Italian phrasebook
  1st ed.
  Includes index.
  ISBN 0 86442 456 6.

  1. Italian language – Conversation and phrase books – English. I. Title.

  458.3421

© Lonely Planet Publications Pty Ltd, 1998
Cover Illustration © Lonely Planet

CONTENTS

4   Contents

About the Author

Maurice Riverso was born in Pistoia and grew up in Tuscany, Trent and later in Melbourne. He has taught Italian Studies at the University of Melbourne and at La Trobe University. He is a writer, freelance editor and a translator.

From the Author

The author wishes to thank his father, Mauro, and Gabriella Baroncelli for their valuable assistance, Stephen Riedel for his helpful suggestions, and his family and friends, notably his mother, Jeanette, Alessia and Claude Riverso and Teresa Anile for their patience and support.

From the Publisher

This book was nurtured to maturity by a number of people. Lou Callan edited it and created the crosswords. Sally Steward, from whose original work this book was written, helped to develop the Grammar chapter and assisted with proofreading. Peter D'Onghia proofread the book, put together the dictionary and provided translations and expertise. The illustrations and design are by Penelope Richardson. Many thanks must go to Professor Andrea Zinato and Matteo Savini, directors of the Zambler Institute in Venice, for their assistance in developing the book. Thanks also to Mirna Cicioni for writing the Dialects chapter and for proofreading the dictionary. Caitlin Stone wrote the section on Travellers' Latin and Wendy Owen provided the crossword clues.

INTRODUCTION

Italian is a Romance language, which means it is descended from Latin (the language of the Romans) and as such it is related to French, Spanish, Portuguese and Romanian. As English and Italian are both Indo-European languages and share common roots in Latin, you'll find many Italian words which you will recognise.

While many and varied dialects are spoken in everyday conversation, standard Italian is the national language of schools, media and literature. This began to be developed in the 13th and 14th centuries, predominantly through the works of Dante, Petrarch and Boccaccio who wrote chiefly in the Florentine dialect. The language drew on its Latin heritage, and the many dialects of Italy, to develop into the standard Italian of today. There are still a great number of dialects spoken in Italy. Some vary greatly, often to the point where they are unintelligible to other Italian speakers, though almost all Italians also speak or, at least understand, standard Italian.

There are around 60 million speakers of Italian in Italy, half a million in Switzerland where it is one of the four official languages, and 1.5 million speakers in France and the former Yugoslavia. As a result of migration, Italian is also widely spoken in the USA, Canada, Argentina, Brazil and Australia.

Opera, film and literature, from the great Renaissance works to modern writers such as Umberto Eco and Alberto Moravia, have all contributed to portraying Italian as the vibrant, melodic and rich language that it is. It is not, however, a difficult language for English-speakers to learn and Italians will welcome your attempts to communicate with them.

Although many Italians speak some English, it is more widely understood in the north, particularly in major centres such as Milan, Florence and Venice, than in the south. You'll find that staff at most hotels and restaurants usually speak some English but you'll always receive a warm welcome if you attempt some Italian.

INTRODUCTION

ARTHUR OR MARTHA?

In this book the feminine form of a word appears first. The alternative masculine ending is separated by a slash. For example la/il bambina/o ('the baby/child') indicates that the feminine form is la bambina and the masculine form is il bambino (see Grammar, page 19, for an explanation of nouns and gender). In cases where the two forms are more complex, both forms of the word appear in full, separated by a slash.

ABBREVIATIONS USED IN THIS BOOK

adj	adjective
f	feminine
inf	informal
lit	literally
m	masculine
n	noun
pl	plural
pol	polite
sg	singular
v	verb

HOW TO USE THIS PHRASEBOOK
You *Can* Speak Another Language

It's true – anyone can speak another language. Don't worry if you haven't studied languages before, or that you studied a language at school for years and can't remember any of it. It doesn't even matter if you failed English grammar. After all, that's never affected your ability to speak English! And this is the key to picking up a language in another country. You don't need to sit down and memorise endless grammatical details and you don't need to memorise long lists of vocabulary. You just need to start speaking. Once you start, you'll be amazed how many prompts you'll get to help you build on those first words.

You'll hear people speaking, pick up sounds from TV, catch a word or two that you think you know from the local radio, see something on a billboard – all these things help to build your understanding.

Plunge In

There's just one thing you need to start speaking another language – courage. Your biggest hurdle is overcoming the fear of saying aloud what may seem to you to be just a bunch of sounds. There are a number of ways to do this.

Firstly, think of some Italian words or phrases you are familiar with, such as ciao, la dolce vita, mamma mia and festa. These are phrases you are already able to say fluently. From these basic beginnings you can start making sentences. You might know that quando means 'when' in Italian (cuando is Spanish, quand is French – they all sound much the same). So, let's imagine you've arranged to meet someone at a party but don't know what time. You could ask Festa quando? Don't worry that you're not getting a whole sentence right first time. People will understand if you stick to the key word. And you'll find that once you're in the country it won't take long to remember the complete sentence.

The best way to start overcoming your fear is to memorise a few key words. These are the words you know you'll be saying again and again, like 'hello', 'thankyou' and 'how much?' Here's an important hint though: right from the beginning, learn at least one phrase that will be useful but not essential. Such as 'good morning' or 'good afternoon', 'see you later' or even a conversational piece like 'lovely day, isn't it?' or 'it's cold today' (people everywhere love to talk about the weather). Having this extra phrase (just start with one, if you like, and learn to say it really well) will enable you to move away from the basics, and when you get a reply and a smile, it'll also boost your confidence. You'll find that people you speak to will like it too, as they'll understand that at least you've tried to learn more of the language than just the usual essential words.

INTRODUCTION

Ways to Remember

There are several ways to learn a language. Most people find they learn from a variety of these, although people usually have a preferred way to remember. Some like to see the written word and remember the sound from what they see. Some like to just hear it spoken in context (if this is you, try talking to yourself in Italian). Others, especially the more mathematically inclined, like to analyse the grammar of a language, and piece together words according to the rules of grammar. The very visually inclined like to associate the written word and even sounds with some visual stimulus, such as from illustrations, TV and general things they see in the street. As you learn, you'll discover what works best for you – be aware of what made you really remember a particular word, and keep using that method.

Kicking Off

Chances are you'll want to learn some of the language before you go. So you won't be hearing it around you. The first thing to do is to memorise those essential phrases and words. Check out the basics (page 47) ... and don't forget that extra phrase (see Plunge In!). Try the sections on First Encounters or Greetings in Meeting People, pages 47 and 48 for a phrase you'd like to use. Write some of these words and phrases down on a piece of paper and stick them up around the place: on the fridge, by the bed, on your computer, as a bookmark – somewhere where you'll see them often. Try putting some words in context – the 'How much is it?' note, for instance, could go in your wallet.

Building the Picture

We include a grammar chapter in our books for two main reasons.
Firstly, some people have an aptitude for grammar and find understanding it a key tool to their learning. If you're such a person, then the grammar chapter in a phrasebook will help you build a picture of the language, as it works through all the basics.

The second reason for the grammar chapter is that it gives answers to questions you might raise as you hear or memorise some key phrases. You may find a particular word is always used when there is a question – check out Questions in Grammar and it should explain why. This way you don't have to read the grammar chapter from start to finish, nor do you need to memorise a grammatical point. It will simply present itself to you in the course of your learning. Key grammatical points are repeated through the book.

Any Questions?

Try to learn the main question words (see page 41). As you read through different situations, you'll see these words used in the example sentences, and this will help you remember them. So if you want to hire a bicycle, turn to the Bicycles section in Getting Around (use the Contents or Index to find it quickly). You'll see the words for 'where' and 'bicycle' a number of times in this book. When you come across the sentence 'Where can I hire a bicycle?', you'll recognise the key words and this will help you remember the whole phrase. If there's no category for your need, try the dictionary (the question words are repeated there too, with examples), and memorise the phrase 'How do you say ...?' (page 56).

I've Got a Flat Tyre

Doesn't seem like the phrase you're going to need? Well, in fact it could be very useful. As are all the phrases in this book, provided you have the courage to mix and match them. We have given specific examples within each section. But the key words remain the same even when the situation changes. So while you may not be planning on any cycling during your trip, the first part of the phrase 'I've got ...' could refer to anything else, and there are plenty of words in the dictionary that, we hope, will fit your needs. So whether it's 'a ticket', 'a visa' or 'a condom', you'll be able to put the words together to convey your meaning.

INTRODUCTION

Finally

Don't be concerned if you feel you can't memorise words. On the inside front and back covers are the most essential words and phrases you'll need. You could also try tagging a few pages for other key phrases, or use the notes pages to write your own reminders.

PRONUNCIATION

Italian has a consistent pattern of pronunciation and the few rules that follow are easy to master. Although some of the clipped vowels and long sound of double letters require a bit of practice, you'll find that it is easy to make yourself understood in Italian. The Italian alphabet has 21 letters. The letters j, w, k, x and y are only found in foreign words that have been adopted by Italian.

VOWELS

Vowels are generally more clipped than in English.

a	as 'a' in 'art'	pasta
e	as 'e' in 'tell'	festa
i	as 'i' in 'bin', but slightly longer	vino
o	as 'o' in 'dot'	donna
o	as 'o' in 'port'	coda
u	as 'oo' in 'book'	sambuca

In Italian each vowel is pronounced. So, the combination ie has two sounds run together 'i' as in 'bin' and 'e' as in 'tell', eg grazie.

DID YOU KNOW ... You may often hear Italians use the word cioè when they speak. This literally means 'that is (to say)' and is a common filler in spoken Italian. Some other 'filler' words you may hear are bene, beh, ecco, mah and diciamolo

PRONUNCIATION

CONSONANTS

The pronunciation of many consonants is the same as in English but there are a few rules you should learn.

c   before a, o, u and h a hard sound as 'k' in 'kick'
            eg camera, zucchini
        before e and i a soft sound as 'ch' in 'choose'
            eg bocce, ciao

g   before a, o, u and h a hard sound as 'g' in 'get'
            eg albergo, spaghetti
        before e and i a soft sound as 'j' in 'job'
            eg gelato, giorno

sc   before a, o, u and h has a hard sound as 'sc' in 'scooter'
            eg scaloppine, scherzo
        before e and i a soft sound as 'sh' in 'sheep'
            eg crescendo, prosciutto

When ci, gi and sci are followed by a, o or u, the i is not pronounced, unless the accent falls on the i. Thus the name Giovanni is pronounced 'jo-VAHN-nee' and ciao is pronounced 'chow'. Think of the i as being there simply to soften the sound.

h   is always silent, eg ho is pronounced as the 'o' in 'hot'
r   a rolled 'rr' sound, as in Spanish, eg supermercato
t, d   a more dental, drier sound than in English.
z   1) voiced as the 'dz' sound in 'beds', eg zero
        2) unvoiced as 'ts' in 'lights', eg stazione
s   1) between two vowels it is voiced as 's' in 'pose', eg casa
        2) everywhere else it is unvoiced, as 's' in 'mouse', eg sì

An exception to the above rule is the word buonasera ('good evening'). The s in this word is unvoiced (ie as the 's' in 'sun'). This is because it is made up of two words that, over time, have come to be written as one word – buona ('good') and sera ('evening').

Combined Letters

Some letters, when combined, produce unusual sounds:

gli   as 'lli' in 'million', eg tagliatelle
gn   as 'ny' in 'canyon', eg gnocchi

Double Consonants

These are pronounced as longer, more emphatic sounds than single consonants. In contrast, the vowel that precedes a double consonant is shortened and clipped:

Pope	papa	(pronounced 'pah-pah')
baby food	pappa	(pronounced 'pup-pa')
dog	cane	(pronounced 'cah-nay')
canes	canne	(pronounced 'cun-ay')

STRESS

Stress generally falls on the second-last syllable, eg spa-GHET-ti. When a word has an accent, the stress is on that syllable, eg citTÀ ('city') should be pronounced with the stress on the last syllable.

Intonation

Intonation is used much as it is in English. Questions are usually addressed with rising intonation:

You're not from here.   Lei non è di qui.
You're not from here?   Lei non è di qui?

While the first makes a statement, delivered in a flat tone, the second asks a question, delivered with rising intonation. See page 40 in Grammar for more on forming questions and for a list of question words.

PRONUNCIATION

DON'T WORRY

One last note about pronunciation: in order to make it easier, it's best to take your time and pronounce each syllable clearly. You'll find that Italians will be patient and helpful if you just make an effort to speak the language.

GRAMMAR

This chapter is designed to give you an idea of how Italian phrases are put together, providing you with the basic rules to help you construct your own sentences.

WORD ORDER
Generally, the word order of sentences follows the same order as English (subject-verb-object).

> We're waiting for the bus.   **(Noi) aspettiamo l'autobus.**
>   (lit: [we] we-wait the bus)

ARTICLES
In English and Italian there are two articles: the definite article ('the' in English) and the indefinite article ('a'). Italian, however, has feminine and masculine, singular and plural forms for each article.

Definite Article
The definite article corresponds to 'the' in English.

Definite Article – Feminine

singular		plural	
the woman	**la** donna	the women	**le** donne
the house	**la** casa	the houses	**le** case

If the word begins with a vowel, the **la** is shortened to **l'**:

the exit	**l'**uscita	the exits	**le** uscite

GRAMMAR

Definite Article – Masculine

singular		plural	
the train	il treno	the trains	i treni
the ticket	il biglietto	the tickets	i biglietti

- When a masculine noun starts with a vowel, the **il** changes to **l'** in the singular, and the plural is **gli** (pronounced /yi/):

singular		plural	
the timetable	l'orario	the timetables	gli orari
the plane	l'aereo	the planes	gli aerei

- When masculine nouns begin with **s-** followed by a consonant and **z-** (and **gn-, ps-, x-** and **y-**), **il** becomes **lo**, and the plural is **gli**:

singular		plural	
the backpack	lo zaino	the backpacks	gli zaini
the studio	lo studio	the studios	gli studi

Indefinite Article

The indefinite article corresponds to 'a/an' in English.

Indefinite Article – Feminine

una – with most nouns:

a woman	una donna
a house	una casa

un' – with nouns starting with a vowel:

an exit	un'uscita
a female friend	un'amica

Indefinite Article – Masculine

un – with most nouns:

a train	**un** treno
a timetable	**un** orario
a dog	**un** cane

uno – when nouns begin with **s-** followed by a consonant and **z-**, and the less common letters **gn-**, **ps-**, **x-**, **y-**:

a studio	**uno** studio
a backpack	**uno** zaino
a gnome	**uno** gnomo

NOUNS

Italian nouns are always either masculine or feminine in gender. They are generally feminine when they refer to a female person or animal, and masculine when they refer to a male person or animal. But even when they refer to things and abstract terms they take either the feminine or the masculine form. These just have to be learned, though there are some ways to recognise which gender a word is.

- Feminine nouns generally end in -a in the singular, and -e in the plural.

| the house | la casa | the houses | le case |
| the woman | la donna | the women | le donne |

- Masculine nouns generally end in -o in the singular, and -i in the plural.

| the train | il treno | the trains | i treni |
| the cart | il carro | the carts | i carri |

GRAMMAR

- Some nouns, however, end in -e in the singular, and these can be either masculine or feminine. This ending changes to -i in both its feminine and masculine plurals. These nouns just have to be learned. Here are a few examples:

the flower	il fiore	the flowers	i fiori
the general	il generale	the generals	i generali
the reason	la ragione	the reasons	le ragioni
the river	il fiume	the rivers	i fiumi
the ship	la nave	the ships	le navi

- Some occupations, though denoted by masculine nouns only, may in fact refer to both women and men.

IRREGULAR PLURAL NOUNS

Nouns that have irregular plural forms include:

il bue (ox)	i buoi (oxen)
il dito (finger)	le dita (fingers)
il lenzuolo (sheet)	le lenzuola (sheets)
la moglie (wife)	le mogli (wives)

Suffixes

The meaning of some nouns (and also adjectives) can be changed slightly with the addition of suffixes, and in spoken Italian these are frequently used. Often words are changed to diminutives, that is, words implying smallness or cuteness:

boy	ragazzo	little boy	ragazzino
piece	pezzo	a little piece	pezzetto
handsome	bello	cute	bellino

GRAMMAR

- Some suffixes imply an increase in size or strength:

| nose | naso | big nose | nasone |
| well | bene | very well | benone |

- Some suffixes imply a negative aspect:

| word | parola | swear word | parolaccia |
| poet | poeta | bad poet | poetastro |

PRONOUNS
Subject Pronouns

The subject pronoun is often omitted in Italian as the subject is understood from the verb form.

I	io	we	noi
you (inf)	tu	you (pl, inf)	voi
you (pol)	Lei	you (pl, pol)	Loro
she, it	lei	they	loro
he, it	lui		

Object Pronouns
Direct Object Pronouns

Direct object pronouns are used in Italian to refer to people as 'him', 'them', etc.

me	mi	us	ci
you (inf)	ti	you (pl, inf)	vi
you (pol)	La	you (pl, pol)	Le (f) Li (m)
her, it	la	them	le (f) li (m)
him, it	lo		

GRAMMAR

The Guccinis know me well.
    I Guccini mi conoscono bene.
        (lit: the Guccinis me they-know well)

Let me know.
    Fammi sapere.
        (lit: make-me to-know)

I've already seen it.
    L'ho già visto.
        (lit: it I-have already seen)

Indirect Object Pronouns

Indirect object pronouns are used to describe 'to her/him', 'to them', etc.

me	mi	us	ci
you (inf)	ti	you (pl, inf)	vi
you (pol)	Le	you (pl, pol)	Loro
her, it	le	them	loro
him, it	gli		

They'll give us a cake.
    Ci danno una torta.
        (lit: to-us they-give a cake)

I talked to him/them.
    Gli ho parlato.
        (lit: to-him/them I-have talked)

DID YOU KNOW ...

If someone or something is in a dangerous situation, the Italians use the expression **navigare in cattive aque**. It literally means 'to sail in troubled waters'.

GRAMMAR

ESSENTIAL LITTLE WORDS

ne

The word ne can mean 'of it/them', 'about it/them', 'from it/them' (translations which in English are often omitted). It can also mean 'some' and 'there':

> We'll speak about it tomorrow.
> > Ne parleremo domani.
> > (lit: about-it we-will-speak tomorrow)

The word ne is always used in Italian to refer to expressions of quantity and to numerals:

> We have three [of them].
> > Ne abbiamo tre.
> > (lit: of-them we-have three)

ci/vi

These two little words have identical meanings including 'to/of/about/on this/that/it/them'. They can take the form ce/ve. Which one to use is simply a matter of preference based on phonetics and style.

The word ci can be used to transform the meaning of individual verbs; as an adverb of place; and used with essere it means there is/there are'.

Do you have it?	Ce l'hai?
	(lit: it it you-have?)
I'll think about it.	Ci penserò.
	(lit: about-it I-will-think)
Shall we go there?	Ci andiamo?
	(lit: to-there we-go?)
There's no-one here.	Non c'è nessuno.
	(lit: not there it-is no-one at this beach)

GRAMMAR

GRAMMAR

si

This word can be used in a number of senses. It may replace the third person to indicate 'one' or 'they', and sometimes is written as se:

You do it like this.	Si fa così.
	(lit: one does like-this)
One never knows!	Non si sa mai!
	(lit: not one knows never)

VERBS

There are three different categories that most Italian verbs fall into, based on the verb endings. These are -are, -ere and -ire. Tenses are formed by taking these endings away and adding various other endings to the verb stem. These tense endings vary according to which category the verb is in. It's useful to learn the regular verb endings, even though there are many exceptions to these. Verbs ending in -ire fall into two divisions – both are listed below.

SAY IT ALL

Remember to pronounce vowels clearly in a word, eg the combination aiuo in the word aiuola ('flower bed'), is four sounds – a, i, u and o – run together quickly. The only vowel not pronounced clearly is the i when it follows c and g. See Pronunciation, page 16, for an explanation of this.

	-are	-er	-ire	-ire
infinitive	amare	credere	seguire	capire
	(to love)	(to believe)	(to follow)	(to understand)
stem	am-	cred-	segu-	cap-

Present Tense

The tense endings are indicated by bold text.

	am(**are**) (to love)	cred(**ere**) (to believe)	segu(**ire**) (to follow)	cap(**ire**) (to understand)
I	am**o**	cred**o**	segu**o**	cap**isco**
you (inf)	am**i**	cred**i**	segu**i**	cap**isci**
she/he/it you (pol)	am**a**	cred**e**	segu**e**	cap**isce**
we	am**iamo**	cred**iamo**	segu**iamo**	cap**iamo**
you (pl)	am**ate**	cred**ete**	segu**ite**	cap**ite**
they/you (pol)	am**ano**	cred**ono**	segu**ono**	cap**iscono**

Future Tense

The future tense is the easiest to learn, as all three verb forms take the same endings. The only thing to remember is that verbs ending in -are change the a of the infinitive to e:

	am(**are**) (to love)	cred(**ere**) (to believe)	segu(**ire**) (to follow)
I	ame**rò**	crede**rò**	segui**rò**
you (inf)	ame**rai**	crede**rai**	segui**rai**
she/he/it you (pol)	ame**rà**	crede**rà**	segui**rà**
we	ame**remo**	crede**remo**	segui**remo**
you (pl)	ame**rete**	crede**rete**	segui**rete**
they/you (pol)	ame**ranno**	crede**ranno**	segui**ranno**

See Key Verbs, page 34, for some common irregular verbs in the future tense.

GRAMMAR

Past Tense

Although there is a simple past tense in Italian, the 'perfect tense' (*passato prossimo*) is most commonly used to express the past. It is made up of the present tense form of either 'to have', **avere** or 'to be', **essere**, together with the 'past participle' of the verb.

A regular past participle is formed by substituting the regular infinitive conjugation endings with:

am(**are**)	am + **ato** = amato	I loved	ho amato
cred(**ere**)	cred + **uto** = creduto	I believed	ho creduto
segu(**ire**)	segu + **ito** = seguito	I followed	ho seguito

Have you seen the [town] centre?	Hai visto il centro?
It cost me twenty thousand lire.	Mi è costato ventimila lire.

Past participles behave like adjectives and agree in gender and number:

- With the subject when **essere** is their auxiliary:

I went. (f)	Sono andata.
They went. (m & f, or just m)	Sono andati.

- With the direct object pronoun when **avere** is their auxiliary:

I saw her yesterday.	L'ho vista ieri.
I've already bought the tickets.	I biglietti, li ho comprati già.

GRAMMAR

Imperfect Tense

	am(are) to love	cred(ere) to believe	segu(ire) to follow
I	amavo	credevo	seguivo
you (inf)	amavi	credevi	seguivi
she/he/it you (pol)	amava	credeva	seguiva
we	amavamo	credevamo	seguivamo
you (pl)	amavate	credevate	seguivate
they/you (pol)	amavano	credevano	seguivano

More commonly used in Italian than in English, the imperfect tense, as its name suggests, refers to a past action or state with an indefinite or 'imperfect' beginning or end. Thus it describes:

- An action or state in the past which is sustained or continued for an indeterminate period of time (English normally uses the verb forms 'was/were (-ing)' or 'would' + verb to express this tense):

  We were watching the TV, when my sister arrived.
  Mentre guardavamo la tivù, è arrivata mia sorella.

- An action or state in the past which is repeated or habitual:

  Every fortnight we would go to the A.A. meeting.
  Ogni quattordici giorni andavamo alla riunione di A.A.

- A psychological state, mental activity, character, health or age in the past:

  Every time I saw them I'd feel queasy.
  Tutte le volte che li vedevo mi veniva la nausea.

• Weather, time, size and colour:

It was raining.	Pioveva.
The dog was brown.	Il cane era grigio.

THE SUBJUNCTIVE TENSE

The subjunctive is a tense frequently used in Italian, and it takes a lot of learning to work out when to use it. However, basically it's used to denote irreality, doubt or desire, often indicated by verbs such as 'to want [that]', volere [che]; 'to think [that]', pensare [che]; 'to be afraid [of]', avere paura [che] or temere [che]. It's also used with expressions such as 'it's possible [that]', è possibile [che]; 'it's necessary [that]', bisogna [che] or è necessario [che]; etc.

Subjunctive Tense

	am(are) (to love)	cred(ere) (to believe)	segu(ire) (to follow)
I	ami	creda	segua
you (inf)	ami	creda	segua
she/he/it you (pol)	ami	creda	segua
we	amiamo	crediamo	seguiamo
you (pl)	amiate	crediate	seguiate
they/you (pol)	amino	credano	seguano

You need to ask someone.	Bisogna che tu chieda a qualcuno.
I'm afraid she's gone.	Ho paura che sia andata.
I think he has a room.	Penso che abbia una stanza.
I hope you succeed.	Spero che tu abbia successo.

GRAMMAR

THE GERUND

The gerund is that verb which, in English, is formed by the addition of '-ing' to a verb stem. In Italian, the equivalent is -ando for -are verbs, and -endo for -ere and -ire verbs. The verb stare is often used with the gerund, see page 33 for stare.

We are going home.   Stiamo andando a casa.
I'm reading a good book.   Sto leggendo un buon libro.
You learn by your mistakes. Sbagliando s'impara.

However you can just use the present tense for the same meaning:

We are going home.   Andiamo a casa.

TO KNOW

There are two words for 'to know': conoscere ('to know someone or a place') and sapere ('to know about/how to do something').

Do you know my brother?   Conosce mio fratello?
Can you read?   Sai leggere? (inf)
Do you know where the   Sa dov'è la fermata
    bus stop is?   dell'autobus?

TO HAVE

The verb 'to have' is avere. As we've already seen, avere is used as an auxiliary verb to form the perfect tense.

Avere	
I have	ho
you (inf) have	hai
she, he, it has, you (pol) have	ha
we have	abbiamo
you (pl, inf) have	avete
they have, you (pl, pol) have	hanno

GRAMMAR

| We have the tickets. | **Abbiamo i biglietti.** |
| Do you have it? | **Ce l'hai?** |

Avere takes **avere** as its auxiliary and its past pasticiple is **avuto**

| I had a nightmare. | **Ho avuto un incubo.** |

A few important phrases that take 'be' in English take **avere** in Italian:

I'm hungry.	**Ho fame.**	(lit: I have hunger)
I'm thirsty.	**Ho sete.**	(lit: I have thirst)
I'm sleepy.	**Ho sonno.**	(lit: I have sleepiness)
I'm cold/hot.	**Ho freddo/caldo.**	(lit: I have cold/hot)

It's important to get these last two right, for it is possible to use the verb 'to be', **essere**, with these two – the meaning then changing to the sexual sense of 'I'm hot' and 'I'm cold (frigid)'.

TO BE
The verb 'to be' has two forms in Italian: **essere** and **stare**, but **essere** is the most common.

Essere
The verb essere is used in situations with a degree of permanence about them:

Essere	
I am	**sono**
you (inf) are	**sei**
she, he, it is, you (pol) are	**è**
we are	**siamo**
you (pl, inf) are	**siete**
they are, you (pl, pol) are	**sono**

- Characteristics of people or things:

    | Giovanna is pretty. | Giovanna è bella. |
    | The book is red. | Il libro è grande. |

- Occupations or nationality

    | I'm a poet. | Sono un poeta. |

- Telling the time and location of events:

    | It's 3.30. | Sono le tre e mezzo. |
    | The party is at my house. | La festa è a casa mia. |

- Mood

    | I'm pleased. | Sono contenta (f). |

Essere takes **essere** as its auxiliary and its past participle is **stato** (borrowed from the verb **stare** which in some cases replaces **essere**).

Stare

The verb **stare** is used with the gerund, and with some feelings (well/unwell). It is also used instead of **essere** in a number of other contexts, but you will still be understood if you use **essere**.

Stare	
I am	sto
you (inf) are	stai
she, he, it is, you (pol) are	sta
we are	stiamo
you (pl, inf) are	state
they are, you (pl, pol) are	stanno

| It's raining. | Sta piovendo. |
| She's fine now. | Sta bene adesso. |

GRAMMAR

andare (to go)
past participle: (essere) andato

	present	perfect	imperfect	future
I	vado	sono andata/o	andavo	andrò
you	vai	sei andata/o	andavi	andrai
he/she/it	va	è andata/o	andava	andrà
we	andiamo	siamo andate/i	andavamo	andremo
you	andate	siete andate/i	andavate	andrete
they/you	vanno	sono andate/i	andavano	andranno

avere (to have)
past participle: (avere) avuto

	present	perfect	imperfect	future
I	ho	ho avuto	avevo	avrò
you	hai	hai avuto	avevi	avrai
he/she/it	hanno	hanno avuto	aveva	avrà
we	abbiamo	abbiamo avuto	avevamo	avremo
you	avete	avete avuto	avevate	avrete
they/you	hanno	hanno avuto	avevano	avranno

bere (to drink)
past participle: (avere) bevuto

	present	perfect	imperfect	future
I	bevo	ho bevuto	bevevo	berrò
you	bevi	hai bevuto	bevevi	berrai
he/she/it	beve	ha bevuto	beveva	berrà
we	beviamo	abbiamo bevuto	bevevamo	berremo
you	bevete	avete bevuto	bevevate	berrete
they/you	bevono	hanno bevuto	bevevano	berranno

capire (to understand)
past participle: (avere) capito

	present	perfect	imperfect	future
I	capisco	ho capito	capivo	capirò
you	capisci	hai capito	capivi	capirai
he/she/it	capisce	hanno capito	capiva	capirà
we	capiamo	abbiamo capito	capivamo	capiremo
you	capite	avete capito	capivate	capirete
they/you	capiscono	hanno capito	capivano	capiranno

comprare (to buy)
past participle: (avere) comprato

	present	perfect	imperfect	future
I	compro	ho comprato	compravo	comprerò
you	compri	hai comprato	compravi	comprerai
he/she/it	compra	hanno comprato	comprava	comprerà
we	compriamo	abbiamo comprato	compravamo	compreremo
you	comprate	avete comprato	compravate	comprerete
they/you	comprano	hanno comprato	compravano	compreranno

conoscere (to know - someone)
past participle: (avere) conosciuto

	present	perfect	imperfect	future
I	conosco	ho conosciuto	conoscevo	conoscerò
you	conosci	hai conosciuto	conoscevi	conoscerai
he/she/it	conosce	hanno conosciuto	conosceva	conoscerà
we	conosciamo	abbiamo conosciuto	conoscevamo	conosceremo
you	conoscete	avete conosciuto	conoscevate	conoscerete
they/you	conoscono	hanno conosciuto	conoscevano	conosceranno

dare (to give)
past participle: (avere) dato

	present	perfect	imperfect	future
I	do	ho dato	davo	darò
you	dai	hai dato	davi	darai
he/she/it	dà	hanno dato	dava	darà
we	diamo	abbiamo dato	davamo	daremo
you	date	avete dato	davate	darete
they/you	danno	hanno dato	davano	daranno

dire (to say)
past participle: (avere) detto

	present	perfect	imperfect	future
I	dico	ho detto	dicevo	dirò
you	dici	hai detto	dicevi	dirai
he/she/it	dice	ha detto	diceva	dirà
we	diciamo	abbiamo detto	dicevamo	diremo
you	dite	avete detto	dicevate	direte
they/you	dicono	hanno detto	dicevano	diranno

dovere (to have to; must)
past participle: (avere) dovuto

	present	perfect	imperfect	future
I	devo	sono dovuta/o	dovevo	dovrò
you	devi	sei dovuta/o	dovevi	dovrai
he/she/it	deve	è dovuta/o	doveva	dovrà
we	dobbiamo	siamo dovute/i	dovevamo	dovremo
you	dovete	siete dovute/i	dovevate	dovrete
they/you	devono	sono dovute/i	dovevano	dovranno

essere (to be)
past participle: (essere) stato

	present	perfect	imperfect	future
I	sono	sono stata/o	ero	sarò
you	sei	sei stata/o	eri	sarai
he/she/it	è	è stata/o	era	sarà
we	siamo	siamo state/i	eravamo	saremo
you	siete	siete state/i	eravate	sarete
they/you	sono	sono state/i	erano	saranno

GRAMMAR

fare (to do; make)

past participle: (avere) fatto

	present	perfect	imperfect	future
I	faccio	ho fatto	facevo	farò
you	fai	hai fatto	facevi	farai
he/she/it	fa	hanno fatto	faceva	farà
we	facciamo	abbiamo fatto	facevamo	faremo
you	fate	avete fatto	facevate	farete
they/you	fanno	hanno fatto	facevano	faranno

mangiare (to eat)

past participle: (avere) mangiato

	present	perfect	imperfect	future
I	mangio	ho mangiato	mangiavo	mangerò
you	mangi	hai mangiato	mangiavi	mangerai
he/she/it	mangia	hanno mangiato	mangiava	mangerà
we	mangiamo	abbiamo mangiato	mangiavamo	mangeremo
you	mangiate	avete mangiato	mangiavate	mangerete
they/you	mangiano	hanno mangiato	mangiavano	mangeranno

potere (to can; be able)

past participle: (avere) potuto

	present	perfect	imperfect	future
I	posso	ho potuto	potevo	potrò
you	puoi	hai potuto	potevi	potrai
he/she/it	può	ha potuto	poteva	potrà
we	possiamo	abbiamo potuto	potevamo	potremo
you	potete	avete potuto	potevate	potrete
they/you	possono	hanno potuto	potevano	potranno

sapere (to know - something)

past participle: (avere) saputo

	present	perfect	imperfect	future
I	so	ho saputo	sapevo	saprò
you	sai	hai saputo	sapevi	saprai
he/she/it	sa	hanno saputo	sapeva	saprà
we	sappiamo	abbiamo saputo	sapevamo	sapremo
you	sapete	avete saputo	sapevate	saprete
they/you	sanno	hanno saputo	sapevano	sapranno

stare (to stay; remain)

past participle: (essere) stato

	present	perfect	imperfect	future
I	sto	sono stata/o	stavo	starò
you	stai	sei stata/o	stavi	starai
he/she/it	sta	è stata/o	stava	starà
we	stiamo	siamo state/i	stavamo	staremo
you	state	siete state/i	stavate	starete
they/you	stanno	sono state/i	stavano	staranno

uscire (to go out; leave)   *past participle:* (essere) uscito

	present	perfect	imperfect	future
I	esco	sono uscita/o	uscivo	uscirò
you	esci	sei uscita/o	uscivi	uscirai
he/she/it	esce	è uscita/o	usciva	uscirà
we	usciamo	siamo uscite/i	uscivamo	usciremo
you	uscite	siete uscite/i	uscivate	uscirete
they/you	escono	sono uscite/i	uscivano	usciranno

venire (to come)   *past participle:* (essere) venuto

	present	perfect	imperfect	future
I	vengo	sono venuta/o	venivo	verrò
you	vieni	sei venuta/o	vehivi	verrai
he/she/it	viene	è venuta/o	veniva	verrà
we	veniamo	siamo venute/i	venivamo	verremo
you	venite	siete venute/i	venivate	verrete
they/you	vengono	sono venute/i	venivano	verranno

vedere (to see)   *past participle:* (avere) visto

	present	perfect	imperfect	future
I	vedo	ho visto	vedevo	vedrò
you	vedi	hai visto	vedevi	vedrai
he/she/it	vede	ha visto	vedeva	vedrà
we	vediamo	abbiamo visto	vedevamo	vedremo
you	vedete	avete visto	vedevate	vedrete
they/you	vedono	hanno visto	vedevano	vedranno

vivere (to live)   *past participle:* (essere) vissuto

	present	perfect	imperfect	future
I	vivo	sono vissuta/o	vivevo	vivrò
you	vivi	sei vissuta/o	vivevi	vivrai
he/she/it	vive	è vissuta/o	viveva	vivrà
we	viviamo	siamo vissute/i	vivevamo	vivremo
you	vivete	siete vissute/i	vivevate	vivrete
they/you	vivono	sono vissute/i	vivevano	vivranno

volere (to want; wish)   *past participle:* (avere) voluto

	present	perfect	imperfect	future
I	voglio	ho voluto	volevo	vorrò
you	vuoi	hai voluto	volevi	vorrai
he/she/it	vuole	hanno voluto	voleva	vorrà
we	vogliamo	abbiamo voluto	volevamo	vorremo
you	volete	avete voluto	volevate	vorrete
they/you	volevano	hanno voluto	volevano	vorranno

MODALS
Must/Have To/Need To

To express having to do something, you can use the verb dovere (see Key Verbs, page 34). Note that sometimes Italians say debbo in place of devo, 'I must'.

I must find a bank.	Devo trovare una banca.

Alternatively you can use the verb bisognare, 'to need'. As a verb, it is only ever used in the third person singular ('one'), otherwise it is used as a noun with the verb avere

I need to change some money.	Ho bisogno di cambiare un po' di soldi.
You need to return at 3.	Bisogna ritornare alle tre.

Can/To Be Able

This is expressed by the verb potere (see Key Verbs, page 34).

I can go now.	Posso andare adesso.
Can you tell me how much it will be?	Mi può dire quanto costerà?

To Want

This is the verb volere (see Key Verbs, page 34).

I want to go there.	Voglio andare lì.
I would like to go there.	Vorrei andare lì.

GRAMMAR

DID YOU KNOW ... Once the word mafia had no underworld crime association. In fact, mafioso was a synonym for 'courageous, excellent, elegant'.

To Like

In Italian, in order to say you like something, you say 'something is pleasing to you'. This form is simple but takes a lot of getting used to when you're used to saying it the other way round. The verb used is piacere, the indirect object pronouns are on page 24.

I like wine.	**Mi piace il vino.**
	(lit: to-me is-pleasing the wine)
We like it.	**A noi piace.**
	(lit: to-us is-pleasing)
They like icecream.	**A loro piace il gelato.**
	(lit: to-them is-pleasing the icecream)
I like you.	**Mi piaci.**
	(lit: to-me you-are-pleasing)

ADJECTIVES

Adjectives agree in gender and number with the nouns they relate to. They are generally placed after the noun, and their endings are generally the same as those of the nouns.

the loose jacket	**la giacca ampia** (f, sg)
the loose jackets	**le giacche ampie** (f, pl)
a new backpack	**uno zaino nuovo** (m, sg)
some new backpacks	**degli zaini nuovi** (m, pl)

They can also follow nouns with a resulting change in meaning, and when they are modified by an adverb. The listings in the dictionary at the back of the book give both meanings when they occur.

the miserable man	**il povero uomo**
the poor (impoverished) man	**l'uomo povero**
a very poor man	**un uomo molto povero**

GRAMMAR

Comparatives

more ... than	più ... che/di
less ... than	meno ... che/di
as ... as	(tanto) ... quanto; (così) ... come

I'm staying more than three weeks.	Resto qua più di tre settimane.
That pensione is as expensive as this one.	Quella pensione è cara come questa.
They have more time than me.	Hanno più tempo di me.

Superlatives

the most ...	la/il più ...
the least ...	la/il meno ...

I'll take the biggest icecream.	Prendo il gelato più grande.
I've seen him less often this year.	L'ho visto meno spesso quest'anno.
It's the fastest car in the world.	È la macchina la più veloce del mondo.

QUESTIONS

As in English, all questions in Italian require a rise in intonation at the end of the sentence. The tag phrases no?/vero?/è vero?/non è vero? (isn't it?/is it?/ aren't they?/are they?, etc.) can be added to the end of a statement to turn it into a question.

LA, LA, LA

The feminine definite article la becomes l' before a noun beginning with a vowel.

GRAMMAR

QUESTION WORDS

What?	Che?; Cosa?; Che cosa?	What would you like? **Cosa/Che cosa desidera?**
Who?	Chi?	Who are those girls? **Chi sono quelle ragazze?**
How?	Come?	How do you get to the country? **Come si arriva in paese?**
Where?	Dove?	Where is the road map? **Dov'è la guida stradale?**
Why?	Perché?	Why has the bus stopped? **Perché si è fermato l'autobus?**
When?	Quando?	When must we meet Mr Ferri? **Quando dobbiamo incontrare il Signor Ferri?**
Why? (How come)?	Come mai?	Why are there never any attendants around? **Come mai questi custodi non ci sono mai?**
Which?	Quale/i?	Which socks are you putting on? **Quali calzini ti metti?**
How much?	Quanta/o?	How much time do we have to wait? **Quanto tempo bisogna aspettare?**
How many?	Quante/i?	How many kilometres have we done? **Quanti chilometri abbiamo fatto?**

GRAMMAR

POSSESSION

Possessives agree with the gender and number of the noun possessed and not, like English, the noun that is possessing. So, 'my bag' will agree in gender with 'bag', not 'me'.

Personal Pronouns

	Feminine		Masculine	
	sg	pl	sg	pl
my/mine	la mia	le mie	il mio	i miei
your/yours (sg)	la tua	le tue	il tuo	i tuoi
her, his / hers, his	la sua	le sue	il suo	i suoi
our/ours	la nostra	le nostre	il nostro	i nostri
your/yours (pl)	la vostra	le vostre	il vostro	i vostri
their/theirs	la loro	le loro	il loro	i loro

These are my bags.	Queste sono le mie borse.
They're mine.	Sono (le) mie.

NEGATIVES

To form the negative in a sentence, you would usually place **non** before the verb:

I don't like it.	Non mi piace.
There aren't any buses today.	Non ci sono autobus oggi.

In Italian, you can use double negatives:

There's never anyone around.	Non c'é mai nessuno.
We've never been to Sardinia.	Non siamo mai andati in Sardegna.
There aren't any buses today.	Non c'è nessun autobus oggi.

Negative Words

none	niente; nessuna/o
never	mai
no-one	nessuno
nothing	niente; nulla
no more	non più
neither ... nor ...	né ... né

Never again!	Mai più!
Nor (do) I.	Neanch'io!

PREPOSITIONS

by, for	per
from, by, at, to	da
in, to	in
of	di
on	su
to, at, in, until	a
with	con

Prepositions with the Article

When the definite article is preceded by certain prepositions, they contract into the following combinations. Note that con, 'with', is also often combined in the forms col, coll' and coi, especially in speech.

Preposition	f, sg		m, sg		f, pl	m, pl	
	la	l'	il	lo	le	i	gli
a 'to' + 'the'	alla	all'	al	allo	alle	ai	agli
da 'from' + 'the'	dalla	dall'	dal	dallo	dalle	dai	dagli
su 'on' + 'the'	sulla	sull'	sul	sullo	sulle	sui	sugli
di 'of' + 'the'	della	dell'	del	dello	delle	dei	degli
in 'in' + 'the'	nella	nell'	nel	nello	nelle	nei	negli

GRAMMAR

GRAMMAR

FALSE FRIENDS

to say ...	use ...	don't use ...	which means ...
accident	incidente	accidente	chance
to accommodate	alloggiare	accomodare	to repair
actually	veramente	attualmente	presently
to annoy	irritare	annoiare	to bore
to arrange	ordinare	arrangiare	to fix up
to assume	supporre	assumere	to appoint
attitude	atteggiamento	attitudine	aptitude
audience	pubblico	udienza	hearing
brave	coraggiosa/o	brava/o	clever
camera	macchina fotografica	camera	bedroom
casual	informale	casuale	fortuitous
college	istituto	collegio	boarding school
comfort	comodità	conforto	moral support
commotion	confusione	commozione	emotion
comprehensive	esauriente	comprensiva/o	understanding
concurrent	coincidente	concorrente	competitor
confident	sicura/o di sé	confidente	confidant
to confront	affrontare	confrontare	to compare
considerate	riguardosa/o	considerata/o	esteemed
consistent	conforme	consistente	substantial
content	soddisfatta/o	contento	happy
demand	pretesa	domanda	question
demonstration	manifestazione	dimostrazione	display
discomfort	scomodità	sconforto	discouragement
discreet	riservata/o	discreto	fairly good
drug	medicina	droga	drugs
educated	istruita/o	educato	well-mannered
exhibition	mostra	esibizione	performance
fabric	stoffa	fabbrica	factory
facile	semplicistica/o	facile	easy
factory	fabbrica	fattoria	farm
familiar	confidenziale	familiare	friendly
fantasy	opera di fantasia	fantasia	imagination
favourite	preferita/o	favorita/o	favoured
fiction	invenzione	finzione	falsity
firm	ditta	firma	signature

FALSE FRIENDS

to say ...	use ...	don't use ...	which means ...
to impress	colpire	impressionare	to shock
incident	episodio	incidente	accident
injury	ferita	ingiuria	insult
instruction	insegnamento	istruzione	education
large	grande	larga/o	wide
lecture	conferenza	lettura	reading
library	biblioteca	libreria	bookshop
local (pub)	il bar vicino	locale	spot/room/club
magazine	rivista	magazzino	warehouse
misery	infelicità	miseria	poverty
morbid	morbosa/o	morbida/o	soft
nervous	agitata/o	nervosa/o	cross
novel	romanzo	novella	short story/tale
to occur	accadere	occorrere	to be needed
operator	centralinista	operatore	broker
paragon	modello	paragone	comparison
parent	genitore	parente	relative
phrase	locuzione	frase	sentence
picture (film)	film	pittura	painting
preoccupied	assorta/o	preoccupata/o	worried
preservative	conservativo	preservativo	condom
question	domanda	questione	matter
quiet	silenziosa/o	quieta/o	still
to realise	accorgersi di	realizzare	to achieve
record	disco	ricordo	memory
to respond	recepire	rispondere	to answer
scales	bilancia	scale	stairs
sensible	sensata/o	sensibile	sensitive
stranger	sconosciuta/o	straniera/o	foreigner
suggestive	allusiva/o	suggestiva/o	evocative
sympathetic	partecipe	simpatica/o	nice/friendly
taste	gusto	tasto	touch
ultimately	in definitiva	ultimamente	lately
unfortunate	sventurata/o	infortunata/o	injured

GRAMMAR

CONJUNCTIONS

also	anche
and	e
as soon as	appena
because, since	siccome
but	ma
however, but	però; comunque
or	o
or	oppure
otherwise	altrimenti
so that	in modo che
so, therefore	dunque; quindi
that is	cioè
until	finché
well then	allora
while	mentre

MEETING PEOPLE

YOU SHOULD KNOW

Although ciao is a common greeting, it is best not to use it when addressing strangers, unless they use it first. Use buongiorno and arrivederci

Hello.	Buongiorno; Ciao.
Goodbye.	Arrivederci; Ciao.
Yes.	Sì.
No.	No.
Excuse me.	Mi scusi; Permesso.
May I? Do you mind?	Posso? Le dispiace?
Sorry. (Excuse me; Forgive me)	Mi dispiace; Mi scusi; Mi perdoni.
Please.	Per favore; Per piacere; Per cortesia.
Thankyou.	Grazie.
Many thanks.	Tante grazie; Grazie mille.
That's fine; You're welcome.	Prego.

GREETINGS & GOODBYES

Good morning/afternoon.	Buongiorno.
Good evening.	Buonasera.
Goodnight.	Buonanotte.
See you later.	A più tardi.
See you tomorrow.	A domani.
How are you?	Come sta? (pol)
	Come stai? (inf)
	Come state? (pl)
Well, thanks.	Bene, grazie.
Not too bad.	Non c'è male.
Not too good.	Non troppo bene.
So-so.	Così, così.

THEY MAY SAY ...

Here are some colloquial terms for 'How are you?' They might be translated as 'How's it going?; What's up?':

Come butta?   Come andiamo?
Come ti va?   Che storie ti fai?
Come te la passi?

FORMS OF ADDRESS

Madam/Mrs/Ms	Signora (Sig.ra)
Sir/Mr	Signore (Sig.)
friend	amica/o
companion	compagna/o

FIRST ENCOUNTERS

What's your name?	Come si chiama?(pol)
	Come ti chiami?(inf)
My name is ...	Mi chiamo ...
I'm a friend of ...	Sono un'/un amica/o di ...
I'd like to introduce you to ...	Vorrei presentarla a ...(pol)
	Vorrei presentarti a ...(inf)
I'm pleased to meet you.	Piacere. Lieto di conoscerla (pol)/ conoscerti(inf).
Haven't we met before?	Non ci siamo già incontrate/i?
I'm here ...	Sono qui ...
on holiday	in vacanza
on business	per affari
to study	per motivi di studio
Where are you staying?	Dove abita(pol)/ abiti(inf) ?

MEETING PEOPLE

How long have you been here?	**Da quanto (tempo) è** (pol)/ **sei** (inf) **qui?**
I've been here ... (days/weeks).	**Sono qui da ... (giorni/ settimane).**
How long are you here for?	**Quanto tempo si fermerà** (pol)/ **ti fermerai** (inf)**?**
I'm/We're here for ...	**Sono/Siamo qui per ...**
This is my ... time in Italy.	**Questa è la mia ... volta in Italia.**
I/We like Italy very much.	**Mi/Ci piace molto l'Italia.**
Are you on your own?	**È** (pol)/ **Sei** (inf) **in viaggio da sola/o?**
No, I'm here with ...	**No, sono qui con ...**
my friend	**la mia amica/ il mio amico**
my partner	**la mia compagna/ il mio compagno**
my business associate	**la miasocia/il mio socio**
my family	**la mia famiglia**
How did you get here?	**Come è** (pol)/ **sei** (inf) **arrivata/o qui?**

NATIONALITIES

Unfortunately we can't list all countries here, however you'll find that many country names in Italian are similar to English. If your country is not listed here, try saying it with Italian pronunciation and you will most likely be understood. For example, Nigeria is pronounced 'nee-jair-EE-ah'.

Where are you from?	**Da dove viene** (pol)/ **vieni** (inf)**?**
Are you from here?	**Lei è di qui?** (pol); **Tu sei di qui?** (inf)

MEETING PEOPLE

I/We come ...	Vengo/Veniamo ...
from Australia	dall'Australia
from Belgium	dal Belgio
from Canada	dal Canada
from Central America	dall'America Centrale
from France	dalla Francia
from Germany	dalla Germania
from Greece	dalla Grecia
from Ireland	dall'Irlanda
from Japan	dal Giappone
from the Middle East	dal Medio Oriente
from New Zealand	dalla Nuova Zelanda
from Pacific Islands	dalle Isole del Pacifico

from Scotland	dalla Scozia
from South Africa	dal Sudafrica
from South America	dal Sud America
from Spain	dalla Spagna
from Thailand	dalla Tailandia
from the Netherlands	dai Paesi Bassi; dall'Olanda
from the UK	dal Regno Unito
from the USA	dagli Stati Uniti
from Wales	dal Galles

MEETING PEOPLE

Have you ever been to my country?	È (pol)/Sei (inf) mai stata/o nel mio Paese?
What is your home town like?	Com'è la Sua (pol)/tua (inf) città?

I live ...
   in the city
   in the countryside
   in the mountains
   by the seaside

Vivo ...
   in città
   in campagna
   in montagna
   lungo la costiera

CULTURAL DIFFERENCES

Is this a local or national custom?	È una tradizione locale o nazionale?
In my country ...	Nel mio paese ...
I don't want to offend you.	Non voglio offenderla (pol)/ offenderti (inf)
I'm sorry. It's not the custom in my country.	Mi dispiace. Non è nostro costume.
I'm not accustomed to this.	Non sono abituato.
I'd prefer not to participate.	Preferisco non partecipare.

My culture/religion doesn't allow me to ...
   practise this
   eat this
   drink this

La mia cultura/religione non mi permette di ...
   fare questo
   mangiare questo
   bere questo

AGE

How old are you?	Quanti anni ha (pol)/hai (inf)?
I'm ... years old.	Ho ... anni.
How old do you think I am?	Quanti anni mi daresti?
You look younger.	Sembra più giovane. (pol)

MEETING PEOPLE

OCCUPATIONS

Where do you work?	Dove lavora (pol)/lavori (inf)?
What (work) do you do?	Che lavoro fa (pol)/fai (inf)?

I'm a/an ...   Sono ...

accountant	ragioniere
artist	artista
banker	banchiere
business person	donna/uomo d'affari
clerk	impiegata/o
computer programmer	programmatore (di computer)
doctor	dottoressa/dottore; medico
electrician	elettricista
engineer	ingegnere
factory worker	operaia/o
farmer	agricoltore
fashion designer	stilista; designer
graphic designer	grafico
hairdresser	parrucchiera/e
homemaker	donna/uomo di casa
journalist	giornalista
lawyer	avvocato
manual worker	manovale
mechanic	meccanica/o
musician	musicista
nurse	infermiera/e
office worker	impiegata/o
scientist	scienziata/o
secretary	segretaria/o
student	studentessa/studente
teacher	insegnante; professoressa/ professore
waiter	cameriera/e
writer	scrittrice/scrittore

I'm ...	Sono ...
retired	in pensione; pensionata/o
unemployed	disoccupata/o

Do you enjoy your work?	Le piace il Suo lavoro? (pol)
	Ti piace il tuo lavoro? (inf)
How long have you been in your job?	Da quanto (tempo) fa (pol)/ fai (inf) queste lavoro?

STUDYING

What are you studying?	Cosa studia (pol)/studi (inf)?

I'm studying ...	Sto studiando ...
art	arte
arts/humanities	lettere
business	economia
computer studies	informatica
drama	arti drammatiche
engineering	ingegneria
Italian	italiano
Italian studies	italianistica
languages	lingue
law	legge; giurisprudenza
medicine	medicina
music	musica
public relations	relazioni pubbliche
science	scienze
sociology	sociologia
teaching studies	studi magistrali

DID YOU KNOW ... Many professions are masculine in gender even though they end in a – elettricista (electrician), giornalista (journalist), artista (artist).

MEETING PEOPLE

Useful Words

amateur	una/un dilettante
college	la residenza universitaria
degree	una laurea
dole	disoccupazione
high school	l'istituto superiore; la scuola superiore
job	un lavoro; un'occupazione
professional	professionale
salary	lo stipendio
school (primary)	la scuola (elementare)
specialist	specialista
university	l'università

RELIGION

About 85% of Italians are Catholic but only about 25% of these attend Mass regularly. Religious festivals always attract a large turnout, however, and many Italians are familiar with the saints and keep an interest in the activities of the Pope. See page 18 for religious festivals.

What is your religion?	Di che religione è Lei? (pol)
	Di che religione sei tu? (inf)

I'm ... **Sono ...**

Anglican	anglicana/o
Buddhist	buddista
Catholic	cattolica/o
Christian	cristiana/o
Hindu	indù
Jewish	ebrea/o
Lutheran	luterana/o
Muslim	musulmana/o
Orthodox	ortodossa/o
Protestant	protestante

MEETING PEOPLE

STRESSED?

Remember that stress in Italian generally falls on the second-last syllable. If a word has an accent, eg **città** (city), the stress falls on that syllable.

I am not religious.	Non sono religiosa/o.
I believe in destiny/fate.	Sono fatalista.
I don't believe in God.	Non credo in Dio.
I'm an atheist.	Sono atea/o.
I'm agnostic.	Sono agnostica/o.

FEELINGS

I (don't) like ...	(Non) Mi piace ...
I'm sorry. (condolence)	Mi dispiace.
I'm well/fine.	Sto bene.
I'm grateful.	La ringrazio.

I am ...	Ho ...
Are you ...?	Ha (pol)/ Hai (inf) ...?
cold	freddo
hot	caldo
hungry	fame
in a hurry	fretta
right	ragione
sleepy	sonno
thirst	sete
wrong	torto

I am ...	Sono ...
Are you ...?	È (pol)/Sei (inf) ...?
angry	arrabbiata/o
happy	felice
sad	triste
tired	stanca/o
worried	preoccupata/o

LANGUAGE DIFFICULTIES

Do you speak English?	Parla (pol)/ Parli (inf) inglese?
Does anyone speak English?	C'è qualcuno che parla inglese?
I speak a little Italian.	Parlo un po' d'italiano.
Excuse my Italian.	Perdona (pol)/ Perdoni (inf) il mio italiano.
I (don't) speak ...	(Non) Parlo ...
I (don't) understand.	(Non) Capisco.
Do you understand?	Capisce? (pol) ; Capisci? (inf)
Could you speak more slowly please?	Può (pol)/ Puoi (inf) parlare più lentamente, per favore?
Could you repeat that, please?	Può (pol)/ Puoi (inf) ripeterlo, per favore?
Could you write that down, please?	Può (pol)/ Puoi (inf) scriverlo, per favore?
How do you say ... ?	Come si dice ...?
What is this called in Italian?	Come si dice questo in italiano?
What does ... mean ?	Che (cosa) vuol dire ...?
How do you pronounce this word?	Come si pronuncia questa parola?

I speak ...	Parlo ...
Chinese	cinese
English	inglese
French	francese
German	tedesco
Japanese	giapponese
Russian	russo
Spanish	spagnolo

GETTING AROUND

DON'T MISS IT!

What time does ... leave/arrive?	A che ora parte/arriva ...?
the (air)plane	l'aereo
the boat	la nave; la barca
the bus	l'autobus
the ferry	il traghetto
the train	il treno

FINDING YOUR WAY

Where is the ...?	Dov'è ...?
bus stop	la fermata del bus
train station	la stazione ferroviarie
taxi stand	il parcheggio dei taxi
port/dock	il porto/la stazione marittima
metro station	la stazione della metro

Excuse me, can you help me please?	Scusi, mi può aiutare per favore?
Where is ...?	Dov'è ...?
I'm looking for ...	Cerco ...
I want to go to...	Vorrei andare a...

How do I get to ...?	Come arrivo a ...?
Is it far/near?	È lontano/vicino?
Can I walk there?	Ci posso andare a piedi?

Where are we now?	Dove siamo adesso?
Can you show me (on the map)?	Può mostrarmi (sulla carta)?
Are there other means of getting there?	Ci sono altri modi per arrivarci?

GETTING AROUND

DIRECTIONS

Go straight ahead.	Si va sempre diritto.
Cross the road.	Si attraversa la strada.
Turn left ...	Gira a sinistra ...
Turn right ...	Gira a destra ...
at the next corner	al prossimo angolo
at the traffic lights	al semaforo
at the intersection	all'incrocio

after	dopo	far	lontano
behind	dietro	near	vicino
between	fra; tra	next to	accanto a
in front of	davanti a	opposite	di fronte a

north   **nord (N)**

west   **ovest (O)**

east   **est (E)**

south   **sud (S)**

What ... is this?	Che ... è questa/o?
street	strada (f)
avenue	viale (m)
square	piazza (f)
suburb	quartiere (m); periferia (f)

DID YOU KNOW ...   There is a law in Rome which guarantees stray cats the right to live where they're born – they cannot be destroyed or chased away.

BUYING TICKETS

SIGNS

BIGLIETTERIA	TICKET OFFICE
ORARIO	TIMETABLE

Excuse me, where is the ticket office?	Scusi, dov'è la biglietteria?
Where can I buy a ticket?	Dove posso comprare un biglietto?
I want to go to ...	Vorrei andare a ...
How much is the fare to ...?	Quanto costa il biglietto per ...?
How long does the trip take?	Quanto è lungo il viaggio?; Quanto ci vuole?
Do I need to book?	Bisogna prenotare (un posto)?
I'd like to book a seat to ...	Vorrei prenotare un posto per ...

I'd like ...	Vorrei ...
a one-way ticket	un biglietto di sola andata.
a return ticket	un biglietto di andata e ritorno.
(two) tickets	(due) biglietti
tickets for all of us	biglietti per tutti noi
a student's fare	uno sconto per studenti
a child's fare	uno sconto per bambini
pensioner's fare	uno sconto per pensionati

I'd like ... (my/our reservation).	Vorrei ... (la mia/la nostra prenotazione).
to cancel	cancellare
to change	cambiare
to confirm	confermare

GETTING AROUND

Is it completely full?
Can we get on the stand-by list?

È completamente pieno?
Possiamo metterci nella lista d'attesa?

Special Requests

I'd like a window seat, please.
Vorrei un posto vicino al finestrino, per favore.

(No) Smoking, please.
Per (non) fumatori.

I require a vegetarian meal.
Vorrei ordinare un pasto vegetariano.

I require a kosher meal.
Vorrei ordinare un pasto kasher.

1st class	**prima classe**
2nd class	**seconda classe**

THEY MAY SAY ...

Deve prenotare.
You need to book.

È pieno; È tutto occupato.
It's full.

Fumatori o non fumatori?
Smoking or non-smoking?

Andata e ritorno?
Return?

AT CUSTOMS

SIGNS

DOGANA	CUSTOMS
IMMIGRAZIONE	IMMIGRATION
CONTROLLO DI PASSAPORTO	PASSPORT CONTROL

I have nothing to declare.
Non ho niente da dichiarare.

This is all my luggage.
Tutti questi bagagli sono miei.

I have (three) pieces of luggage.
Ho (tre) colli di bagaglio.

May I/we go through?
Posso/Possiamo passare?

Do I/we have to declare this?
Devo/Dobbiamo dichiarare questo?

I'd like to declare ...
Vorrei dichiarare ...

May I call my embassy/consulate?
Posso chiamare l'ambasciata/il consolato del mio paese?

AIR

Is there a flight to ...?	C'è un volo per ...?
When is the next flight to ...?	A che ora parte il prossimo volo per ...?
How long does the flight take?	Quanto tempo impiega il volo?
Is it a direct flight?	È un volo diretto?
What is the flight number?	Qual è il numero del volo?
What time do I have to check in?	A che ora devo presentarmi per la registrazione?
I'd like to check in my luggage.	Vorrei registrare i miei bagagli?
Is there a departure tax?	C'è una tassa d'imbarco da pagare?
What's the charge for each kilo of excess baggage?	Quant'è il sovratassa per ogni chilo di bagaglio in eccesso?
My luggage hasn't arrived.	I miei bagagli non sono arrivati.
Is there a bus to/from the airport?	C'è un autobus che va all'/dall'aeroporto?

SIGNS

ARRIVI	ARRIVALS
PARTENZE	DEPARTURES
POSTO/BANCO DI CONTROLLO BIGLIETTI	CHECK IN
RECLAMO BAGAGLI	BAGGAGE CLAIM
DEPOSITO BAGAGLI	LEFT-LUGGAGE OFFICE
REGISTRAZIONE	REGISTRATION
VOLI INTERNI/NAZIONALI	DOMESTIC FLIGHTS
VOLE INTERNAZIONALI	INTERNATIONAL FLIGHTS
CAMBIO	EXCHANGE

Useful Words

airport	l'aeroporto
airport tax	la tassa aeroportuale
boarding pass	la carta d'imbarco
duty-free shop	lo duty-free
flight	il volo
gate	la porta d'imbarco
luggage	i bagagli
plane	l'aereo
transit lounge	la sala d'attesa

ABBREVIATIONS

AA (Assistenza Automobilistica)	Automobile Association
ac (anno corrente)	this year
AC (Avanti Cristo)	BC (Before Christ)
ANAS	National Road Board
ANSA	Italian News Agency
CC (Carabinieri)	military police
cm	this month
cp	postcode
DC (Dopo Cristo)	AD (Anno Domini)
ENIT	Tourist Information Office
FS (Ferrovie dello Stato)	National Railway
L.; l	lire (local currency)
ONU	UN
PP	parcel post
RAI	Italian Broadcasting Network
S.	Saint
SS (Santi; Santissimi)	holy
sec	century
SRL; Srl; Spa	Pty Ltd
UE (Unione Europea)	EU (European Union)

TRAIN

Travelling by train in Italy is simple, cheap and usually efficient. After you have bought a ticket, you must validate it (vidimare) in one of the yellow machines found at the entrance to platforms.

SIGNS

STAZIONE FERROVIARIA	TRAIN STATION
BINARIO	PLATFORM

Where is the nearest station?	Dov'è la stazione più vicina?
Is it a/an ... train?	È un treno ...?
direct	diretto
express	espresso; rapido
local	locale
fast	super rapido; TEE
Is this the right platform for ...?	È questo il binario per ...?
Do I have to change trains/ platforms?	Devo cambiare treno/binario?
Passengers must change trains/ platforms.	I passeggeri devono cambiare treni/binari.
The train leaves from platform number ...	Il treno parte dal binario numero ...
dining car	il vagone ristorante
sleeping car	il vagone letto
ticket collector	la/il controllore; la/il bigliettaia/o
train	il treno

TRAIN TRAVEL

Intercity (IC) trains run between the major cities in Italy.
There are several types of trains in Italy:

regionale	usually stops at all stations and can be very slow
interregionale	runs between the regions
diretto	indicates you do not need to change trains to reach the final destination
espresso	stops only at major stations

On the Train

Is that seat taken?	**È occupato quel posto?**
Do you mind if I smoke?	**Le dispiace se fumo?**
Do you mind if I open/close the window?	**Le dispiace se apro/fermo il finestrino?**
I'm sorry, I can't find the ticket.	**Sono spiacente, ma non trovo il biglietto.**

DID YOU KNOW ... Some say pasta was invented by the Chinese and introduced to Italy by Marco Polo in the 13th century. Others believe it was introduced by the Arabs who ruled Sicily in the Middle Ages. And there is mention of a mixture resembling pasta in a book on cooking from 1st century AD Rome. Types of pasta were also known in Ancient Greece.

BUS & TRAM

Buses are usually slightly cheaper than trains and can get you to more out-of-the-way places. You should make reservations in high tourist season and for long trips.

SIGN	
FERMATA DELL'AUTOBUS/ DEL TRAM	BUS/TRAM STOP

Where is the bus/tram stop?	Dov'è la fermata dell'autobus/ del tram?
Which bus goes to ...?	Quale autobus va a ...?
Does this bus go to ...?	Questo autobus va a ...?
How often do buses/trams pass by?	Ogni quanto tempo passano gli autobus/i tram?
What time is the ... bus?	A che ora passa ... autobus?
next	il prossimo
first	il primo
last	l'ultimo
When's the bus/tram for ...?	A che ora passa l'autobus/ il tram per ...?
the beach	la spiaggia
the city centre	il centro
the station	la stazione
Do you stop at ...?	Si ferma a ...?
Could you let me know when we get to ...?	Mi può dire quando arriviamo a ...?
I want to get off!	Vorrei scendere!
local/city bus	autobus; pullman
long-distance bus	corriera

METRO

Milan, Naples and Rome are the only cities in Italy which have metros.

SIGNS	
METRÒ	METRO/UNDERGROUND
USCITA	WAY OUT
DA QUESTA PARTE PER ...	THIS WAY TO ...

Which line takes me to ...?	**Qual è la linea per andare a ...?**
What's the next station?	**Qual è la prossima stazione?**
Where do I/we change for ...?	**Dove devo/dobbiamo cambiare per ...?**

small change	**gli spiccioli**
destination	**la destinazione**
line	**la linea**
ticket machine	**la biglietteria automatica**

TAXI

SIGN	
POSTEGGIO TAXI	TAXI STAND

Are you free?	**È libero?**
Please take me ...	**Mi porti ..., per piacere.**
to this address	**a questo indirizzo**
to the airport	**all'aeroporto**
to the city centre	**in centro**
to the railway station	**alla stazione ferroviaria**

GETTING AROUND

How much is it to go to ...?	Quanto costa andare a ...?
Does the price include luggage?	La tariffa comprende anche i bagagli?
Can you take five people?	Può portare cinque persone?
Do you have change for ... lira?	Ha da cambiare ... lire?
Is this the most direct route?	È questa la strada più breve?
This is not the way to ...	Questa non è la strada per ...

Instructions

Here is fine, thankyou.	Qui va benissimo, grazie.
The next corner, please.	Al prossimo angolo, per favore.
Keep going!	Avanti!
The next street to the left/right.	È la prossima strada a sinistra/destra.
Stop here!	Si fermi qua!
Please hurry.	Può accelerare, per favore?
Please slow down.	Può rallentare, per favore?
Please wait here.	Mi aspetti qui.
How much do I owe you?	Quanto Le devo?

USEFUL WORDS & PHRASES

The (train) is delayed/ cancelled.	Il (treno) è in ritardo/ cancellato.
There is a delay of ... minutes/hours.	Ci sarà un ritardo di ... minuti/ore.
Services will be reduced.	La circolazione sarà ridotta.
How long does the trip take?	Quanto dura il viaggio?
Is it a direct route?	È un itinerario diretto?
Excuse me. (pushing through a crowd)	Permesso.

boat	la barca; la nave; il battello
driver	l'autista
ferry	il traghetto
to hitchhike	fare l'autostop
hydroplane	l'aliscafo
motor boat	il motoscafo
port	il porto
visa	il visto
waiting room	la sala d'aspetto

QUESTIONS

The easiest way to turn a statement in to question is to just change the intonation of your voice. (See page 40.)

CAR

Cars are now banned from most city centres in an effort to reduce pollution and damage to buildings. Roads in Italy range from toll-paying autostrade (freeways) to serviceable strade statali (state roads) to picturesque strade provinciali (regional roads).

Where can I rent a car?	Dove posso noleggiare una macchina?
How much is it daily/weekly?	Quanto costa al giorno/alla settimana?
Does that include insurance?	È compresa l'assicurazione?
Does that include mileage?	È compreso il costo per chilometro?
Where's the next petrol station?	Dov'è la prossima stazione di servizio?
I want ... litres of petrol/gas.	Vorrei ... litri (di benzina).
Please fill the tank.	Il pieno, per favore.
Please check the oil, water and air.	Può controllare l'olio, l'acqua e la pressione dei pneumatici, per favore?
How long can I park here?	Per quanto tempo posso parcheggiare qui?
Does this road lead to ...?	Questa strada porta a ...?

GETTING AROUND

ROAD SIGNS

ACCESSO PERMANENTE	24-HOUR ACCESS
ATTENZIONE	CAUTION
AUTOSTRADA	FREEWAY
DARE LA PRECEDENZA	GIVE WAY
DEVIAZIONE	DETOUR
DIVIETO DI ACCESSO	NO ENTRY
DIVIETO DI SORPASSO	DO NOT OVERTAKE
LAVORI IN CORSO	ROADWORKS
PARCHEGGIO	PARKING
PASSAGGIO PEDONALE	PEDESTRIANS
PERICOLO GENERICO	DANGER
RALLENTARE	SLOW DOWN
SENSO UNICO	ONE WAY
SOSTA VIETATA	NO PARKING
STOP; ALT	STOP
USCITA	EXIT

air (for tyres)	l'aria
battery	la batteria
brakes	i freni
breath test	l'alcoltest
clutch	la frizione
diesel	il gasolio
driver's licence	la patente (di guida)
engine	il motore
garage	il garage; l'autorimessa
headlights	gli anabbaglianti
high beam lights	gli abbaglianti
indicator	la spia
leaded/unleaded	con/senza piombo
main road	la strada principale
motorway	l'autostrada

oil	l'olio
puncture	la foratura
radiator	il radiatore
road map	la carta stradale
seatbelt	la cintura di sicurezza
speed limit	il limite di velocità
super	il super
tail lights	i fanalini di coda
tyre/s	la/le gomma/e
windscreen	il parabrezza

TIP BOX

Don't park your car where there's a sign saying **Zona Rimozione** This is a towaway zone.

Car Problems

SIGNS	
STAZIONE DI SERVIZIO	PETROL STATION
MECCANICO	MECHANIC
RIPARAZIONI	REPAIRS

I need a mechanic.	Ho bisogno di un meccanico.
What make is it?	Che tipo di macchina è?
My car's broken down at ...	La mia auto si è fermata a ...
The battery is flat.	La batteria è scarica.
The radiator is leaking.	Il radiatore perde acqua.
I have a flat tyre.	Ho la gomma bucata.
It's overheating.	Si sta surriscaldando.
It's not working.	Non funziona.
I've lost my car keys.	Ho perso le chiavi della macchina.
I've run out of petrol.	Ho esaurito la benzina.

DID YOU KNOW ... Some slang words for car are **un carro; una carriola** (a slow car), **una bomba** (a fast car) and **una barca** (a big and slow car).

BICYCLE

Where can I hire a bicycle?	Dove posso noleggiare una bicicletta?
How much is it for an hour/day?	Quanto costa all'ora/al giorno?
Where can I leave my bike?	Dove posso lasciare la mia bicicletta?
Can I take my bike on the train/bus?	Posso portare la bicicletta sul treno/sull'autobus?
Where is a good bike repairer?	Dove trovo un bravo meccanico per biciclette?
Is this road OK for bikes?	Si può percorrere in bici questa strada?
Is there a cycling track?	C'è una pista per le biciclette?

bike	una bici
bicycle pump	una pompa
chain	la catena
frame	il telaio
handlebars	il manubrio
helmet	il casco
motorbike	un motociclo; una moto
mountain bike	una bici da montagna; una mountain bike
padlock	un lucchetto
puncture	una foratura
racing bike	una bici da corsa
seat	la sella
spokes	i raggi
wheel	la ruota
wheel hub	il mozzo

See also Cycling, page 207.

ACCOMMODATION

SIGNS

PENSIONE	GUESTHOUSE
ALBERGO	HOTEL
OSTELLO DELLA GIOVENTÙ	YOUTH HOSTEL
VILLA; CASOLARE	VILLA
LOCANDA	BUDGET HOTEL
CAMPING; CAMPEGGIO	CAMPING GROUND

FINDING ACCOMMODATION

I'm looking for ...	Sto cercando ...
Where is a ... hotel?	Dov'è un albergo ...?
cheap	a basso prezzo; economico
good	buono
nearby	vicino
clean	pulito
What is the address?	Qual è l'indirizzo?
Could you write the address down, please?	Mi può scrivere l'indirizzo, per favore?

For phrases on camping, see page 193.

DID YOU KNOW ... By law, you must have a **permesso di sogiorno**, from police stations, if you plan to stay at the same address for more than a week. Tourists who stay in hotel are not required to do this.

ACCOMMODATION

BOOKING AHEAD

Do you have any rooms free?	Ha delle camere libere?
I'm not sure how long I'm staying.	Non sono sicura/o quanto tempo resterò.
My name is ...	Il mio nome è ...
I'll be arriving at ...	Arriverò il ...

I'd like ...	Vorrei ...
a bed	un letto
a single room	una camera singola
a room with twin beds	una doppia a due letti
a room with a double bed	una doppia matrimoniale
to share a room	dividere una stanza

I want a room with a ...	Vorrei una camera con ...
bathroom	bagno
shower	doccia
television	televisore
view	vista
window	finestra

THEY MAY SAY ...

Ha un documento d'identità?	Do you have identification?
La sua tessera, per favore.	Your identification card, please.
Mi dispiace, è completo.	Sorry, we're full.
Non c'è posto.	There are no vacancies.
Quanto tempo vuole restare?	How long will you be staying?
Per quante notti?	How many nights?
Costa ... al giorno/ per persona.	It's ... per day/per person.

ACCOMMODATION

It must be ...	Dev'essere ...
quiet	silenziosa
light	luminosa

I'm going to stay for ...	Resto per ...
one day	un giorno
two days	due giorni
one week	una settimana

ACCOMMODATION

CHECKING IN

I have a reservation.	Ho una prenotazione.
How much is it per night/ per person?	Quanto costa per una notte/ per persona?
May I see it?	Posso vederla?
Are there any others?	Ce ne sono altre?
Are there any cheaper rooms?	Ci sono altre camere che costano di meno?
May I see the bathroom?	Posso vedere il bagno?
Is there a reduction for students/children?	C'è uno sconto per studenti/ bambini?
Do you charge for the baby?	Quanto paga il bambino?
Does the price include breakfast?	La colazione è compresa nel prezzo?
It's fine, I'll take it.	Va bene, la prendo.

REQUESTS & QUERIES

The key for room ..., please.	La chiave per la camera ..., per piacere.
Please wake me up at ...	Mi svegli all'/alle ..., per favore.
The room needs to be cleaned.	La camera dovrebbe essere pulita.

DID YOU KNOW ...

The usual way to form an ethnic adjective is to add the endings -ese or -ano to the name of the country, eg 'Italian' is italiano 'French' is francese. Some, however, do not follow this rule:

German	tedesco
Polish	polacco

Please change the sheets.	Cambi le lenzuola, per piacere.
Can you give me an extra blanket, please?	Può darmi un'altra coperta, per piacere?
Is there a lift?	C'è un ascensore?
Where is the bathroom?	Dov'è il bagno?
Is there hot water all day?	C'è l'acqua calda tutto il giorno?
Do you have a safe?	C'è una cassetta di sicurezza?
Is there a laundry?	C'è una lavanderia?
Can I use the kitchen?	Posso usare la cucina?
Do you change money here?	Si possono cambiare i soldi in questo albergo?
Can I ask for meals to be served in my room?	Potete servire i pasti in camera?
Do I leave my key at reception?	Devo lasciare la chiave al banco?
Is there a message board?	C'è una bacheca per i messaggi?
Can I leave a message?	Posso lasciare un messaggio?
Is there a message for me?	C'è un messaggio per me?
Can I receive mail here?	Posso ricevere posta qui?

ACCOMMODATION

COMPLAINTS

I can't open/close the window.
Non posso aprire/chiudere la finestra.

I've locked myself out of my room.
Mi sono chiusa/o fuori dalla mia camera.

The toilet won't flush.
Il gabinetto non funziona.

I don't like this room.
Questa camera non mi piace.

CE, CI = CH

Remember that c is hard as in 'cat' before a, o, u and h but soft as in 'church' before e and i:

Hello. Ciao (chow)
Hot. Caldo (kull-doh)

ACCOMMODATION

It's too ...	È troppo ...
small	piccola
noisy	rumorosa
dark	scura
expensive	cara
cold	fredda
hot	calda

PAPERWORK

address	indirizzo
age	età
birth certificate	certificato di nascita
border	frontiera
car owner's title	titolo di proprietà
car registration	registrazione
customs	dogana
date of birth	data di nascita
divorced	divorziata/o
driver's licence	patente (di guida)
form	modulo
identification (card)	(carta d') identiftà
immigration	immigrazione
marital status	stato civile
married	sposata/o
name	nome
nationality	nazionalità
passport	passaporto
passport number	numero del passaporto
place of birth	luogo di nascita
profession	professione
reason for travel	motivi di viaggio
religion	religione
sex	sesso
single	nubile (f)/celibe (m)
visa	visto consolare

CHECKING OUT

When is checkout time?	A che ora si deve lasciar libera la camera?
I am/We are leaving now.	Parto/Partiamo adesso.
I'd like to pay the bill.	Vorrei pagare il conto.
Can I pay by credit card?	Posso pagare con la carta di credito?
May I leave my backpack at reception until tonight/ tomorrow?	Posso lasciare il mio zaino a reception fino a stasera/domani?
Please call a taxi for me.	Mi chiama un taxi, per piacere?

RENTING

I'm here about the room for rent.	Sono qui per la camera che date in affitto.
I'd like to rent the room for ...	Vorrei prendere la camera in affitto per ...
I'm looking for an apartment to let for ...	Cerco un appartamento da prendere in affitto per un periodo di ...
I'm looking for something close ...	Sto cercando un posto vicino ...
to the city centre	al centro
to the beach	alla spiaggia
to the railway station	alla stazione (ferroviaria)
Is there anything cheaper?	C'è qualcosa di meno caro?
Is there anything better?	C'è qualcosa di meglio?
Could I see it?	Potrei vederla?
How much is it per week/ month?	Quant'è alla settimana/ al mese?
Do you require a deposit?	Richiede una caparra/ un acconto?

ACCOMMODATION

estate agent	un agente immobiliare
furnished	ammobiliato
heating	il riscaldamento
landlady/landlord	la/il proprietaria/proprietario di casa
lease	una locazione
tenant	un'inquilina/un inquilino
owner	un proprietario

LOOKING FOR ...

I'm looking for ...	Sto cercando ...
the art gallery	la galleria d'arte (mainly contemporary art); la pinacoteca (fine art)
a bank	la banca
the church	la chiesa
the city centre	il centro (città)
the consulate	il consolato
the ... embassy	l'ambasciata ...
my hotel	il mio albergo
the market	il mercato
the museum	il museo
the police	la polizia
the post office	la posta; l'ufficio postale
a public toilet	i gabinetti; i servizi igienici
a restaurant	un ristorante
the telephone centre	un centro telefonico
the tourist information office	l'Ente del Turismo
What time does it open?	A che ora apre?
What time does it close?	A che ora chiude?

For directions, see Getting Around, page 57.

DID YOU KNOW ... When a number ends with the suffix -ina it indicates an approximation. So ottantina means 'about 80'; quarantina means 'about 40', etc.

STREET LIFE

What's this?	Cos'è questo?
What's happening?	Cosa sta succedendo?
What's happened?	Cosa è successo?
What's she/he doing?	Cosa sta facendo?
What do you charge?	Quanto fa pagare?
How much is it?	Quanto costa?
Can I have (one), please?	Me ne dà (una/o), per cortesia?

street	la strada
festival	il festival
street demonstration	la manifestazione
newspaper kiosk	l'edicola
tobacco kiosk	la tabaccheria

The People

artist	l'artista
clown	il pagliaccio
crowd	una folla
beggar	il mendicante
busker	la suonatrice/il suonatore girovaga/o
flower seller	la/il fioraia/o
fortune teller	l'indovina/o
magician	la/il maga/o
performing artist	l'artista ambulante
street performer	l'artista di strada
portrait sketcher	la/il ritrattista; la/il caricaturista
street-seller	la/il venditrice/venditore ambulante

See page 156 for things to buy.

AROUND TOWN

AT THE BANK

Italy's currency is the lira (plural: lire). The smallest useful denomination is L100 and the largest is L100,000. Credit cards can be used in ATM machines to obtain cash 24 hours a day, as long as you have a PIN number.

Can I change money here?	Si cambia denaro qui?
I want to exchange some money/travellers' cheques.	Vorrei cambiare del denaro/ dei travellers' cheques.
What is the exchange rate?	Quant'è il cambio?
How many lire to the dollar?	A quanto si cambia il dollaro?
Please write it down.	Può scriverlo, per favore?
What is your commission?	Qual è la vostra commissione?
Where do I sign?	Dove devo firmare?
Can I have smaller notes?	Mi può dare banconote più piccole?
Can I transfer money overseas?	Posso mandare denaro all'estero?
The automatic teller has swallowed my credit card.	Il Bancomat ha trattenuto la mia carta di credito.
Can I use my credit card to withdraw some money?	Si può usare la carta di credito per fare prelievi?
Can I have money transferred here from my bank?	Posso trasferire del denaro dalla mia banca a questa?
How long will it take to arrive?	Quanto tempo ci vorrà per il trasferimento?
Has my money arrived yet?	È arrivato il mio denaro?

AROUND TOWN

DID YOU KNOW ... In the 4th century BC about 40 languages were spoken in Italy and there were several written languages. Almost all gave way to Latin as the language of the Romans triumphed.

account	il conto corrente
ATM	il Bancomat
ATM card	la tessera bancomat
bank draft	una cambiale
cashier	la cassa
coins	le monete
credit card	una carta di credito
deposit	il deposito
exchange	il cambio
identification	l'identificazione
loose change	gli spiccioli
signature	la firma
withdrawal	un prelievo

NO I, NO YOU

You don't need to use the subject pronoun in Italian as it is understood from the verb form. You can use it for extra emphasis, however, at the end of a sentence:

Che fai tu?
(lit: what are you doing (you?)

AT THE POST OFFICE

Italy's postal service can sometimes be unreliable – occasionally letters will take longer than normal to arrive at their destination. So, take this into account when sending letters or parcels home.

I'd like to send ...	Vorrei mandare ...
an aerogram	un'aerogramma
a box	una scatola
a letter	una lettera
a parcel	un pacchetto
a postcard	una cartolina
a telegram	un telegramma
I'd like some stamps, please.	Vorrei dei francobolli, per favore.
How much to send this to ...?	Quant'è l'affrancatura per ...?
Where is the poste restante section?	Dov'è il fermoposta?
Is there any mail for me?	C'è posta per me?

WHERE AM I ?

Everywhere:

Vicolo (V.lo)	alley; lane
Viale (V.le)	avenue; boulevard
Borgo (B.go)	district
Corso (C.so)	main street; avenue
Via (V.)	road; street
Piazza (P.za)	square
Largo (L.go)	little square

In Venice:

calle	street
campo	square with a church
campiello	square without a church
fondamenta; riva	street

In Genoa:

carrugio	little street

In Medieval Cities:

contrà; contrada	street

air mail	via aerea
envelope	una busta
mailbox	la cassetta postale
parcel	un pacchetto
postcode	il codice postale
poste restante	il fermo posta
printed matter	le stampe
registered mail	(la posta) raccomandata
insured mail	(la posta) assicurata
surface mail	la posta ordinaria
express	espressa

See page 118 for how to write letters.

AROUND TOWN

TELECOMMUNICATIONS
Telephone

There are different types of public phones in Italy. Some just take coins but others may take tokens (gettoni) or phone cards (carte telefoniche). These can be bought from post offices, tobacconists, newspaper stands and vending machines.

I want to ring ...	Vorrei telefonare a [+ city]/ in [+ country] ...
The number is ...	Il numero è ...
I want to speak for three minutes.	Voglio parlare per tre minuti.
How much does a three-minute call cost?	Quanto costa una telefonata di tre minuti?
How much does each extra minute cost?	Quanto costa ogni minuto in più?
Is there a cheap rate for evenings and weekends?	Le chiamate serali e fine-settimanali sono a tariffa ridotta?
What's the area code for ...?	Qual è il prefisso per ...?
I'd like to make a reverse-charges phone call.	Vorrei fare una chiamata a carico del destinatario.
Is it OK to use my mobile phone here?	Posso usare il telefonino qui?
Where can I rent a mobile phone?	Dove posso noleggiare un telefonino?
dial tone	un segnale (acustico)
directory assistance	gli informazioni telefoniche
operator	la/il centralinista; l'operatore/l'operatrice
phone book	l'elenco telefonico
phone booth	una cabina telefonica

phone card	una carta telefonica
telephone	il telefono
telephone number	il numero di telefono
telephone office	i telefoni pubblici
telephone token	un gettone

Making a Call

Hello!	Pronto!
It's ...	Sono ...
May I speak with ...?	Posso parlare con ...?
Is ... there?	C'è ...?
I'd like to speak to Mr Bertuzzi.	Vorrei parlare con il signor Bertuzzi.
Who am I speaking to?	Con chi parlo?
What time will she/he be back?	A che ora sarà di ritorno?
I'll call at ...	Telefonerò all'/alle ...
Yes, please tell her/him I called.	Sì, dille/digli che ho telefonato, per favore?
No thanks, I'll call back later.	No grazie, richiamerò più tardi.
It's engaged.	La linea è occupata.
I've been cut off.	È caduta la linea.

AROUND TOWN

THEY MAY SAY ...

Chi è?
   Who is it?
Un attimo, gliela/glielo passo.
   Just a minute, I'll put her/him on.
Mi dispiace, non c'è in questo momento.
   I'm sorry, she's/he's not here right now.
Desidera lasciare un messaggio?
   May I take a message?
Lasci un messaggio sulla segreteria (automatica).
   Leave a message on the answering machine.

Fax & Email

Faxes are a very expensive mode of communication in Italy. Telegrams are also expensive but are a sure way of having messages delivered within a day.

I want to send a fax.	Vorrei spedire un fax.
How much per page?	Quanto costa per pagina?
Where can I use email?	Dove posso usare l'Email?
Where can I use the Internet?	Dove posso usare l'Internet?
fax number	numero di fax
telex number	numero di telex

COMMON EXPRESSIONS

OK	D'accordo; OK.
Of course!	(Di) Certo; Certamente; Naturalmente!
Sure!	Come no; Di certo!
Good/Great!	Bene; Benissimo; Ben fatto; Brava/o!
Good luck!	Buona fortuna!
Good idea!	Buona idea!
Let's go!	Andiamo!
Go on!	Forza; Dai; Su!
Come on!	Via; Su; Forza!
Hurry up!	Affrettati!; Sbrigati!
Ready?	Sei pronta/o?
I'm ready.	Sono pronta/o.
See you.	Ci vediamo!
What's up?	Che c'è?
Doesn't matter.	Non importa; (Non) Fa niente.
Don't worry.	Non preoccuparti!
No problem.	Nessun problema.
It's nothing.	Non è niente; Non c'è di che.

AROUND TOWN

SIGHTSEEING

Do you have a local map?	Ha una pianta locale?
What are the main attractions?	Quali sono le maggiori attrazioni?
What's that?	Cos'è?
How old is it?	Quanti anni ha?; Di che epoca è?
Can I take photographs?	Posso fare fotografie?
What time does it open/close?	A che ora apre/chiude?

AROUND TOWN

Is there an admission charge?	C'è un prezzo d'ingresso?
Is there a discount for ...?	C'è uno sconto per ...?
children	i bambini
students	gli studenti
pensioners	i pensionati

AROUND TOWN

SIGNS

VIETATO CONSUMARE CIBI O BEVANDE	NO EATING OR DRINKING ALLOWED
APERTO/CHIUSO	OPEN/CLOSED
CALDO/FREDDO	HOT/COLD
GABINETTI; SERVIZI PUBBLICI	TOILETS
INFORMAZIONI	INFORMATION
INGRESSO GRATUITO	FREE ADMISSION
INGRESSO/ENTRATA	ENTRANCE
NON CALPESTARE L'ERBA	KEEP OFF THE GRASS
RISERVATO; PRENOTATO	RESERVED
PROIBITO; VIETATO	PROHIBITED
SPINGERE	PUSH
TELEFONO	TELEPHONE
TIRARE	PULL
USCITA	EXIT
USCITA DI SICUREZZA	EMERGENCY EXIT
VIETATO FOTOGRAFARE	DO NOT TAKE PHOTOGRAPHS
VIETATO FUMARE	NO SMOKING
VIETATO L'INGRESSO	NO ADMITTANCE
VIETATO TOCCARE	DO NOT TOUCH
VIETATO USARE FLASH	DO NOT USE FLASH
VIETATO/NON ENTRARE	NO ENTRY

ancient	antica/o
archaeological	archeologica/o
arches	i portici
art gallery	la galleria d'arte; la pinacoteca
beach	la spiaggia
bell tower	il campanile
building	l'edificio
castle	il castello
cathedral	la cattedrale; il duomo
caves	le grotte
church	la chiesa

UNA/UN

The feminine indefinite article , una, changes to un' before a noun beginning with a vowel. The masculine indefinite article, un, changes to uno before nouns beginning with st, z, gh, ps, x and y.

city walls	le mura
concert hall	la sala per concerti; il teatro comunale
convent	il convent
dome	un duomo
fountain	la fontana
gardens	i giardini
library	la biblioteca
main square	la piazza principale
monastery	il monastero
monument	il monumento
mosque	la moschea
old city	la cittadella
opera house	il teatro dell'opera
palace	il palazzo
park	il parco
ruins	le rovine
stadium	lo stadio
statues	le statue
synagogue	la sinagoga scola in Venice)
temple	il tempio
zoo	lo zoo; il giardino zoologico

AROUND TOWN

TRAVELLERS' LATIN

Inscriptions & Dedications

While a knowledge of Italian will help you in your travels through the Italy of today, it is a knowledge of Latin which will help you to understand the Italy of the past. Although Latin is a far more complex language than modern Italian, a knowledge of a few words and phrases will enable you to make sense of simple inscriptions and dedications you'll come across when you're sightseeing.

Ancient Roman inscriptions are often in a heavily abbreviated form, with words and abbreviations separated by a dot (·). The inscription on the front of the Pantheon, for example, reads:

M · AGRIPPA · L · F · COS · TERTIVM · FECIT
Marcus Agrippa, Luci filius, consul tertium, fecit.
Marcus Agrippa, son of Lucius, consul for the third time, built it.

Some of the most common abbreviations found on Roman inscriptions are:

AED	*aedilis*	aedile
ANN	*annos; anni*	years
COL	*colonia*	colony
COS	*consul*	consul
COSS	*consules*	consuls
C R	*cives Romani*	Roman citizens
CVR	*curavit*	attended to; took care of
D	*dat; dedit*	he gives; he gave
DEC	*decreto*	by decree
DED	*dedit*	gave
D M	*dis manibus*	to the spirits of the dead
EX S C	*ex senatus consulto*	by a decree of the Senate
F	*fecit; faciundum; filius; filia*	did; to be done; son; daughter
FID	*fidelis*	faithful

TRAVELLERS' LATIN

IMP	*imperator*	general; emperor
I O M	*Iuppiter Optimus Maximus*	Jupiter Best and Greatest
P C	*Patres conscripti*	senators
P(ONT) M(AX)	*Pontifex Maximus*	chief priest
P R	*Populus Romanus*	the People of Rome
R	*Romanus*	Roman
REST	*restituit*	restored
R P	*res publica*	state; republic
S C	*senatus consulto*	by decree of the Senate
S P Q R	*Senatus Populusque Romanus*	The Senate and the People of Rome

Names

Roman names are often abbreviated. Some of the most common are:

AVG	Augustus		SP	Spurius
L	Lucius		CN	Gnaeus
Q	Quintus		MAM	Mamius
A	Aulus		T	Titus
M	Marcus		D	Decimus
S	Servius		P	Publius
C	Gaius		TI	Tiberius
M'	Manius			

Roman Emperors

The Romans expressed dates in one of two ways; either by giving the number of years since the founding of the city (tradition-ally dated to 753 BC), or by giving the names of the two consuls for that year.

TRAVELLERS' LATIN

The following list of emperors and the years of their rule will help you to date ancient Roman inscriptions.

AUGUSTUS	27 BC-AD 14
TIBERIUS	AD 14-37
GAIUS (CALIGULA)	37-41
CLAUDIUS	41-54
NERO	54-68
GALBA	68-69
OTHO	69
VITELLIUS	69
VESPASIAN	69-79
TITUS	79-81
DOMITIAN	81-96
NERVA	96-98
TRAJAN	98-117
HADRIAN	117-38
ANTONINUS PIUS	138-61
MARCUS AURELIUS	161-80
COMMODUS	180-92
SEPTIMIUS SEVERUS	193-211
CARACALLA	212-17
ELAGABALUS	218-22
SEVERUS ALEXANDER	222-35

AROUND TOWN

Roman Numerals

The ancient Romans did not use our familiar Arabic system of numbers (1, 2, 3 and so on). Instead they used a system of letters and symbols. You will see Roman numerals used on ancient tombs and milestones as well as on statues, churches, bridges, and other monuments from later periods.

I	1	IIII; IV	4	VII	7
II	2	V	5	VIII	8
III	3	VI	6	IX	9

TRAVELLERS' LATIN

X	10	LXX	70
XI	11	LXXX	80
XII	12	XC	90
XIII	13	C	100
XIV	14	CC	200
XV	15	CCC	300
XVI	16	CCCC	400
XVII	17	D	500
XVIII	18	DC	600
XIX	19	DCC	700
XX	20	DCCC	800
L	50	DCCCC; CM	900
LX	60	M	1000

You may already be familiar with Roman numerals but sometimes it's difficult to decipher the bigger numbers. There are some rules which can help you to work them out. In general, a smaller number to the left of a larger number should be subtracted from that number (eg IX = 9; XL = 40), but a smaller number to the right of a larger number should be added to that number (eg XI = 11; LX = 60). The year 1998, for example, is made up of:

1000	M
900	DCCCC
90	XC
8	VIII

It would be expressed in Roman numerals as MDCCCCXCVIII or MCMXCVIII. Other examples are:

MDCCCCLXXXV	1985	MDCCIII	1703
MCCCXLII	1342	DXXIX	529

CROSSWORD – AROUND TOWN

AROUND TOWN

Across

1. Not here. Please leave a message
3. The place to go for a visa.
4. If you lose it all, your only alternative may be to become one
6. You'll need one if you have foreign money

Down

2. Subterranean, sometimes blue, always rocky
5. Would you cross one with your eyes closed?
7. Smiling on the outside...funny man
8. It's where the action is in town.

Answers on page 324

GOING OUT

WHERE TO GO?

The entertainment sections of local newspapers will tell you what's on, where and when.

What's there to do in the evenings?	Cosa si fa di sera?; Come vi divertite la sera?
Where can I find out what's on?	Come ci si informa su quel che c'è in programma?
Is there a local entertainment guide?	C'è una guida agli spettacoli locale?
What's on tonight?	Che c'è in programma stasera?
What are you doing tonight?	Cosa fai (sg)/fate (pl) stasera?
What are you doing this weekend?	Cosa fai (sg)/fate (pl) questo finesettimana?
I feel like going to ...	Ho voglia di andare ...
the cinema	al cinema
the opera	all'opera
the theatre	al teatro
a bar	al bar
a café	al caffè
a concert/a gig	a un concerto
a disco	a una discoteca
a nightclub	in un nightclub
a restaurant	in un ristorante
I feel like ...	Ho voglia di ...
a stroll	fare una passeggiata
going dancing	andare a ballare
something to eat	fare uno spuntino
a drink	bere qualcosa

INVITES

Do you want to go out tonight?	Vuoi uscire stasera?
Do you know a good restaurant?	Conosci un buon ristorante?
Would you like to go for a drink/meal?	Vuoi (sg)/Volete (pl) andare a prendere qualcosa?
It's on me.	Pago io; Offro io.
We're having a party. Would you like to come?	Facciamo una festa. Vuoi (sg) Volete (pl) venire?

Responding to Invites

Yes, I'd love to.	Sì, mi piacerebbe; Sì, lo gradirei.
Sure! Where shall we go?	Sì, perché no. Dove andiamo
Great!	Come no!
No, I'm afraid I can't. What about tomorrow?	No, temo di no. Domani che ne dici?
Tomorrow I can't.	Domani non posso.

NIGHTCLUBS & BARS

Nightclubs and discos are more popular during winter. Som even close down over the summer months.

Are there any discos/clubs?	Ci sono delle discoteche/ dei clubs?
Shall we check out the local club scene?	Perché non saggiare la vita notturna locale?
What type of music do they play?	Che tipo di musica suonano dànno?
What time do I/we have to be there?	A che ora devo/dobbiamo esserci?
Are drinks expensive?	Sono alti i prezzi delle bevande?
What time does it shut?	A che ora chiude?
What's the best night?	Qual è la migliore serata?

GOING OUT

there a women-only night?	**C'è una serata dedicata esclusivamente alle donne?**
there a door charge?	**L'ingresso è libero?**
ow much is it to get in?	**Quanto si paga?**
o you want to dance?	**Ti va di ballare?**
m a terrible dancer.	**Faccio pena.**
can't dance.	**Non so ballare.**

Who's the best DJ?	**Chi è il miglior DJ?**
What stuff does she/he play?	**Che musica suona?**
What time does she/he come on?	**A che ora comincia?**
Does she/he play really cool records?	**Suona dischi proprio forti?**

PEOPLE ARE PEOPLE

Did you check out that girl/guy!	**Hai adocchiato quella/ quello?**
She/He is ...!	**È ...!**
You're so ...!	**Sei così ...!**
amazing	**stupenda/o**
bad/nasty	**brutta/o** (literally 'ugly')
crazy	**pazza/o**
cool	**forte; arrapante**
gorgeous	**figa/o; bona/o**
sick	**sconvolgente**
with it/cool person	**figa/o; fichissima/o**
a good guy	**un figlio (di puttana)** (lit: 'son of a bitch')
annoying person	**rompiballe; scassacazzi**
awkward person	**imbranata/o; intoppata/o**
boring person	**borsa; palla; piaga; pizza; pippa**
cool person	**draga/o; druga/o; ganza/o; spada; toga/o**
stupid/idiotic person	**gnocca/o; bamba; micca/o; biscotto; lince; tonno; pesce**

GOING OUT

ARRANGING TO MEET

What time shall we meet?	A che ora ci vediamo?
Where shall we meet?	Dove ci vediamo?
Let's meet at …	Facciamo alle …
OK. I'll see you then.	Va bene. Ci vediamo allora.
OK!	D'accordo!
I'll come over at …	Vengo/Sarò là alle …
I'll pick you up at …	Ti (sg)/Vi (pl) vengo a prendere alle …
I'll try to make it.	Cercherò di farcela.
If I'm not there by …, don't wait for me.	Se non ci sono entro le …, non aspettarmi.
I'll join you later. Where will you be?	Ti (sg)/Vi (pl) raggiungerò più tardi. Dove ti troverai (sg)/ vi troverete (pl) ?
See you later/tomorrow.	A più tardi; A domani.
Sorry I'm late.	Scusi. Sono in ritardo.

AFTERWARDS

I had a great day/evening.	Mi sono proprio divertita/o oggi/stasera.
It was nice talking to you.	Abbiamo fatto una bella chiacchierata.
I have to get going now.	Adesso devo andare.
Hope to see you again soon.	Spero di rivederti presto.
Next time it's on me.	**La prossima volta offro io.**
See you soon.	**A presto.**
We must do this again sometime.	**Bisogna ripetere questa esperienza presto.**

COMBOS

The combination **gli** is pronounced as the 'lli' in million. So **Dirgli!** (Tell him!) is pronounced *deerlyee*.

GOING OUT

DATING & ROMANCE
Breaking the Ice

Would you like ...? | Prendi ...?
a drink | qualcosa da bere
a cigarette | una sigaretta
something to eat | qualcosa da mangiare

What would you like? | Cosa prendi?
What's your name? | Come ti chiami?
My name's ... | Mi chiamo ...

Do you mind if I sit here? | Posso sedermi qui?
Are you here alone? | Sei qui da solo?
Do you have a girlfriend/boyfriend? | Hai una ragazza/un ragazzo?
Here's my telephone number. | Ecco il mio numero di telefono.

CLASSIC PICK-UP LINES

Do you want to dance? | Vuoi ballare?
Do you have a light? | Hai d'accendere?
Do you have a cigarette? | C'hai mica una svampa/svapora?

Do you come here often? | Vieni spesso qua?
Let's get some fresh air? | Andiamo a prendere un po' d'aria fresca?

May I take you home? | Posso accompagnarti a casa?
Do you want to come to my place? | Vuoi venire a casa mia?

GOING OUT

CLASSIC REJECTIONS

I'm waiting for my girlfriend/boyfriend.	Sto aspettando la mia ragazza/il mio ragazzo.
You're not my type.	Non sei il mio tipo.
I'm not interested.	Non sono interessata/o.
No, thank you.	No, grazie.
Thanks, but I'd rather not.	Grazie, ma preferirei di no.
Maybe some other time.	Un'altra volta.
Leave me alone!	Lasciami in pace!
I'm gay.	Sono gay.
Get lost!	Vattene!
Fuck off!	Vaffanculo!

The Date

Do you want to do something ...?	Vuoi fare qualcosa ...?
tomorrow	domani
tonight	stasera
at the weekend	questo finesettimana

Yes, I'd love to.	Sì lo gradirei molto.

Where do you want to go?	Dove vuoi andare?

THEY MAY SAY ...

Ti chiamo io.
   I'll call you.

boyfriend	un ragazzo
girlfriend	una ragazza
affair	un'avventura; una storia
date	l'appuntamento
kiss	un bacio
lover	un'amante

GOING OUT

DID YOU KNOW ...

When you're planning what to do and where to go, don't confuse casinò (casino) with casino (brothel). (In either case, it's a strain on your pocket!)

Afterwards

I had a great time.	Mi sono divertita/o tanto.
Will you take me home?	Mi porti a casa?
May I see you again?	Posso rivederti?
May I call you?	Posso chiamarti?
I'll call you tomorrow.	Ti chiamerò domani.
Goodnight.	Buonanotte.
Would you like to come inside for a while?	Vuoi entrare per un po'?

Making Love

You're very attractive.	Sei molto attraente.
You're beautiful!	Sei bellissima/o!
You turn me on.	Mi ecciti.
I want you.	Ti desidero.

I really like your ...	Mi piace (sg)/ Mi piacciono (pl) molto ...
hands	le tue mani (pl)
eyes	i tuoi occhi (pl)
lips	le tue labbra (pl)
mouth	la tua bocca (sg)
smile	il tuo sorriso (sg)
skin	la tua pelle (sg)

Kiss me.	Baciami.
May I kiss you?	Posso baciarti?
I want to make love to you.	Voglio fare l'amore (con te).
Let's go to bed/the bathroom.	Andiamo a letto/in bagno.
Take your clothes off.	Spogliati.

Do you have a condom?	Hai un preservativo/condom?
I'd like you to use a condom.	Voglio che ti metta il preservativo.
I only have safe sex.	Io pratico solo sesso sicuro.

GOING OUT

INTIMATE ITALIAN

This feels good.	Questo mi piace; Mi fai godere.
This is wonderful!	Questo è stupendo/ magnifico!
I (don't) like this.	(Non) mi piace questo.
Please stop!	Basta, per favore!
Please don't stop!	Continua!; Sì, così va bene.
Do it again!	Fallo ancora!
Go on!; Come on!	Su!; Dai!

Faster!	Più veloce!
Slower!	Più lentamente!
Harder!	Più forte!
Softer!	Più dolcemente!

Naughty Italian

erection	erezione
fetish	feticcio
oral sex	pompino; bocchino; sesso orale
orgasm	orgasmo
quickie	la sveltina; la botta
S&M	sadomaso(chismo)
to chat up	adescare
to pick (someone) up	rimorchiare
to kiss	baciare
to fuck	scopare; chiavare; sbatter(si)
to get laid	fare il porco
to have a hard on	averlo duro; averlo ritto

Sexuality

I am ...	Sono ...
bisexual	bisessuale
gay	gay; omo
heterosexual/straight	etero(sessuale)
a lesbian	lesbica
queer	diversa/o
celibate	celibe
a transexual	transessuale
a transvestite	una/o travestita/o
a drag king/queen	una/un travestita/o

Afterwards

That was great.	È stato fantastico.
Let's do it again!	Facciamolo di nuovo!
Was it good for you?	Ti è piacuto?
I'd like to see you again.	Voglio verderti ancora.
When can I see you again?	Quando possiamo rivederci?
I must go now.	Adesso devo andare.
May I stay over?	Posso restare/passare la notte?
You can't stay here tonight.	Non puoi restare qui stanotte.
Do you want breakfast here?	Vuoi fare colazione qui?

Love

I'd like to keep seeing you.	Vorrei frequentarti.
I really like you.	Mi piaci davvero.
I love you.	Ti amo.
I'm fond of you.	Ti voglio bene.
I'm in love with you.	Sono innamorata/o di te.
I've fallen in love with you.	Mi sono innamorata/o di te.
I'm really happy with you.	Sono felice con te;
	Mi sento felice con te.
Do you love me?	Mi ami?
I'd love to have a relationship with you.	Vorrei tanto avere una relazione con te.

GOING OUT

Do you want to go out with me?	Vuoi uscire con me?
Let's move in together.	Perché non conviviamo?
Will you marry me?	Vuoi sposarmi?;
	Vuoi sposarti con me?

MY LITTLE CHOOK

There are many endearing names in Italian which are used both with affection and irony. Sometimes they are a little tongue in cheek.

mia cara/mio caro;	my darling; my dear
cara mia/caro mio	
amore mio	my love
tesoro mio	my treasure
pollastrella/o mia/o	my little chook
ciccina/o mia/o	my little fleshy thing
gioia mia	my joy
dolcezza	honey; sugar
delizia	delicious one

Leaving & Breaking Up

I have to leave tomorrow.	Devo andarmene domani
I'll miss you.	Mi mancherai.
I'll come and visit you.	Verrò a trovarti.
I want us to stay in touch.	Voglio che ci teniamo in contatto.
I don't think it's working out between us.	Non credo che stia funzionando fra noi due.
I want to end the relationship.	Voglio finirla (fra noi due).
I want us to remain friends.	Voglio che restiamo amici.

GOING OUT

QUESTIONS

It could be said that the family is the cornerstone of Italian society, a reliable emotional and cultural reference point in the face of endemic political and institutional instability. But the fact remains that apart from the ever-declining number of marriages, Italy has for many years had the lowest birth rate of any country in Europe.

Are you married?	**Sei sposata/o?**
Is your wife/husband here?	**Tua moglie/Tuo marito è qui con te?**
Do you have a girlfriend/ boyfriend?	**Hai una ragazza/un ragazzo?**
Do you have any children?	**Hai figli?**
How many children do you have?	**Quanti figli hai?**
How many sisters/brothers do you have?	**Quante sorelle/Quanti fratelli hai?**
How old are they?	**Quanti anni hanno?**
Do you live with your family?	**Abiti con i tuoi?**
Do you get along with your family?	**Vai d'accordo con la tua famiglia?** (inf)

DID YOU KNOW ... Italians have always been seen by others as being very involved with family and having children. But you may be surprised to hear that Italy, with a population of 58 million, has the lowest birthrate in Europe.

FAMILY

REPLIES

I'm ...	**Sono ...**
single	**nubile** (f); **celibe** (m); **scapolo** (m)
separated	**separata/o**
divorced	**divorziata/o**
a widow/widower	**vedova/o**

I have a partner.	**Ho una/un compagna/o.**
We live together (but we're not married).	**Conviviamo (ma non siamo sposati).**
I don't have any children.	**Non ho figli.**
I have a daughter/a son.	**Ho una figlia/un figlio.**

FAMILY MEMBERS

aunt	**la zia**
baby	**la/il bimba/bimbo; bebé**
boy	**il bambino**
brother	**il fratello**
brother-in-law	**il cognato**
children	**i figli; i bambini**
cousin	**la/il cugina/o**
dad	**il papà**
daughter	**la figlia**
daughter-in-law	**la nuora**
family	**la famiglia**
father	**il padre**
father-in-law	**il suocero**
girl	**la bambina**
grandfather	**il nonno**
grandmother	**la nonna**
husband	**il marito**
mother	**la madre**
mother-in-law	**la suocera**
mum	**la mamma**

nephew	il nipote
niece	la nipote
sister	la sorella
sister-in-law	la cognata
son	il figlio
son-in-law	il genero
stepbrother	il fratellastro
stepdaughter	la figliastra
stepfather	il patrigno
stepmother	la matrigna
stepsister	la sorellastra
stepson	il figliastro
uncle	lo zio
wife	la moglie

See also Tracing Roots & History, page 245, for phrases about the family.

FAMILY

TALKING WITH PARENTS

What a cute baby!	Che bella bimba/Che bel bimbo!
He's a real darling!	È proprio carino!
How old is she?	Quanto anni ha?
What's his name?	Come si chiama?
How many children do you have?	Quanti figli ha?
How old are they?	Quanti anni hanno?
How old is the eldest?	Quanto età ha la/il più grande?
How old is the youngest?	Quanto età ha la/il più piccola/o?
She/He is very like you.	Le somiglia molto.
He is very like his mother.	Somiglia molto a sua madre.

KIDS' TALK

mum/mummy	mamma; mammina
dad	papà; babbo
grandad	nonno; nonnino; nonnetto
granny	nonna; nonnina; nonnetta
aunt/auntie	zia; zietta; ziuccia
uncle	zio; zietto; ziuccio
nanny/nanna	la tata
food (meat)	la ciccia
to be hurt/have a pain	avere la bua
swear word/naughty word	la parolaccia
beddy-byes	ciao-ciao!
puppy dog	il bau-bau; il cagnolino
pussy cat	il micino
train	il ciuf-ciuf
poo-poo	la cacca; la popò
pee-pee	la pipì
to sleep	(fare la) nanna

KIDS' TONGUE TWISTERS

Sopra la panca la capra campa, sotto la
panca la capra crepa.
*(literally, 'on the bench the goat lives, under
the bench the goat dies.')*

Trentatré trentini entrarono in Trento tutti i
trentatré trottando.
*(literally, 'thirty-three Trentini entered into Trent,
all of them on the trot.')*

Do they go to school or kindergarten?	Vanno a scuola o all'asilo?
Who looks after the children?	Chi bada ai bambini?
When is the baby due?	Quando aspetta il bambino?

TALKING WITH CHILDREN

What an adorable little girl!	(Ma) Che bella bambina!; Che bella femminuccia!
What an adorable little boy!	(Ma) Che bel bambino!; Che bel maschietto!
How old are you?	Quanti anni hai?
Do you go to school yet?	Vai ancora a scuola?
Do you like school?	Ti piace andare a scuola?
Is your teacher nice?	È brava/o la tua maestra/ il tuo maestro?
Do you have a pet at home?	Hai un animale domestico a casa?
Do you play sport?	Fai dello sport?
What do you do after school?	Cosa fai dopo la scuola?
When's your birthday?	Quand'è il tuo compleanno?
Do you have any brothers and sisters?	Hai fratelli o sorelle?
Do you learn English?	Stai imparando l'inglese?

FAMILY

PETS

Do you like animals?	**Ti piacciono gli animali?**
What's it called?	**Come si chiama?**
How old is it?	**Quanti anni ha?**
What breed is it?	**Di che razza è?**
Is it a cross-breed/a half-breed?	**È un incrocio/una mezza razza?**
What sort of temperament does it have?	**Che temperamento ha?**

Is it ...?	**È ...?**
docile	**docile**
domesticated	**addomesticata/o**
ferocious	**feroce**
friendly	**amichevole**
lovable	**socievole; affettuoso/a**
restless	**irrequieta/o**
tamable	**domabile**
trained	**ammaestrata/o**
wild	**selvatica/o**

Does it bite?	**Morde?**
Does it scratch?	**Graffia?**
May I pat/pet it?	**Posso accarezzarla/o?**

I have ...	**Io ho ...**
a bird	**un uccellino**
a budgerigar	**una cocorita; un pappagallino**
a canary	**un canarino**
a cat	**un gatto; micio**
a cow	**una mucca; vacca**
a dog	**un cane**
a donkey	**un asino**
a duck	**un'anatra**

SSSSSSS

The combination **ss** is always pronounced as the 's' in 'sun'. A single **s** between two vowels is pronounced as the 'z' in 'zoo'.

a frog	**una rana**
a goldfish	**un pesciolino rosso**
a hamster	**un criceto**
a horse	**un cavallo**
a kitten	**un gattino; micino**
a lizard	**una lucertola; un ramarro**
a mule	**un mulo**
a parrot	**un pappagallo**
a pig	**un maiale**
a pony	**un pony**
a puppy	**un cucciolo**
a salamander	**una salamandra**
a snake	**un serpente**
a toad	**un rospo**
a turtle	**una tartaruga**

FAMILY

CROSSWORD – FAMILY

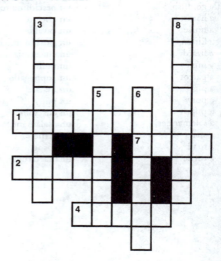

Across

1. Your brother loves her, your son calls her Auntie
2. You bring them up and they bring you down to earth
4. It's hard to find one in a rocking chair now
7. Stubborn beast of burden.

Down

3. A mixed up kid (like no. 7)
5. What every woman needs to be a good wife
6. Wears pink ribbons
8. Sibling

Answers on page 324

COMMON INTERESTS

What do you do in your spare time?	Cosa fai nel tuo tempo libero?
Do you like ...?	Ti piace ...?
art	l'arte
dancing	la danza
going to the cinema	andare al cinema
cooking	cucinare
music	la musica
shopping	fare lo shopping
photography	la fotografia
going out	uscire
the theatre	il teatro
travelling	viaggiare
reading	leggere
writing	scrivere
sport	lo sport

STAYING IN TOUCH

Let's keep in touch!	Teniamoci ai contatto!
Let's swap addresses.	Scambiamoci l'indirizzo.
What's your address?	Qual è il tuo indirizzo?
What's your phone/fax number?	Qual è il tuo numero di telefono/fax?
If you're ever in ..., you must look me up.	Se mai ti trovi in ..., devi venire a trovarmi. (sg);
	Se mai vi trovate in ..., dovete venire a trovarmi. (pl)
When you comt to ..., you can stay with me.	Quando vienia ..., puoi stare da me. (sg)
	Quando venite a ..., potete stare da me. (pl)

INTERESTS

Do you have an email address?	Hai un indirizzo di posta elettronica?
Do you have a fax?	Hai un fax?
I'll write first.	Ti scriverò per prima/o io.
I'll send you copies of the photos.	Ti spedirò le copie delle foto
Don't forget to write!	Non dimenticarti di scrivere!
Let's keep in touch!	Teniamoci ai contatto!

Writing

If you want to write your new friends in Italian when you get back home, here are some useful words and phrases.

Dear ...	Cara/o; Carissima/o (more affectionate)
I'm sorry it's taken me so long to write.	Mi scuso d'aver tardato così tanto a scriverti.
Why don't you drop me a line now and then?	Perché non mi butti giù una riga ogni tanto?
It was great to meet you.	È stato bello aver fatto la tua conoscenza.
Thank you so much for your hospitality.	Ti ringrazio tanto per la tua ospitalità.
I miss you.	Mi manchi molto.
I had a fantastic time in Italy.	Mi sono divertita/o moltissimo in Italia.
I hope to visit Italy again soon.	Spero di ritornare in Italia molto presto.
Say 'Hi' to ... for me.	Saluti ... da parte mia.
I'd love to see you.	Vorrei tanto rivederti.
Write soon!	Scrivi presto!

THE FORMAL LETTER

When writing a formal letter, don't forget to use the correct titles together with honorifics. Masculine professional titles are increasingly being used for female professionals.

INTERESTS

Titles

Mrs/Ms/Miss	Signora/Signorina (Sig.ra)
Mr/Sir	Signor (Sig.)
Messrs	Signori (Sigg.)

Honorifics

Dear	Egregia/o (Egr.)
Respectable	Spettabile (Spett.) – especially used for companies
Esq./excellent	Pregiatissima/o (Preg.ma/mo)
Distinguished	Chiarissima/o (Ch.ma/mo)
Kind	Gentile/Gentilissima/o (Gent.ma/mo)

Professional Titles

architect	Architetta/Architetto (Arch.)
lawyer	Avvocatessa/Avvocato (Avv.)
doctor	Dottoressa/Dottor(e) (Dott.)
professor	Professoressa/Professor(e) (Prof.)
engineer	Ingegnera/Ingegner(e) (ing.)
accountant	Ragioniera/Ragionier(e) (Rag.)

Useful Words

sender	mittente (Mitt.)
addressee	destinatario (Dest.)

INTERESTS

ART

One of the most prestigious art events on the calendar, the Venice Biennale, always attracts a large number of visitors. The Italian public is generally quite art-conscious and accords respect to its artists and critics.

Talking About It

Where are the galleries in this town/city?	Dove sono concentrate le gallerie in questa città?
Which works are exhibited here?	Quali sono le opere qui esposte?
Where can I see the work of ...?	Dove sono esposte le opere di ...?
What time is the opening?	A che ora è l'inaugurazione della mostra?
Where is the opening?	Dov'è l'inaugurazione della mostra?
I like this gallery space.	Trovo bello questo spazio.

EVERYONE'S A CRITIC I

I think this ... is ...	Trovo ... ...
work	quest'opera
painting	questo quadro; dipinto
installation	questa installazione
beautiful	bella/o
challenging	provocante
engrossing	avvincente
expressive	espressiva/o
fascinating	affascinante
innovative	innovatrice/innovatore
interesting	interessante
silly	fatua/o; sciocca/o
ugly	brutta/o

Doing It

Are you an artist?	Sei un'/un artista?
I am an artist.	Sono artista.
What is your medium?	Quale mezzo impieghi?
What are the main themes in your work?	Qual è la tematica dominante nella tua opera?
• paint	dipingere
• sculpt	scolpire
• draw	disegnare
• photograph	fotografare
brushstroke	una pennellata
paintbrush	un pennello
palette	una paletta

ARCS, ARCHANGELS & ARCHES

INTERESTS

Any traveller to Italy won't be able to help being struck by the magnificent architecture and the abundance of beautiful art. To help you to appreciate the arts in Italy, here are some common terms referring to architecture, both modern and ancient, and to the arts, especially religious.

affresco	fresco
andron	ground-floor hall behind the water-gate entrance of a Venetian house
apse	domed or arched area at the altar end of a church
arcade	a series of arches
arco	arch
badia	abbey
baldacchino	canopy supported by columns over the altar in a church
barocco	Baroque; style of architecture and decorative arts, characterised by extensive ornamentation
basilica	in ancient Rome, a building used for public administration, with a rectangular hall flanked by aisles and an apse at the end; later, a Christian church built in the same style
battistero	baptistery
borgo	suburb or arterial road
bottega	workshop
bugnato; bugnatura	rustication; protruding masonry on an exterior wall
buttress	support or prop for a wall
bizantino	Byzantine; architectural style characterised by massive domes with square bases, rounded arches, spires and minarets, and mosaics

ARCS, ARCHANGELS & ARCHES

campanile	bell tower
cappella	chapel; often just a small room or altarpiece in a church aisle
cattedrale	cathedral
cenacolo	supper room or refectory; also refer to the fresco of the Last Supper
chiesa	church
chiostro	cloister; covered walkway, usually enclosed by columns, around a quadrangle
circo	oval or circular arena
cofano	coffer; a recessed panel in a ceiling or vault
colonna	column
colonnade	a row of columns
comune	medieval city state; modern municipality
cortile	courtyard
cupola	dome (of cathedral)
cupolone	big dome
curia	arcade of columns on the ground and first floors of a Venetian Byzantine palace
duomo	dome; also means 'cathedral'
exedra	a semicylindrical architectural space or shape surmounted by a half-dome
fascia	frieze; an ornamental band or strip on a wall
fontana	fountain
foro	forum
fresco	(lit: fresh); a painting on a wall usually done on wet plaster so painting and plaster dry at the same time
fresco a secco	a fresco done on an already-dry wall
gonfalone	banner of a medieval free city
gotica/o	Gothic; style of architecture, characterised by the lancet arch, the ribbed vault and the flying buttress

INTERESTS

ARCS, ARCHANGELS & ARCHES

intarsia	inlaid wood, marble or metal
intonaco	the plaster surfacing of a wall
liagò	a roofed terrace or an enclosed balcony
lintel	a horizontal beam spanning an opening
loggia	covered area on the side of a building; porch; can also be a small garden cottage
maesta	Madonna and Child on a throne
minaret	the slender tower of a mosque having one or more balconies
navata centrale	nave; central part of the church
opera	a work of art; may be in process
pala d'attare	altarpiece; a religious image that stands on and behind an altar
palazzo	a large building of any type, including apartment blocks
pali	the larch pilings driven as foundations for Venetian buildings; also mooringpoles
palio	banner of a medieval free city
persiane	louvre shutters
piazza	square
piazzale	large open square
pieta	Virgin with dead Christ
pietra forte	fine sandstone used in Florence
pietra serena	fine dark sandstone used for carving
pietre dure	semi-precious stones embedded in a mosaic
ponte	bridge
portico	covered walkway, usually attached to the outside of buildings
predella	pedestal of an altarpiece, usually decorated with narrative scenes
putti	cherubs
refettorio	refectory; dining hall of a monastery

ARCS, ARCHANGELS & ARCHES

rilievo	relief; sculpture or painting which projects from a flat surface
rocca	fortress
romanica/o	Romanesque; architectural style characterised by rounded arches, massive-masonry wall construction and some use of mouldings
sala	room or hall
sassi	stone houses
scale	stairs
scalinata	stairway
scavi	excavations
serliana	a three-light opening, the centre one surmounted by an arch
serrande	roller blinds for windows
sestiere	city sections
sinopia	the etched layout of a fresco
sottoportego	street continuing under a building (like an extended archway)
studiolo	small decorated chambers in Renaissance palazzi where books, words of art and important objects were kept
terrazzo	terrace; balcony
tondo	round painting
torre	tower
travertino	light-coloured limestone, used extensively as a building material in both ancient and modern Rome because of large deposits in the area
trittico	triptych — a painting, often an altarpiece, in three sections
trompe d'oeil	painting designed to deceive the eye, creating the impression that the image is real

INTERESTS

INTERESTS

Useful Words

architecture	l'architettura
artist	un'/un artista
conceptual art	l'arte concettuale
graphic art	l'arte grafica
industrial art	l'arte industriale
multimedia	il multimedia
painter	la pittrice/il pittore
painting	la pittura
performance art	l'arte d'esibizione
pop art	la pop art
post-modernism	il postmoderno
retro	retró
sculptor	la scultrice/lo scultore
sculpture	la scultura
studio	lo studio
technique	la tecnica
technological art	l'arte tecnologica

MEDIA

canvas	la tela
charcoal	il carboncino
crayon	il gessetto
ink	l'inchiostro
lead	la grafite; la mina
oil painting	un dipinto a olio
paper	la carta
pen	la penna
pencil	il lapis; la matita
wash-drawing	la tempera
watercolour	l'acquarello

MUSIC
Talking About It

Do you like ...?	Ti piace ...?
listening to music	ascoltare la musica
dancing	ballare
this singer	questa/o cantante
this band	questo gruppo; complesso; questa band
this orchestra	questa orchestra
this conductor	questo direttore (d'orchestra)
this piece	questa/o passo
Do you like this riff/ arrangement?	Ti piace questo pezzo/ arrangiamento?
What style of music do you like?	Quale stile di musica ti piace?
Which bands do you like?	Quali gruppi/complessi ti piacciono?
I like ...	Mi piacciono ...
Have you heard the latest CD/record by ...?	Hai sentito l'ultimo cidì/ disco di ...?

INTERESTS

TYPES OF MUSIC

Most musical styles keep their original English name in Italian. Some exceptions are:

light/easy listening	la musica leggera
funk	la musica funky
lounge	la musica cocktail
classical	la musica classica

INTERESTS

Doing It

Do you play an instrument?	Suoni uno strumento?
I play ...	Suono ...
I strum/pound/twang as best as I can.	Strimpello/Pesto/Pizzico come meglio posso.
Do you sing?	Canti?

Musical Instruments

bass guitar	il basso
cello	il violoncello
double-bass	il contrabbasso
drums	la batteria
flute	il flauto
guitar (classic/electric/acoustic)	la chitarra (classica/elettrica/acustica)
harp	l'arpa
keyboard	la tastiera
piano	il pianoforte
saxophone	il sassofono
trumpet	la tromba
viola	la viola
violin	il violino

Useful Words

audience	gli spettatori
band	un gruppo; una band
concert	un concerto
live	dal vivo
musician	un musicista
orchestra	una orchestra
performance	l'esibizione musicale
show	uno spettacolo
singer	un cantante

ZZZZZZZZZ

At the beginning of a word **z** is pronounced as the 'ds' in 'beds'. In the middle of a word **z** is pronounced as the 'ts' in 'hits'.

INTERESTS

singer-songwriter	una cantautrice/un cantautore
song	la canzone
venue	un locale
voice	la voce

Going to a Concert

Do you want to go to a concert tomorrow night?	Vuoi (sg)/Volete (pl) andare a un concerto domani sera?
Is there a concert on today?	C'è un concerto stasera?
When are ... playing?	Quando dànno lo spettacolo di ...?
Which band is playing here tonight?	Quale gruppo suona qui stasera?
Where do the young local alternative bands play?	Dove si esibiscono le giovani band alternative?
What time does the concert start?	A che ora inizia il concerto?
How much is it to get in?	Quant'è l'ingresso?
Shall we go closer to the stage?	Ci avviciniamo al palco?
What a fantastic concert!	Che concerto sensazionale!
She's/He's great!	È forte!
She's/He's terrible!	È terribile; Fa pena.

Radio

Which station plays ...?	Quale stazione suona ...?
On what frequency is ....?	Su quale frequenza è ...?
broadcast	la trasmissione
DJ	il deejay; il DJ
radio announcer	l'annunciatrice/annunciatore
radio programme	il programma radiofonico
radio news	il giornale radio
talkback	il talk show

INTERESTS

CINEMA

The Italian movie industry is a great success story and has produced such international stars as Rodolfo Valentino, Marcello Mastroianni, Anna Magnani, Gina Lollobrigida and, of course, Sophia Loren. Great film directors include Frederico Fellini, Bernado Bertolucci and Sergio Leone.

I feel like seeing a film.	Avrei voglia d'andare a vedere un film.
I'd like to see ...	Vorrei vedere ...
What's on at the cinema tonight?	Cosa dànno al cinema stasera?
Where can I find a cinema guide?	Dove posso trovare una guida agli spettacoli/ai film?
Which type/genre do you like?	Quale tipo/genere di film ti piace?
Have you seen ...?	Hai mica visto ...?
Do you like films by ...?	Ti piacciono i film di ...?
Who's in it?	Chi sono i protagonisti?
Who is it by?	Chi è il regista?
At which cinema is this film being shown?	A quale cinema dànno questo film?
Is it in English?	È in inglese?
Does it have English subtitles?	Le didascalie sono in inglese?
Is there a short before the film?	C'è un cortometraggio prima del film?
Are these seats taken?	Sono liberi questi posti?

DID YOU KNOW ... The 'spaghetti western' stars, Bud Spencer and Terence Hill used pseudonyms. These famous cowboys are, in fact, Italian.

EVERYONE'S A CRITIC II

Did you like the film?	Ti è piaciuto il film?
I liked it very much.	Mi è piaciuto davvero.
I didn't like it very much.	Non mi è piaciuto granché.

I found it ...	L'ho trovato ...
boring	noioso
excellent	magnifico
interesting	interessante
OK	passabile

I had a few problems with the language.	Ho trovato il linguaggio un po' difficile da capire.

INTERESTS

Useful Words

actor	un'attrice/un attore
to act	recitare
cinema critic	un critico; un recensore
direction	la regia; la direzione
director/film maker	la/il regista
to direct	dirigere
film	un film
producer	la/il direttore di produzione
review	una recensione
screen	lo schermo
script	il copione
scriptwriter	la sceneggiatrice/ lo sceneggiatore
short	un cortometraggio
stage	il palcoscenico
subtitles	le didascalie; i sottotitoli

INTERESTS

WHAT'S YOUR POISON?

action	**azione**
adventure	**avventura**
black comedy	**tragicomico**
comedy	**commedia; film brillante**
drama	**drammatico**
espionage	**spionaggio**
fantasy	**fantastico**
film noir	**film noir**
horror	**orrore**
humour	**umoristico**
musical	**musical**
neorealist	**neorealista**
police drama	**poliziesco**
science fiction	**fantascienza**
sentimental	**sentimentale**
suspense	**suspense; thriller**
thriller	**giallo**
war	**film di guerra**
western	**western**

THEATRE

If you enjoy the theatre, winter is the best time to see shows as this is the height of the theatre season.

What's on at the theatre tonight?	Cosa dànno al teatro stasera?
I feel like going to see a play.	Avrei voglia d'andare a vedere una recita/commedia.
Do you have a favourite playwright?	Hai una commodiografo/a preferita/o?

INTERESTS

THEY MAY SAY ...

In bocca al lupo; In culo alla balena!	Break a leg!

art direction	la direzione artistica
costume	il costume
costume designer	la/il costumista
rehearsal	la prova
rendition/performance	l'interpretazione
scene	la scena
set	lo scenario; lo set
set designer	la/lo scenografa/o
stage	il palcoscenico
stalls	la platea
theatrical production	una produzione drammatica

LITERATURE
Books

Who is your favourite author?	Chi è la tua autrice preferita?/Chi è il tuo autore preferito?
What kind of books do you read?	Quale tipo di libri leggi?
Have you read ...? **Hai letto ...?**	
Can you recommend a book to me? **Mi potrebbe consigliare un libro?**	
Do you read in other languages? **Leggi in altre lingue?**	

SUFFIXES

Suffixes are used a lot in Italian to change slightly the meaning of nouns and adjectives. These suffixes usually indicate cuteness or smallness. (See page 22.)

INTERESTS

EVERYONE'S A CRITIC III

What did you think of ...?	Che ne pensi di ...?
I thought it was better/worse than the previous book.	Penso che sia migliore/ peggiore del libro precedente
I thought it was ...	Penso che sia ...
badly-written	mal scritta/o
boring	noiosa/o
excellent	brillante
good	discreta/o
great	ottima/o
interesting	interessante
really bad	pessima/o
well-written	ben scritta/o

I like ...	Mi appassiona (sg)/ Mi appassionano (pl) ...
the classics	la letteratura classica
comics	i fumetti
contemporary literature	la letteratura contemporanea
crime/detective novels	i gialli
erotic literature	la letteratura erotica
fantasy literature	la letteratura fantastica
fiction	la narrativa; novellistica
hypertext	ipertesto
nonfiction	la saggistica
novels	i romanzi; le novelle
plays	la drammaturgia
poetry	la poesia
romance literature	letteratura romantica/rosa
sciencefiction	la fantascienza
short stories	i racconti; le novelle
travel writing	i libri di viaggio

Books & Newspapers

Did you hear about ...?	Hai sentito di ...?
I read it in ...	L'ho letto su ...
Did you see the news yesterday?	Hai visto il telegiornale ieri?
Who is the reporter from ...?	Chi è l'inviata/o da ...?
This column is well-written.	Questa rubrica è ben scritta.
I don't like this journalist's opinions.	Non apprezzo le opinioni di questa/o giornalista.

INTERESTS

HOBBIES

Do you have any hobbies?	Hai qualche hobby/passatempo?
I make ...	Faccio ...
I like ...	Mi piace/piacciono ...
bird-watching	il bird-watching
body building	il body building
cooking	cucinare
dancing	ballare
drawing	disegnare
embroidery	il ricamo
fencing	la scherma
fishing	pescare
gardening	il giardinaggio
genealogy	la genealogia
martial arts	le arte marziali
painting	dipingere
photography	fotografare
pottery	la ceramica
reading	leggere
sewing	cucire
singing	cantare
trainspotting	osservare i treni
travelling	viaggiare
woodwork	il modellismo (su legno)

INTERESTS

I collect ...	Fare collezioni di ...
antiques	antiquariato
books	libri
coins	monete
comics	fumetti
miniature cars	auto in miniature; automodelli
stamps	francobolli

TRAVEL

Have you travelled much?	Hai viaggiato molto?
Where have you been?	Dove sei stato/a?
I've been to ...	Sono stato/a a ...
What do you think of ...?	Che cosa pensi di ...?

I thought it was ...	Trovo che sia ...
awful	orrendo/a
boring	noioso/a
exciting	stimulante
expensive	costoso/a
great	grande

There are too many tourists.	Ci sono troppo turisti.
Is it safe to go alone?	È prudente andarci da sole/i?
Is it safe for women travellers on their own?	È sicuro per donne che viaggiano sole?
When is the best time to go?	Quale è il periodo migliore per andarci?
Is it expensive?	È costoso?

DID YOU KNOW ...   Pranzo is used to mean the noon meal, while cena refers to the evening meal. Colazione is breakfast but a colazione d'affari is a business lunch.

STARS
Astrology

What sign of the zodiac are you?	Di quale segno dello zodiaco sei?

INTERESTS

I am a/an ...	Sono ...
Aries	Ariete
Taurus	Toro
Gemini	Gemelli
Cancer	Cancro
Leo	Leone
Virgo	Vergine
Libra	Bilancia
Scorpio	Scorpione
Sagittarius	Sagittario
Capricorn	Capricorno
Aquarius	Acquario
Pisces	Pesci

BLACK CATS

Adjectives are generally placed after the noun, and their endings are generally the same as those of the noun:

the black cat
il gatto nero

the black cats
i gatti neri

(Leos) are very ...	I (Leoni) sono molto ...
aggressive	aggressivi
ambitious	ambiziosi
calm	calmi
caring	attenti
insecure	insicura/o
imaginative	alla fantasia
jealous	gelosi
loyal	leali
outgoing	estroversi
practical	pratica/o
romantic	romantica/o
selfish	egoisti
sensual	sensuali
shy	timidi
stubborn	ostinati

INTERESTS

COMMON EXPRESSIONS

At last!	Finalmente; Alla fine!
It's bothering me; It shits me.	Mi sfava; Mi rompe; Mi scassa!
It's easy.	Cosa da niente.
It's great/cool!	Che sballo; Che slego; Che flebo; Che fine; Che sbrago!
It's useless!	È una boccia!
That's really bad!	Che boiata; Che porcata; Che stronzata; Che cesso; Che vaccata!
That's annoying.	Questo m'aggrava.
Too bad; What a shame!	Tanto peggio; Peggio così; Che peccato!

Astronomy

I'm interested in ...	Mi affascina ...
Do you have a telescope?	Hai un telescopio?
What star/ planet is that?	Che stella/pianeta è?
Is there a planetarium/ observatory nearby?	C'è un planetario/ osservatorio qui vicino?

asteroids	gli asteroidi	Moon	la Luna
astronaut	l'astronauta	planet	un pianeta
astronomer	l'astronoma/o	solar system	il sistema solare
black hole	il buco nero	spaceship	l'astronave
comet	la cometa	star	una stella;
constellation	la costellazione		un astro
galaxy	la galassia	Sun	il Sole
meteorite	la meteorite	telescope	un telescopio
Milky Way	la Via Lattea	Universe	l'Universo

THE PLANETS

Mercury	Mercurio
Venus	Venere
Earth	Terra
Mars	Marte
Jupiter	Giove
Saturn	Saturno
Uranus	Urano
Neptune	Nettuno
Pluto	Plutone

THE UNKNOWN

Do you believe in ...	Credi ...
UFOs	negli ufo
extraterrestrials	negli extraterrestri
flying saucers	nei dischi volanti
strange/unexplained phenomena	ai fenomeni strani/inspiegabili
ghosts	nei/ai fantasmi
life after death	nella vita dopo la morte
reincarnation	nella reincarnazione
telepathy	nella telepatie
witchcraft	alle streghe
life on Mars	nella vita su Marte
Satan	in Satana/al diavolo

People here tend to be ...	La gente tende ...
imaginative	alla fantasia
superstitious	alla superstizione
scientific	al pragmatismo
sceptical	allo scetticismo

Have you ever seen one?	**Ne hai mai visto uno?**
I believe in destiny/fate.	**Io credo nel destino/fato.**
space travel/exploration	**il viaggio nello spazio**
time travel	**il viaggio nei tempi**
the future	**il futuro**
science fiction	**la fantascienza**

SOCIAL ISSUES

POLITICS

What do you think of the (new) government?	Che te ne pare del (nuovo) governo?
I (don't) agree with their policy/line of action on ...	(Non) Sono d'accordo con la loro politica/linea d'azione ...
the budget	sulla finanziaria
defence	sulla difesa
drugs	sulla droga
the economy	sull'economia
education	sull'istruzione
foreign aid	sull'assistenza estera
immigration	sull'immigrazione
military service	sul servizio militare
privatisation	sulla privatizzazione
separatism	sul separatismo
unemployment	sulla disoccupazione
Who do you vote for?	Per chi voti?
I support the ... party.	Appoggio il partito ...
communist	comunista
democratic	democratico
green	verde
labor	laburista
liberal	liberale
radical	radicale
republican	repubblicano
socialist	socialista
I'm an anarchist.	Sono un'/un anarchica/o.
I abstain.	Mi astengo.

THEY MAY SAY ...

Tutti i politici sono uguali.
  Politicians are all the same.
Non ci si può mai fidare dei politici.
  Politicians can never be trusted.

Useful Words

constitution	la costituzione
corrupt	corrotta/o
democracy	una democrazia
demonstration	una manifestazione; una dimostrazione
election	un'elezione
electorate	l'elettorato
exploitation	lo sfruttamento
foreign politics	la politica estera
government	il governo
left(-wing)	(di) sinistra
legalisation	la legalizzazione
legislation	la legislazione
legislature	la legislatura
local politics	la politica interna
ministry	il ministero
monarchy	la monarchia
opposition	l'opposizione
parliament	il parlamento
policy	la politica
political campaign	la campagna elettorale
polls	i sondaggi
premier	il premier
president	il presidente
prime minister	il primo ministro
propaganda	la propaganda
rally	un comizio; un raduno
republic	la repubblica
right(-wing)	(di) destra
seat	il seggio
term of office	il periodo in carica
vote	un voto
vote counting	lo scrutinio
voter	la/il votante

SOCIAL ISSUES

SOCIAL ISSUES

... elections	le elezioni ...
local council	communali
regional	amministrative
general	politiche
national	nazionali
European	europee

STATING YOUR CASE

I agree.	Sono d'accordo; Condivido.
Absolutely!	Assolutamente!
Exactly!	Esattamente!
Of course!	Certamente!; (Di) Certo!
Really!	Davvero!
You're kidding!	Lei scherza!; Tu scherzi! (inf)/ Voi scherzate! (plur)
Yes, but actually ...	Sì, ma veramente ...
Even so ...;	Eppure ...; Tuttavia ...;
All the same ...	Comunque ...
In any case ...	In ogni caso ...; Ad ogni modo ...
To be brief ...	Insomma ...
I disagree.	Non sono d'accordo; Non la vedo così.
That's not true!	Non è affatto vero!
No way!	Per nulla/niente; Neanche per sogno!
Yes, and I'm the Pope!	Sì, e io sono il Papa!
In your dreams/As if!	Immaginiamoci; Immaginati!
Come off it!	Vien via; Come no!
Yeah right!	Figuriamoci; Figurati!
Get out of here!	Ma va' là!
Like hell!	Col cazzo; Una sega! (rather strong)
Shut up!	Chiudi!; Sta' zitta/o!

Italian Politics

Italy is a parliamentary republic, headed by a president who appoints a prime minister. The parliament consists of two houses – the Senate and the Chamber of Deputies – which have equal legislative power and are elected every five years. Executive power is exercised by the government and judiciary power by the Magistrature. The President of the Republic, elected for seven years, is in charge of the Constitution. The seat of Government is in Rome.

Chamber/Lower House	La Camera
Senate/Upper House	Il Senato
Local Government	la giunta regionale/comunale
Senate	Il Senato della Repubblica
Chamber of Deputies	La Camera dei Deputati
Cabinet	Il Consiglio dei Ministri
Public Administration	La Pubblica Amministrazione
Magistrature	La Magistratura
Constitutional Court	La Corte Costituzionale
Constitutional Assembly	L'Assemblea Costituente

SOCIAL ISSUES

MAJOR POLITICAL PARTIES IN ITALY

PDS	Partito Democratico della Sinistra
PPI	Partito Popolare Italiano
RC	Partito della Rifondazione Comunista
Verdi	Partito Ecologista
Ulivo	Coalizione Politica di Centro Sinistra
Forza Italia	Partito di Silvio Berlusconi
Alleanza Nazionale	Partito di Destra Conservatore
CCD	Centro Cristiano Democratico
CCU	Centro Cristiano-Unitario
Polo Delle Libertà	Coalizione di Centro Destra
Lega Nord	Movimento Secessionista

SOCIAL ISSUES

THE ENVIRONMENT

Pollution problems exist throughout Italy, especially in the more industrialised north and in major cities where car emissions poison the atmosphere. Italians are not very litter conscious. The Ministry for the Environment was only created in 1981 and many of its laws are not adequately enforced.

I'm concerned about ...	Mi preoccupa/preoccupano ...
I'm active in the campaign ...	Prendo parte attiva nella campagna ...
for ...	per ...
against ...	contro ...
to save ...	per salvare ...
deforestation	la deforestazione
endangered species	le specie in via d'estinzione
nuclear energy	l'energia nucleare
nuclear rain	la pioggia nucleare/acida
nuclear testing	gli esperimenti nucleari
pollution	l'inquinamento

DID YOU KNOW ... Administratively, Italy is divided into 20 regions. Five of these — Sicily, Sardinia, Trentino-Alto Adige, Friuli-Venezia Giulia and Valle d'Aosta — are autonomous or semi-autonomous, with special powers granted under the constitution. They have a wider range of economic and administrative powers than the other 15 regions.

recycling	il riciclaggio
toxic waste	i rifiuti nucleari; gli scarti tossici
woodchipping	la truciolatura (la riduzione di alberi secolari in trucioli)

Do you have a recycling programme in this town?	Esiste un programma di riciclaggio in questa città?
Is this a protected ...	È ... protetta/o questa/o?
forest	una foresta
park	un parco
species	una specie
What kind of pollution problems does this town have?	Che tipo di problemi d'inquinamento ha questa città?

SOCIAL ISSUES

Is there an unemployment problem?	C'è il problema della disoccupazione?
Do you have adequate social welfare?	L'assistenza sociale provvede in modo adeguato?
What do people think about ...?	Cosa pensa la gente di ...?
Is there assistance for the homeless?	C'è assistenza sociale per i senzatetto.
What do the statistics tell us about the economy?	Cosa dicano le statistiche sull'economia?

JEE OR GHEE

Remember that the letter g is hard as in 'goat' before a, o, u and h but soft as in 'gentle' before e and i.

SOCIAL ISSUES

I am against/in favour of ...	Sono contro/a favore di ...
abortion	l'aborto
citizenship	la cittadinanza
class system	il sistema delle classi sociali
equality	l'eguaglianza
euthanasia	l'eutanasia
gay rights	i diritti omosessuali
homeless people	i senzatetto
human rights	i diritti umani
inequality	l'ineguaglianza
inflation	l'inflazione
migrants	gli immigrati
minorities	le minoranze
political exiles	gli esiliati politici
racism	il razzismo
refugees	i rifugiati
sexism	il sessismo
sexual harassment	le molestie sessuali
social security	la previdenza sociale
social welfare	l'assistenza sociale
street kids	i ragazzi di strada
strike	lo sciopero
tax	la tassa
the Rom people (gypsies)	il popolo Rom; i nomadi
trade union	il sindacato; l'unione
unemployment benefit	il sussidio di disoccupazione

DID YOU KNOW ...

Mare vivo, literally 'living sea', is an environmental organisation dedicated to protecting the Mediterranean Sea. Among other things, it prevents industrial pollution and the killing of dolphins.

DRUGS

The possession of any amount of any drugs in Italy is illegal and penalties are harsh. If you find yourself in a situation where drugs are being discussed, the following phrases may help you to understand the conversation, but if referring to your own interests, use discretion.

Do you smoke pot?	**Fumi l'erba?**
Would you like a drag on this joint?	**Vuoi un tiro di questo spinello?**
I take (coke) occasionally.	**Prendo (la coca) di tanto in tanto.**
I'm stoned.	**Sono rimbata/o; stonata/o; fatta/o.**
I'm out of it.	**Sono sballata/o.**
My friend has taken an overdose.	**La mia amica/Il mio amico ha preso un overdose.**
This drug is for personal use only.	**Questa droga è esclusivamente per uso personale.**

SOCIAL ISSUES

DOPE

Here are some colloquial terms — if you hear them in use around you, you're probably in the wrong bar.

grass/pot	**la marijuana; l'erba; il basilico; l'insalata; la rimba**
to roll a joint	**rollare; fare uno spinello**
hashish	**la nera**
trip	**un viaggio; uno sballo**
coke	**la neve**
speed	**lo speed; l'amfe**
smack/heroin	**il bicarbonato**
to shoot up	**bucarsi; farsi**
cut	**tagliata**

SOCIAL ISSUES

THEY MAY SAY ...

Vuoi dell'erba?
Ti interessa un po' di coca?
C'ho un po' di hascisc.
Che ne dici di una pasticca?

Do you want some pot?
Are you interested in some cocaine?
I've got some hash.
What would you say to an e?

Saying 'No'

I'm not interested in drugs.
La droga non mi interessa.

I don't take/do drugs anymore.
Non prendo più la droga; Non mi faccio più. (inject)

Getting Help

I'm addicted to ...
Sono dedita/o ...

acid/LSD — all' acido; LSD
cocaine — alla cocaina
ecstasy — all' ecstasy
hash — all' hashish
heroin — all' eroina
speed — all'anfetamina

I'm trying to get off it/detox.
Sto cercando di smettere/ disintossicarmi.

Where can I get help for a drug problem?
Dove posso cercare aiuto per il mio problema di (tossico)dipendenza?

Do you have a methadone programme?
Avete un programma di disintossicazione al metadone?

Can I register?
Posso partecipare?

Useful Words

addiction	la dipendenza
cocaine addict	la/il cocainomane
cold turkey	l'astinenza seca; la crisi di astinenza
dealer	una spacciatrice/uno spacciatore
to detox	disintossicarsi
disintoxication	la disintossicazione
drug	una droga; una roba
drug addict	una/un drogata/o; tossicomane; tossicodipendente
drug addiction	la tossicomania
to hallucinate	allucinare
hallucinogen	l'allucinogeno
heroin addict	un'/un eroinomane
to inject	iniettarsi; farsi
junkie	una/un drogata/o; rimbata/o
narcotic	un narcotico
overdose	overdose; iperdosaggio; abuso di stupefacenti
pure	pura/o
to smoke	fumare; svampare
to sniff	sniffare; fare uno sniffo
syringe	una siringa; spada; sprizza

CROSSWORD – SOCIAL ISSUES

SOCIAL ISSUES

Across
1. These people are like a snail without a shell.
2. Family first, then genus, then ...
6. The conservative factions are at this end of the political spectrum
4. Your own finances usually fluctuate with this

Down
3. It may look like putty, but you can smoke it
5. Civilians all in the same boat?
7. It's as inevitable as death
8. All politicians are capable of being?

Answers on page 324

SHOPS

Where can I buy ...?	Dove posso comprare ...?
Where is the nearest ...?	Dov'è la/il più vicina/o ...?
bakery	fornaio; panetteria
bank	banca
bookshop	libreria
camera shop	fotografo
clothing store	negozio di abbigliamento
computer shop	negozio di informatica
chemist	farmacia
craft shop	bottega d'artigianato
delicatessen	pizzicheria; salumeria
department store	grande magazzino
fish shop	pescheria
furniture store	negozio di mobili
grocery store	negozio di alimentari; drogheria
hardware shop	ferramenta
health shop	erboristeria
hypermarket	ipermercato
launderette	lavanderia
market	mercato
newsagency; stationer's	edicola
optician	ottico
pharmacy	farmacia
record shop	negozio di dischi
shoeshop	negozio di scarpe
shopping centre	centro commerciale
souvenir shop	negozio di souvenir
supermarket	supermercato
travel agency	agenzia di viaggi
video shop	videoteca

MAKING A PURCHASE

I'd like to buy ...	Vorrei comprare ...
I'm just looking.	Sto solo guardando.
How much is it?	Quanto costa?
Can you write the price down, please?	Può scrivere il prezzo, per cortesia?
Can I look at it?	Posso dare un'occhiata?
Do you have others?	Ne ha altre/i?
I don't like it.	Non mi piace.
I will (not) buy it.	(Non) la/lo compro.
Do you accept credit cards?	Accetta la carta di credito?
Can I have a receipt, please?	Può darmi una ricevuta, per cortesia?
Does it have a warranty?	Ha la garanzia?
Can I have it sent overseas?	Posso spedirlo all'estero?

sale	la svendita; i saldi
lay-by	il pagamento a rate
deposit	una caparra; un deposito
discount	uno sconto

THEY MAY SAY ...

Posso aiutarla?	Can I help you?
Cosa desidera?	What would you like?
Desidera altro?	Will that be all?
Nient'altro?; Qualcos'altro?	Anything else?
La/Lo vuole imballata/o?	Would you like it wrapped?
Mi dispiace, è l'unica/o.	Sorry, this is the only one.
Quanto/i ne vuole?	How much/many do you want?

Returning Goods

I'd like to return this, please.	Vorrei restituire questa/o, per favore.
It's faulty.	È difettosa/o.
It's broken.	È rotta/o.
I'd like my money back.	Vorrei indietro il mio denaro.

BARGAINING

Bargaining is common in Italian markets but not in shops.

Really? Come on!	Ma via! Scherza!
That's very expensive!	È troppo cara/o!
Do you have something cheaper?	Ha qualcosa di meno costoso?
Could you lower the price?	Può farmi lo sconto?
I don't have much money.	Non ho molti soldi.
I'll give you ...	Le offro ...
No more than ...	Non più di ...

ESSENTIAL GROCERIES

batteries	le pile
bread	il pane
cereal	i cereali
chocolate	il cioccolato
coffee	il caffè
dishwashing liquid	il detergente per i piatti
fruit juice	il succo di frutta
gas cylinder	la bombola a gas
matches	i fiammiferi
milk	il latte
mineral water	l'acqua minerale
sugar	lo zucchero
tea	il tè
tissues	i fazzolettini di carta
toothpaste	il dentifricio; la pasta dentrifica
washing powder	il detersivo

SOUVENIRS

blown glass	il vetro soffiato
brooch	una spilla
ceramics	la ceramica
earrings	gli orecchini; le buccole
embroidery	il ricamo
handicraft	il lavoro artigianale
jewellery	la bigiotteria
lace	il merletto
leather bag	una borsa di cuoio
miniature statue	una statuetta
necklace	una collana
ornament	un soprammobile
plate	un piatto
pottery	gli oggetti in ceramica
ring	un anello
rug	un tappeto
vase	un vaso
woodcarving	un legno intagliato

CLOTHING

belt	una cintura
boots	gli stivali
clothing	gli abiti; i vestiti; l'abbigliamento
coat	un cappotto
dress	un vestito
jacket	una giacca
jeans	i jeans
jumper/sweater	un maglione; un golfino
hat	un cappello
raincoat	un impermeabile
sandals	i sandali
shirt	una camicia
(sports) shoes	le scarpe (da ginnastica)

shorts	i pantaloni corti; i pantaloncini
skirt	una gonna; una sottana
socks	i calzini
stockings/pantyhose	le calze; i collant
swimsuit	un costume da bagno
T-shirt	una maglietta; un T-shirt
umbrella	un ombrello
trousers	i pantaloni
underwear	la biancheria intima

May I try it on?	Potrei provarmela/o?
My size is ...	Io porto la/il ...; La mia misura/taglia è ...
It doesn't fits.	Non mi va bene.
It doesn't suit me/you.	Non mi/ti sta bene.

It is too ...	È troppo ...
big	grande
small	piccola/o
short	corta/o
long	lunga/o
tight	aderente; stretta/o
loose	larga/o

SHOPPING

Shoe Repairs

Is there a shoe repairer near here?	C'è un calzolaio de queste parti?
I'd like to have my shoes resoled.	Vorrei farmi risuolare le scarpe.
I'd like to have my shoes reheeled.	Vorrei rifarmi i tacchi.
When will they be ready?	Quando saranno pronte?
shoelaces	i lacci per scarpe
shoe polish	crema/lucido per scarpe

AT THE JEWELLER'S

What metal/stone is it?	Che metallo/pietra è?
This metal/stone is ...	Questo metallo/Questa pietra è ...
This is made of ...	Questa/o è di ...

MATERIALS

What is it made of?	De che cos'è fatta/o?
It's handmade.	È fabbricata/o a mano

It's made of ...   È fatta/o di ...

brass	ottone
bronze	bronzo
ceramic	ceramica
cotton	cotone
glass	vetro
gold	oro
leather	pelle; cuoio
linen	lino
lycra	licra
marble	marmo
metal	metallo
nylon	nailon

SHOPPING

DID YOU KNOW ...   By law you must obtain receipts for all goods and services in Italy. This applies to everything from a litre of milk to a haircut. Although it is uncommon, you could be asked by the Fiscal Police to produce a receipt immediately after you've bought something at a shop.

paper	carta
plastic	plastica
polyester	poliestere
porcelain	porcellana
copper	rame
satin	raso
silk	seta
silver	argento
stone	pietra
velvet	velluto
wood	legno
(pure, new) wool	(pura) lana (vergine)

COMMON EXPRESSIONS

At last!	Finalmente; Alla fine!
How lucky!	Che fortuna!
At once; Straight away.	Subito.
Wait!	Aspetta!
Watch out!; Careful!	Attenzione; Attenta/o!
What?	(Che) Cosa?
Not again!	Ancora!
Never again!	Mai più!
Everything's all right.	Tutto fila (liscio).
It's important.	È importante.
It's not important.	Non è importante.
It's possible.	È possibile.
It's (not) possible.	Non è possibile.
It's impossible to ...	Non c'è modo che ...
I don't care!	Non m'importa!
I don't give a damn/fuck!	Non me ne frega una sega/un cazzo!

SHOPPING

SHOPPING

COLOURS

dark	scura/o
light	chiara/o
black	nera/o
(dark) blue	blu
(mid) blue	azzurra/o
(light) blue	celeste
brown	marrone
burgundy	bordò/a
green	verde
grey	grigia/o
maroon	cardinale
orange	arancione
pink	rosa
purple	viola
red	rossa/o
white	bianca/o
yellow	gialla/o

LIKING

When you want to say that you like something in Italian you must literally say that something is pleasing to you. When you use the verb **piacere**, the person or thing liked is the subject and the person doing the liking is the object:

Ti piace l'arte?
Do you like art?
(lit: to you is pleasing the art?)

TOILETRIES

aftershave	il dopobarba
comb	un pettine
condoms	i preservativi
dental floss	il filo interdentale
deodorant	il deodorante
hairbrush	una spazzola (per i capelli)
conditioner	il balsamo per i capelli
moisturising cream	la crema idratante
nailclippers	il tagliaunghie
perfume	il profumo
pregnancy test kit	il test per la gravidanza
razor (electric)	un rasoio (elettrico)
razor blades	le lamette da barba
sanitary napkins	gli assorbenti igienici
shampoo	lo shampoo

shaving cream	la crema da barba
scissors	le forbicine
soap	il sapone
sunblock cream	la crema solare
talcum powder	il borotalco
tampons	i tamponi
tissues	i fazzolettini di carta
toilet paper	la carta igienica
toothbrush	lo spazzolino da denti
toothpaste	il dentifricio

See page 232 for more toiletries.

FOR THE BABY

baby chair	il seggiolino
baby food	gli omogeneizzati
baby powder	il borotalco
crib	il bavaglino
disposable nappies	i pannolini usa e getta
dummy	il ciuccio
feeding bottle	il biberon
nappy rash cream	la crema per l'irritazione da pannolini
playpen	il box; il recinto per bambini
potty	il vasino
pram/baby carriage	la carrozzina
pusher/stroller	il passeggino
teat	la tettarella
toy	il giocattolino; il gingillo

SHOPPING

DID YOU KNOW ... When the preopsition da is used before an infinitve, it indicates a goal – un libro da leggere means 'a book to be read'

AT THE HAIRDRESSER

Where can I get a haircut?	Dove posso tagliarmi i capelli
I like your haircut.	Mi piace il tuo taglio.
I want a haircut like this.	Vorrei un taglio come questo
I want it short.	Lo vorrei corto.
I just want a trim.	Vorrei solo una spuntatina.
I want to colour my hair.	Vorrei tingermi i capelli.

hairdresser	la parrucchiera/il parrucchiere; il barbiere (for men)
haircut	un taglio
hairstyle	la pettinatura
blonde	biondo
more/less blonde	piu/meno biondo
dark	scuro
more/less dark	piu/meno scuro

STATIONERY & PUBLICATIONS

The two major dailies are Rome's *La Repubblica* and Milan's *Corriere della Sera*. There are also a number of English-language newspapers available.

Is there an English-language bookshop?	C'è una libreria specializzata in lingua inglese?
Where is the English-language section?	Dov'è la sezione di lingua inglese?
Do you have the latest novel/book by ...?	Ha l'ultimo romanzo/libro di ...?
Do you have a copy of ...?	Ha una copia di ...?
Do you stock ...?	Tenete ...?
Can you recommend a good Italian book that's been translated into English?	Può consigliarmi un buon libro italiano tradotto in inglese?
Do you know if this author is translated into English?	Mi sa dire se questa/o scrittrice/scrittore è stata/o tradotta/o in inglese?

Useful Words

a map	una cartina ...; una pianta ...
city	della città
regional	della regione; zona
road	stradale
dictionary	un dizionario
envelope	una busta
newspaper in English	un giornale in inglese
newsagent	il giornalaio
novel in English	un romanzo in inglese
paper	la carta
pen (ballpoint)	una penna (a sfera)
postcards	le cartoline
scissors	le forbici

SHOPPING

MUSIC

I'm looking for a CD by ...	Cerco un cidì di ...
What is her/his best recording?	Qual è la sua migliore incisione?
What's the latest recording by ...?	Qual è l'ultima incisione di ...?
Where can I find the ... section?	Dov'è la sezione ... ?
Do you have this on ...?	Questo è inciso su ...?
CD	cidì
record	disco
cassette/tape	cassetta
May I listen to this CD here?	Potrei ascoltare qui questo cidì?
I want to buy a blank tape.	Vorrei comprare una cassetta vuota.
I want to buy a CD player.	Vorrei comprare un lettore cidì.

PHOTOGRAPHY

How much is it to process this film?	Quanto costa sviluppare questa pellicola?
When will it be ready?	Quando saranno pronte le foto?
I'd like to have some passport photos taken.	Vorrei delle foto formato tessera.
I'd like a film for this camera.	Vorrei una pellicola per questa macchina fotografica.
Would you put the film in for me, please?	Potrebbe inserire la pellicola Lei, per favore?
Do you have one-hour processing?	Avete un servizio di sviluppo istantaneo?

These photos have come	Queste foto sono venute
out really ...	davvero ...
out of focus	sfuocate
faint	sfumate
dark	opache; scure

battery	una pila
B&W	bianco e nero
camera	una macchina fotografica
colour	il colore
film	una pellicola
film speed	la sensibilità; la durata di esposizione
flash	il flash
lens	l'obiettivo
light meter	l'esposimetro
movie camera	una cinepresa
slides	le diapositive
telephoto lens	un teleobiettivo
video camera	una videocamera
videotape	un videonastro

LOSING YOUR COOL

Damn you!	Va' al diavolo!
Piss off!	Lèvati dai piedi!; Tògliti di torno!; Lèvati dai coglioni!
Go to hell!	Ma va' all'inferno!
Get fucked!	Vaffanculo!; Va' a cacare!
Fuck off!	Fottiti!; Va' a farti fottere/sbattere!
I can't stand you!	Mi stai sui coglioni. Mi stai sulle palle!
You're getting on my nerves!	Mi rompi!; Mi scocci!

SHOPPING

SMOKING

A packet of cigarettes, please.	Un pacchetto di sigarette, per favore.
Are these cigarettes strong/ mild?	Queste sigarette sono forti/ leggere?
Do you have a light?	Mi fai accendere?
Please don't smoke.	Per favore non fumare (inf)/ fumi (pol).
No, thank you. I don't smoke.	No, grazie. Non fumo.
I'm trying to give up.	Sto cercando di smettere.
Do you have an ashtray?	Hai un portacenere?

carton	una scatola
cigarette papers	le cartine (per sigarette)
cigarette machine	un distributore di sigarette
cigarettes	le sigarette
cigar	un sigaro; un toscano
filtered/unfiltered	con/senza filtro
lighter	un accendino
matches	i fiammiferi; i cerini
menthol	alla menta
pipe	una pipa
tobacconist	la tabaccheria
... tobacco (pipe)	il tabacco (da pipa) ...
dark	secco
light	dolce

SIZES & COMPARISONS

small	piccola/o
big	grande; grossa/o
heavy	pesante
light	leggera/o
more	(di) più
less	(di) meno
too much/too many	troppa/o/e/i

SHOPPING

many	tante/i
enough	abbastanza
also	anche
a little (bit)	un po'
a lot	molta/o; tanta/o
as ... as	(tanto) ... quanto;(così) ... come
few	poca/o; poche/i
some	alcune/i
neither ... nor ...	né ... né
either ... or ...	o ... o

CROSSWORD – SHOPPING

SHOPPING

Across
1. Make your purchases here
2. The best time to buy
3. Linked with time and arsenic
4. If you take advantage of them you'll save money

Down
2. Not enough light
3. Not his, not hers, not theirs nor yours.
5. ....with age.
6. Keep them on if you don't want trouble.
6. Social climbing for the upwardly mobile

Answers on page 324.

Eating is considered one of life's great pleasures in Italy. Cooking styles vary from region to region and there is plenty of room to be adventurous. Italians are still so busy discovering every region's rich and luscious cooking traditions that they haven't been quick to relish international cuisines.

MEALS

Lunch is traditionally the main meal of the day, and shops and businesses close for three to four hours each afternoon to accommodate the meal and the siesta which usually follows.

breakfast	**la (prima) colazione**
lunch	**il pranzo; la colazione**
dinner	**la cena**
meal	**il pasto**
entree	**il principio**
first course	**il primo piatto**
second/main course	**il secondo piatto**
dessert	**il dolce; il dessert**

Vegetarian & Special Meals

Vegetarians will have no trouble eating in Italy. Vegetables are a staple of the Italian diet. **Contorni** are vegetable dishes prepared in various ways. **Antipasti** (see page 177) consist mainly of vegetables, and there are many vegetarian pasta sauces to choose from (see page 178).

I'm a vegetarian.	**Sono vegetariana/o.**
Does this dish have meat?	**C'è carne in questo piatto?**
Could you cook this without meat?	**Potreste preparare questo piatto senza carne?**

FOOD

169

I don't eat ...	Non mangio ...
meat	carne
chicken	pollo
poultry	pollame
fish	pesce
seafood	frutti di mare
pork	maiale
cured/processed meats	salumi; insaccati

I'd like a kosher meal.	Vorrei un pasto kasher.

Is it ...?	È ...?
gluten-free	senza glutine
lactose-free	senza lattosio
wheat-free	senza frumento; senza grano
salt-free	senza sale
sugar-free	senza zucchero
yeast-free	senza lievito

BREAKFAST

Breakfast usually consists of a quick cappuccino and a pastry, gulped down while standing at the bar.

pastry	il cornetto
cereal	i fiocchi
corn flakes	i fiocchi di mais
muesli	il müesli
bacon & eggs	le uova alla pancetta
eggs Benedict	le uova alla Benedict
eggs florentine	le uova alla fiorentina
... eggs	le uova ...
scrambled	strapazzate
soft-boiled	alla coque
fried	fritte

See page 186 for your favourite coffee.

FOOD

EATING OUT

Table for ..., please.	Un tavolo per ..., per favore.
Do you have a highchair for the baby?	Ha mica un seggiolino per la bimba/il bimbo?
May I see the menu?	Potrei vedere il menù?
I'd like the set lunch, please.	Vorrei il menù del giorno/turistico, per favore.
What does it include?	Cosa è compreso?
Does it come with salad?	L'insalata è compresa?
Is service included in the bill?	Il servizio è compreso nel conto?
What is the soup of the day?	Qual è la zuppa/minestra del giorno?
What's the speciality here?	Qual è la vostra specialità?

PLACES TO EAT

Pizzerie and ristoranti speak for themselves, but you may like to try eating at one of these:

tavola calda
Literally 'hot table', these offer cheap self-service with a selection of hot dishes.

taverna
A small restaurant of a rustic nature, though not always cheap.

trattoria; osteria
These offer simple local dishes. They generally cater for locals rather than tourists, and are cheaper than ristoranti.

rosticceria
This place specialises in grilled meat and is often takeaway only.

FOOD

What can you recommend?
Cosa mi consiglia?

What's that?
Cos'è?

What's in this dish?
Quali sono gli ingredienti in questo piatto?

Not too spicy please.
Non troppo piccante, per favore.

Do you want anything to drink?
Cosa vuole (sg)/**volete** (pl) **da bere?**

Would you like ... ?
Vuole (sg)/**Volete** (pl) **dell'/del ... ?**

Please bring me ...?
Mi porta ... per favore?
some water **dell'acqua**
some wine **del vino**
some salt **del sale**
some pepper **del pepe**
some bread **del pane**

The bill, please.
Il conto, per favore.

Let's (not) give her/him a tip.
(Non) Diamole/Diamogli la mancia.

Thank you, that was delicious.
Grazie, era squisito.

FOOD

DID YOU KNOW ...   You usually need to order vegetables or salad as extras. **Insalata** is simply lettuce. **Insalata mista** is a tossed salad.

MENU DECODER

aceto	vinegar
addensare con farina e burro	to make a roux
affumicato	smoked
aglio	garlic

alghe marine giapponesi	(Japanese) sea vegetables
aneto	dill
antipasto	appetizers; hors d'oeuvres
arista	cured, cooked pork meat
aromatica/o	spicy
aromi	aromatic herbs; spices
arrosto	roast
arundo	arrowroot
avena	oats
baccalà	dried salt cod with garlic, parsley and sometimes tomatoes
bagna cauda	anchovy, olive oil and garlic dip served with raw vegetables
bagnomaria	bainmarie style
basilico	basil

ben cotta/o	well done
besciamella	white sauce
bietola	beet
biroldo	pig blood sausage
bollita/o	boiled
braciola	chop
brasata/o	braised
bresaola	thin slices of cured raw beef
brodo	broth
bruschetta	toasted bread with olive oil and various toppings
budino	pudding
buridda	fish soup with spices
al burro	in butter (sauce)
cacciucco	seafood stew with wine, garlic and herbs
(in) camicia	poached
cannella	cinnamon
cantucci	hard almond biscuits served with vin santo (a dessert wine)
caponata	eggplant with a tomato sauce
capperi	capers
carabaccia	onion soup
cardo	chard
carpaccio	raw sliced beef/fish
casseruola	casserole; saucepan
cedro	lime
cerfoglio	chervil
cicoria	chicory
cipolline	chives

MENU DECODER

coda alla vaccinara	braised oxtail with herbs and tomatoes (from Rome)	cuocere sulla gratella all'aperto	to barbecue
		curcuma	turmeric
codone	rump	cuscus	couscous
collo	neck	al dente	firm to the bite
condimento	condiment; seasoning; dressing	dolce	sweet
		dolci	desserts; sweets
condita/o	seasoned	dorata/o	golden brown
contorni	side dishes; vegetables	dragoncello	tarragon
		erba medica	alfalfa
coperto	cover charge	farcita/o	stuffed
coppa	fatty cured pork meat	fare un infuso	to infuse
		farinata	thin, crunchy bread made from oil and chickpea flour
coriandolo	coriander		
cosciotto	leg		
costata	entrecôte		
costoletta	cutlet; chop	filetto	fillet
cotechino	spicy pork sausage	foglia d'alloro	bay leaf
		fonduta	fondue
cotogna	quince	forno	oven
cotoletta alla milanese	veal cutlets in breadcrumbs (Wiener schnitzel)	frattaglie	offal
		fresca/o	fresh
		fritto	fried
		fritto misto	fried seafood
		frittura	fry up; fried food
cottura	cooking	frumento	wheat
crespa	crêpe	frutta	fruit
al creta	in a clay pot	frutta secca	dried fruit
in crosta	in pastry	glassa	icing; frosting
crostata	tart; flan	grano	wheat
crostino	savoury toast with various toppings	grano di pepe	peppercorn
		grano saraceno	buckwheat
		granturco	corn; maize
		grasso	fat; grease
cruda/o	raw	gratinata/o	au gratin
cuocere al forno	to bake	griglia	grill
		guarnito	garnished
cuocere alla griglia	to grill	guava	guava
		impanata/o	in breadcrumbs
cuocere in camicia	to poach	insalata	salad

MENU DECODER

involtini	parcels; roulade	pancia	stomach
involtini siciliani	rolled meat in breadcrumbs, stuffed with egg, ham and cheese	panzanella	tomato, onion, garlic, olive oil, bread and basil salad
lessata/o	boiled	pastella	batter
lombata;	loin	pasticcio	pie; pastry
lonza		pasto	meal
luganega	long, thin sausage	pelato	peeled
maggiorana	marjoram	peperoncini	chillies
mais	maize; corn	pesto	paste made from garlic, basil, pine-nuts and Parmesan
mandarino	mandarine/ tangerine		
mango	mango	pezzo	piece
marinata/o	marinated	piatto	dish; plate
menta	mint	piatto prelibato	choice dish
mettere sott'aceto	to pickle	piccante	spicy
migliaccio	pig blood pancake	(alla) pizzaiola	pizza-style (with tomatoes and red peppers)
miglio	millet	poco cotta/o	undercooked
minestra brodosa	watery soup; broth	polenta	made from cornmeal; often grilled and served with a sauce
mirtilli	blueberries		
mista	mixed		
mortadella	cured horse meat		
nespola	loquat	polpette	meatballs; rissoles
noce	walnut; rumpsteak	polpettone	meatloaf
		pomodori secchi	sundried tomatoes
noce moscata	nutmeg		
non troppo cotta/o	medium rare	popone verde	honeydew
		portafoglio	pocket
origano	oregano	prezzemolo	parsley
orto	vegetable	primavera	spring vegetable sauce
orzo	barley		
ossobuco	veal shanks in a ragoût sauce, rice and peas	primo piatto	first course
		principio	entree
		prosciutto cotto	boiled/cooked ham
pancetta	bacon		

MENU DECODER

prosciutto crudo	cured ham	sarde in saor	grilled sardines in sweet and sour sauce
prugna	prune		
puntine	ribs	scamone	rump
raffermo	stale (of bread)	scottata/o	blanched; scorched
ragù	meat sauce	scottiglia di cinghiale	wild boar chops
ribes neri	blackcurrants		
ribes rossi	redcurrants	secca	dried; dry
ripieno	stuffed	secondo piatto	second/main course
rigatino	cured pork strips		
riso (scuro/ integrale)	rice (brown)	segale	rye
		semisecchi	semidried
risotto	rice dish	semolino	semolina
risotto alla milanese	rice dish with onion, saffron, stock and Parmesan	servizio	service charge
		spalla	shoulder
		spicchio	segment; slice
		spiedini	kebabs; skewers
risotto alla romana	rice dish with liver, sweet- breads and Marsala	stantia/o	stale
		stracotta/o	overcooked
		stufato	stew
		sugo	sauce
risi e bisi	rice with peas	supplì di riso	fried balls of rice stuffed with mozzarella
riungere	to baste		
rosmarino	rosemary		
rosolato	browned	tagliata/o	sliced; chopped
rotolo	roll	teglia di pasta	pasta bake
rucola	rocket	timo	thyme
salame	dry-cured pork sausage	tritata/o	minced; ground
		torta	cake; tart; flan
salamoiare	to pickle (in brine)	tortino	pie
salsa	sauce	troppo cotta/o	overcooked
salsiccia	sausage	al vapore	steamed
saltata/o	sautéed	verdure	vegetables
saltimbocca alla romana	veal with ham, cheese and sage	verdure di mare	sea vegetables
		al vino	in wine (sauce)
		vino della casa	house wine
al salto	sautéed	zafferano	saffron
salvia	sage	zampone	stuffed pig's trotter
al sangue	rare; undercooked	zenzero	ginger
sapore	taste; flavour	zuppa	soup
saporita/o	tasty; seasoned		

FOOD

TYPICAL DISHES
Appetisers (Antipasti)

antipasto misto	assortment of cold appetisers
bruschetta	crisp baked bread slices in oil, often with tomato on top (Florence, Tuscany)
caponata (alla siciliana)	eggplant dish with capers, olives, onion and anchovies (Sicily)
ceci con origano	marinated chickpeas with oregano
condimento al pepe	pepper relish
prosciutto e melone	melon with cured ham
olive ascolane	stuffed, deep-fried olives
sottaceti	pickled vegetables

Soup (Zuppa; Brodo)

cappelletti	a form of ravioli with various stuffings in broth
cuscucu	fish soup (Sicily)
minestrone	vegetable soup, often with beef stock and pork
stracciatella	egg in broth
zuppa pavese	Pavian soup of bread, butter, chicken broth and eggs
paparot	spinach soup (Istria)

Rice (Riso)

bomba di riso	rice with pigeon (Parma)
polenta	cornmeal, often sliced and deep-fried
risi e bisi	risotto with green peas (Venice/Veneto)
risotto in capro roman	risotto with mutton (Venice)
sartù	savoury rice dish (Naples)
supplì	deep-fried balls of rice with mozzarella cheese and tomato sauce inside

FOOD

Pasta Sauces

Italian sauces are delicious, and it is quite acceptable to use the unsalted bread provided to mop up your sauce. Pastasciutta is the collective name for over 500 varieties of products made from flour, water and sometimes eggs. If you want your pasta to be cooked to perfection, ask for it to be al dente which means 'to the tooth'.

Note that pasta dishes are generally larger than main dishes, so this is the course to fill up on if you're very hungry.

aglio e olio	garlic and olive oil
alfredo	butter, cream, Parmesan cheese and parsley
alla checca	cold summer sauce of ripe tomatoes, olives, basil, capers and oregano (Rome)
alla bolognese	minced beef, tomatoes, onions and herbs

alla carbonara	cured bacon (pancetta), cream, paprika, egg and parmesan cheese
all'amatriciana	spicy tomato and bacon
misto di mare	mixed seafood, often in cream and wine
alla pescatora; marinara	mixed seafood, often in tomato sauce
al pesto	basil, pine nuts, parmesan and garlic
alla puttanesca	spicy tomato sauce with anchovies, olives and basil
al ragù	chunks of meat, tomatoes, onions and herbs
alla siciliana	eggplant, anchovies, olives, capers, tomato and garlic
al tonno e funghi	tuna and mushrooms in tomato and cream sauce

Main Dishes (Piatti Principali)

anelletti gratinati	crumbed fried cuttlefish rings (Sicily)
baccalà mantecato	purée of salt cod, served with polenta (Veneto)
burrida; ciuppa; zimmo sfogie in saòr	fish stew (Genoa, Liguria) sole with herbs and garlic (Venice, Veneto)
abbacchio	young lamb (Rome, Lazio)
bistecca alla fiorentina	huge grilled T-bone steak; often priced all'etto, per hundred grams, (Florence)
bollito	various meats boiled and served with vegetables (Turin, Piedmont)
busella	tripe dish (Milan, Lombardy)
calzone	folded pizza (Naples)
capon magro	salad of vegetables and fish (Genoa, Liguria)
cima	cold veal, stuffed with pork, sweet breads, nuts, peas and eggs (Genoa)
cotechino	sausage, stuffed with raw spice pork (Emilia-Romagna)

FOOD

fasœil al fûrn	oven-baked beans (Piedmont)
finocchiona	spicy salami, with fennel seeds (Florence, Tuscany)
involtini	stuffed veal rolls (Bologna, Emilia-Romagna)
polenta e osei	small roasted birds, served with polenta (Milan, Lombardy)
tacchino con sugo di melagrana	turkey with pomegranate sauce (Venice, Veneto)
testarelle di abbacchio	lamb's heads (Rome, Lazio)
tortino	flat omelette with vegetables (Florence, Tuscany)
zampone	pig's trotters, stuffed with raw spiced sausage (Modena)

Desserts (Dolci)

bignè alla cioccolata	puff pastry filled with cream and covered with chocolate
cannoli	tubes of sweet pastry filled with a rich cream
cassata	pudding of sponge, cream, fruit and chocolate; also an ice-cream
crema inglese/ all'uovo	custard
granita di limone	lemon-water ice
macedonia	fruit salad
panettone	large, dry yeast cake
panna cotta	type of cheesecake
paste di mandorle	almond pastries
tiramisù	trifle dessert with a chocolate, coffee and marscarpone base
zabaglione; zabaione	egg yolks whipped with sugar and Marsala
zuccotto	almond and hazelnut cake with brandy
zuppa inglese	trifle

SELF CATERING

Where can I find ...?	**Dove trovo ...?**
biscuits	**i biscotti**
bread	**il pane**
butter	**il burro**
cheese	**il formaggio**
chocolate	**il cioccolato**
eggs	**le uova**
flour	**la farina**
frozen foods	**i surgelati**
fruit & vegetables	**la frutta e verdura**
honey	**il miele**
ice-cream	**il gelato**
jam	**la marmellata;**
	la confettura di frutta
margarine	**la margarina**
mayonnaise	**la maionese**
mustard	**la senape; la mostarda**
olive/sunflower oil	**l'olio d'oliva/di girasole**
pepper	**il pepe**
salt	**il sale**
sugar	**lo zucchero**
vinegar	**l'aceto**
yoghurt	**l'yogurt**

bottle	**una bottiglia**	packet	**un pacchetto**
box	**una scatola**	sachet/bag	**un sacchettino**
can	**una lattina**	tin	**una scatoletta**

DID YOU KNOW ... For a quick and cheap snack, try a **panino** (sandwich) — served at most bars and caffès — or **pizza al taglio** (pizza by the slice).

FOOD

BREAD OF LIFE

Italian bread comes in all varieties. Here's a guide so you won't be too confused at the bakery.

focaccia	flat bread
schiacciata	crunchy, flat bread
ciabatta	crisp, long loaf
casereccio	firm, floury loaf
pane salato	savoury bread
pane all'olio	oil bread
pane aromatico	herb or vegetable bread
pagnotta; coppia	loaf
filoncino	breadstick
panino; pagnottella	breadroll
pane integrale	wholemeal bread
pane a lievito naturale	sourdough bread
pane al sesamo	sesame bread
pane di segale	rye bread
pane di mais	corn bread
pane scuro	brown loaf
pan di frutta	fruit bread
pan di zucchero	sugar loaf

AT THE MARKET
Meat (Carne)

beef	il manzo
brains	le cervella
chop	la braciola
pork	il maiale
hare	la lepre
horse meat	la carne equina
kid (goat)	il capretto
lamb	l'agnello

FOOD

liver	il fegato
offal	le interiora
mutton	il montone
steak	la bistecca
tongue	la lingua
tripe	la trippa
veal	il vitello
venison	il cervo
wild boar	il cinghiale
game	la selvaggina;
	la cacciagione (large game)

Poultry & Wildfowl (Pollame & Selvaggina)

capon	il cappone
chicken	il pollo
duck	l'anitra
goose/geese	l'oca/le oche
pheasant	il fagiano
partridge	la pernice
pigeon	il piccione
quail	la quaglia
turkey	il tacchino
fowl	i volatili

Fish & Seafood (Pesce & Frutti di Mare)

anchovies	le acciughe
bream	l'abramide
calamari	i calamari
cockles	le vongole
cod	il baccalà; il merluzzo; lo stoccafisso
crab	il granchio
crayfish	il gambero
eel	l'anguilla
fish	il pesce
hake	il nasello
herring	l'aringa

FOOD

lobster	l'aragosta
mackerel	lo sgombro
mussels	le cozze
octopus	il polipo
oysters	le ostriche
prawns	i gamberoni
red mullet	la triglia
salmon	il salmone
shrimp	gli scampi
spider crab	la granceola; la grancevola
trout	la trota
tuna	il tonno

Vegetables (Verdure)

artichoke	il carciofo
asparagus	gli asparagi
avocado	l'avocado
bean shoots	i germogli di fagiolo
beetroot	la barbabietola
broccoli	i broccoli
cabbage	il cavolo
capsicum	il peperone
carrot	la carota
cauliflower	il cavolfiore
celery	il sedano
cucumber	il cetriolo
eggplant/aubergine	la melanzana
endive	l'indivia
fennel	il finocchio
green/string beans	i fagiolini
leek	il porro
lettuce	la lattuga
mushrooms	i funghi
onion	la cipolla
potato	la patata
pumpkin	la zucca

radish	il ravanello
shallots	le scalogne
tomato	il pomodoro
truffles	i tartufi
turnip	la rapa
silverbeet	la bietola
spinach	gli spinaci
zucchini	gli zucchini

... olives	le olive ...
green	verdi
black	nere
stuffed	ripiene

Fruit (Frutta)

apple	la mela
apricot	l'albicocca
banana	la banana
blackberries	le more
cherries	le ciliegie
coconut	la noce di cocco
date	il dattero
fig	il fico
grapefruit	il pompelmo
grapes	l'uva
kiwifruit/s	il kiwi
lemon	il limone
melon	il melone
nectarine	la nocepesca
orange	l'arancia
persimmon	il cachi
peach	la pèsca
pear	la pera
pineapple	l'ananas
plum	la susina

SHHHHH

The combination **sc** is hard as the 'sc' in 'scooter' before **a**, **o**, **u** and **h** but soft as the 'sh' in 'sheep' before **e** and **i**.

FOOD

raisins	**l'uva secca**
raspberries	**i lamponi**
sultana	**l'uva sultanina; l'uvetta**
strawberries	**le fragole**
watermelon	**il cocomero**

COFFEE HEAVEN

The Italians have many ways of drinking their coffee. Here's a guide so you'll know what to ask for when you order yours.

caffè latte
coffee with milk. A breakfast drink.

caffè macchiato
strong coffee with a little milk

cappuccino   named after the Capuchin monks who wore robes of chocolate and cream colours; considered a morning drink by Italians

espresso   very strong black coffee served in small cups and drunk at any time of the day

ristretto   very concentrated, even stronger than the espresso; strictly for the initiated only

corretto   with a dash of liqueur; drunk especially after meals

doppio   long and black; also known as **americano**

latte macchiato   hot milk with a little coffee; enjoyed by children.

FOOD

DRINKS (BEVANDE)

Nonalcoholic

almond milk	l'orzata
bitter coke	il chinotto
fruit juice	il succo di frutta
milk	il latte
mineral water	l'acqua minerale
plain water	l'acqua non gassata/naturale
orange juice	il succo d'arancia/l'aranciata
soft drink	la bibita
tamarind drink	il tamarindo
.. tea	il tè ...
chamomile	alla camomilla
peppermint	alla menta
rosehip	alla rosa
lemon	al limone
milk	al latte
herbal	alle erbe
decaffeinated	decaffeinato

AT THE BAR

Shall we go for a drink?	Andiamo a prendere qualcosa da bere?
I'll buy you a drink.	Ti offro una bevanda.
Okay.	D'accordo; Okay; Va bene.
Thanks, but I don't feel like it.	Grazie, (ma) non mi va.
What would you like?	Cosa prendi?
Cheers!	Cin cin!
I'll have ...	Prendo ...
an anise	una sambuca
a beer	una birra
a (bitters/digestive) liqueur	un amaro; un digestivo
a brandy	un cognac; un'acquavite

FOOD

a champagne	uno champagne; uno spumante
a cocktail	un cocktail; un aperitivo
a coke	una coca
a cider	un sidro
a grappa	una grappa
a martini	un martini
a mineral water	un'acqua minerale
a rum	un rum
a whisky	un whisky
a glass of wine	un bicchiere di vino

I'll have a rum and coke.	Mi dia un rum e coca?
I'll have a vodka and orange.	Prendo una vodka e arancia.
I don't drink.	Non bevo.

Getting Attention In The Bar

I'm next!	Dopo sta a me!; La/Il prossima/o sono io!
Excuse me!	Scusi!
I was here before this lady/ gentleman.	C'ero prima io di questa/o signora/e!

Cheers!

It's my round.	Mi occupo io di queste.
It's on me.	Pago io; Offro io.
You can get the next one.	La prossima la paghi tu.
Same again, please.	Facciamo il bis; Un altro, per favore.

FOOD

DID YOU KNOW ...   Be aware that the prices double, and sometimes triple, if you sit down to eat or drink in a bar.

One Too Many?

I'm a bit tired, I'd better get
   home.
Where is the toilet?
Is food available here?

Sono un po' stanca/o, è
   meglio che vada a casa.
Dove sono i servizi?
Servite cibi qua?

FOOD

I'm feeling tipsy.	**Mi sento un po' brilla/o**
I'm feeling drunk.	**Mi sento un po' ubriaca/o.**
I think I've had one too many.	**Sento d'aver bevuto troppo.**
I'm pissed.	**Sono ciucca/o; Sono ubriaca/o.**
I feel ill.	**Non mi sento bene;**
	Mi sento male.
I feel like throwing up.	**Mi viene da vomitare.**
She/He's passed out.	**È svenuta/o.**
I'm hung over.	**Ho la sbornia.**

THEY MAY SAY ...

Italian has many words for 'hangover', though they can't easily be translated literally.

la ciucca	**la piomba**
la stoppa	**la toppa**

WINE

Wine is an essential accompaniment to any meal. Most people tend to order the house wine **(vino della casa)** or the local wine **(vino locale)** when they go out to dinner.

May I see the wine list, please?	**Mi fa vedere la lista dei vini, per favore?**
What is a good year?	**Qual è una buona annata?**
May I taste it?	**Posso degustarlo?**
Which wine would you recommend with this dish?	**Quale vino è consigliabile con questo piatto?**
I'd like a glass of ... wine.	**Vorrei un bicchiere di vino ...**
red	**rosso**
white	**bianco**
rosé	**rosat**

FOOD

This wine has a nice/bad taste.	Questo vino ha un buon/ cattivo sapore.
This wine has a nice/bad colour.	Questo vino ha un bel/ brutto colore.

very dry	molto secco
dry	secco
semi-dry/full	rotondo
fruity	amabile
lightly sweet	dolcigno
sweet	dolce
very sweet	molto dolce

WINE

There is a classification system for wines in Italy. The class of wine is marked on the label:

enominazione d'origine controllata (DOC)
> this wine is produced subject to certain specifications, although the label doesn't certify quality.

denominazione d'origine controllata e garantita (DOCG)
> this wine is subject to the same requirements as DOC but it is also tested by government inspectors

vino da tavola (table wine)
> these wines are generally of a lower standard although some can be of excellent quality

FOOD

CHEESE FORMAGGIO

besciamella
not really a cheese, it i
used in many dishes
as a sauce

caprino
tart goat cheese
often mixed at the
table   into a paste
with oil, pepper and a
drop of sweet vinegar

fontina	creamy kind of Gruyère (Piedmont)
gorgonzola	soft, rich, blue-veined cheese
mascarpone	mild creamy cheese; often used in desserts
mozzarella	traditionally made from buffalo's milk
parmigiano	parmesan; often simply called **grana**
pecorino	hard cheese, usually made from ewe's milk; popular at the end of a meal
provolone	rich and piquant cheese made from cow's milk
ricotta	soft ewe's-milk cheese
sardo	popular, sharply flavoured cheese (Sardinia)
stracchino	very soft, subtly flavoured cheese eaten with fruit
taleggio	a soft, subtle cheese (Piedmont)

CAMPING

Facilities range from major complexes with swimming pools, tennis courts, restaurants and supermarkets to simple camping grounds. Free camping is generally not permitted. Always get permission from the landowner if you want to camp on private property.

SIGN	
VIETATO CAMPEGGIARE	NO CAMPING

Am I allowed to camp here?	Si può piantare la tenda qui?
Is there a campsite nearby?	C'è un campeggio qui vicino?
Where's the nearest campsite?	Dov'è il campeggio più vicino?
How much is it per night?	Quant'è per notte?
Are the showers free?	Le docce sono somprese nel prezzo?
Where can I hire a tent?	Dovo posso noleggiare una tenda?
Where can I get drinking water?	Dove trovo dell'acqua potabile?

can opener	un'apriscatole
canvas	la tela
firewood	la legna da ardere; per il fuoco
gas cylinder	una bombola a g as
hammock	un'amaca
mat	una stuoia
mattress	un materasso
penknife	un temperino
rope	una corda
tent	una tenda

tent pegs	i picchetti (per la tenda)
torch (flashlight)	una torcia elettrica
sleeping bag	un sacco a pelo
stove (portable)	un fornellino; una stufa (a gas)
water bottle/flask	una borraccia

HIKING & MOUNTAINEERING

The Alps and Appenines have many well-marked trails and strate gically placed rifugi (refuges) along the way where you can sta and buy food. Most rifugi are open only from July to September

What hiking routes are in this region?	Quali sono i sentieri in questa regione?
How long is the trek?	Quanto è lungo il sentiero?
Is it a difficult walk?	È un percorso difficile?
Is it a scenic walk?	È un percorso panoramico?
Does this path go to ...?	Questo sentiero va verso ...?
How many kilometres to ...?	Quanti chilometri
Where can we spend the night?	Dove possiamo passare la notte?
We've lost our way.	Ci siamo perduti.

antiglare sunglasses	gli occhiali antiriflesso
backpack	lo zaino
binoculars	il binocolo
bivouac	il bivacco
boots	gli scarponi
to climb	scalare; arrampicarsi
compass	una bussola
crampons	i ramponi; le grapinette
first aid kit	un set di pronto soccorso
gloves	i guanti
hiking	lo hiking; l'escursionismo
ice-axe	una piccozza
map (topographical)	una carta topografica
mountaineering	l'alpinismo

multipurpose knife	un coltellino multifunzioni
rope	la corda
stove (portable)	il fornellino
tracks/slopes	le piste
trekking	il trekking

AT THE BEACH

SIGN	
VIETATO NUOTARE	NO SWIMMING

Do you feel like going for a swim?	Ti va di andare a nuotare?
Is it safe to swim?	È sicuro da nuotare?
What time is high/low tide?	A che ora è l'alta/bassa marea?

bather	una/un bagnante
beach bag	una sacca da spiaggia
changing booth	la cabina; lo spogliatoio
coast	la costa; la riviera
hat	un cappello
lifeguard	una/un bagnina/o
rocks	gli scogli
sand	la sabbia
sea	il mare
sunblock	la crema solare
sunglasses	gli occhiali da sole
surfboard	una tavola da surf
swimsuit	un costume da bagno
towel	l'asciugamano
waterskiing	lo sci acquatico
wave	l'onda; l'ondata

See also Aquatic Sports, page 209.

GEOGRAPHICAL TERMS

agriculture	l'agricoltura
bridge	il ponte
caves	le grotte
cliff	la scogliera; il dirupo
creek	la insenatura; la baia
crops	il raccolto
forest	la foresta

hill	la collina
lake	il lago
mountain pass	il passo di montagna; un valico
mountains	le montagne
nature reserve	una riserva naturale
peak	il picco; la vetta
pond	lo stagno; il bacino
river	il fiume
scenery	il paesaggio; il panorama
trail	il sentiero
waterfall	la cascata

FAUNA
Farm Animals

What's that ... called?	Come si chiama ...?
animal	quell'animale
bird	quell'uccello
insect	quell'insetto

ant	la formica
butterfly	la farfalla
cat	il gatto; il micio
chicken	il pollo
cow	la mucca; la vacca
dog	il cane
donkey	l'asino
duck	l'anatra
fly	la mosca
goat	la capra
goldfish	il pesciolino rosso
horse	il cavallo
ox	il bue
pig	il maiale
sheep	la pecora

See also Pets, page 114.

IN THE COUNTRY

WEATHER

As in English, the present tense is also used in Italian when referring to future weather conditions, so long as a future word is used in the sentence, eg **domani** (tomorrow).

The weather is ... today.	**Oggi è ...**
Will it be ... tomorrow?	**Domani ... sarà?**
cloudy	**nuvoloso**
cold	**freddo**
drizzly	**piovigginoso**
foggy	**nebbioso**
hot	**caldo**
sultry	**afoso**
sunny	**soleggiato**

How is it?

It's overcast.	**E coperto.**
It's raining.	**Piove.**
It's snowing.	**Nevica.**
It's hailing.	**Grandina.**
It's windy.	**Tira vento; È ventoso.**
It's drizzling.	**Pioviggina.**
It's sleeting.	**Nevischia.**
It's hazy.	**C'è foschia.**

It's a beautiful day.	**Fa bel tempo.**
The weather's bad.	**Fa brutto tempo.**
The sun's out.	**C'è il sole.**
It's cool outside.	**È fresco fuori.**

Wildlife

badger	il tasso
bear	l'orso
chamois	il camoscio
deer	il cervo
dolphin	il delfino
fallow deer	il daino
fox	la volpe
frog	la rana
hare	la lepre
heron	l'airone
ibex (wild goat)	lo stambecco
lynx	la lince
marmot	la marmotta
porcupine	il porcospino
rabbit	il coniglio
roe-deer	il capriolo
seal	la foca
shark	lo squalo; il pescecane
snake	il serpente
spider	il ragno
squirrel	lo scoiattolo
toad	il rospo
turtle	la tartaruga
viper	la vipera
wild	selvaggia/o; selvatica/o
wild boar	il cinghiale
wolf	il lupo
woodpecker	il picchio

DID YOU KNOW ... I farinacei is used to refer to any food made from flour, eg pasta and bread as well as beans. It comes from the word farina ('flour').

IN THE COUNTRY

Birds

bird	l'uccello
canary	il canarino
cormorant	il cormorano
crow	la cornacchia
eagle	l'aquila
falcon	il falcone
flamingo	il fenicottero
hawk	il falco
pheasant	il fagiano
pigeon	il piccione
quail	la quaglia
sparrow	il passero
swallow	la rondine
vulture	l'avvoltoio

GENDER

You can often recognise the gender of a noun from its ending. Feminine nouns usually end in a in the singular and e in the plural; masculine nouns usually end in o in the singular and i in the the plural. There are a few exceptions, however. (See page 21.)

FLORA

What kind of plant/tree is that?	Che (tipo di) pianta/fiore è quello?
beech	il faggio
birch	la betulla
fir	l'abete
maple	l'acero
marshland	la palude
oak	la quercia
pine	il pino
plane	il platano
spruce	l'abete rosso

Plants & Flowers

azalea	l'azalea
buttercup	il ranuncolo
cornflower	il fiordaliso

deadly nightshade
  la belladonna
cyclamen
  il ciclamino
edelweiss
  la stella alpina
nettle
  l'ortica

SEASONS	
summer	l'estate
autumn	l'autunno
winter	l'inverno
spring	la primavera

bluebell	la campanula
gentian	la genziana
heather	l'erica
holly	l'agrifoglio
honeysuckle	il caprifoglio
juniper	il ginepro
lavender	la lavanda
lily	il giglio
lily of the valley	il mughetto
mistletoe	il vischio
narcissus	il narciso
poppy	il papavero
primrose	la primula
rhododendron	il rododendro
snapdragon	la bocca di leone
snowdrop	il bucaneve
thistle	il cardo (alpestre)
wild rose	la rosa selvatica

IN THE COUNTRY

CROSSWORD – IN THE COUNTRY

Across
1. A tin of anything is useless without it
2. Too wet to walk in
3. The day we're always waiting for
4. Built to get us over the top

Down
2. You need good shoes for this
4. It always does when you organise a picnic
5. Temporary shelter
6. Social climbing for the upwardly mobile

Answers on page 324.

TYPES OF SPORT

I like .../Do you like ...	Mi piace .../Ti piace ...?
I play .../Do you play ...?	Pratico .../Pratichi ...?
athletics	l'atletica
baseball	il baseball
basketball	la pallacanestro
boxing	il pugilato; la boxe
car racing	l'automobilismo
cricket	il cricket
cycling	il ciclismo
diving	il tuffo
equestrian sports	l'equitazione
fencing	la scherma
fishing	la pesca
football	il football
golf	il golf
gymnastics	la ginnastica
hockey	l'hockey
horse racing	la corsa ippica
rollerblading	il roller in linea
rowing	il cannottaggio
rugby	il rugby
skiing	lo sci
sailing	la vela
skateboarding	lo skateboard
soccer	il calcio
squash	la pallaelastica
surfing	il surf
swimming	il nuoto
tennis	il tennis
volleyball	la pallavolo
waterpolo	la pallanuoto
weight training	il culturismo

ACTIVITIES

recreational sports	gli sport ricreativi
competitive sports	gli sport competitivi
extreme sports	gli sport estremi
indoor sports	gli sport al coperto; indoor

TALKING ABOUT SPORT

Do you like sport?	Ti piace lo sport?
Yes, very much.	Sì, moltissimo.
No, not at all.	No, niente affatto.
I like watching, rather than participating.	Mi piace assistere, piuttosto che partecipare.
Which sport do you like?	Quale sport ti piace?
What sport do you play?	Quale sport pratichi?
Which sport do you follow?	Quale sport segui?
I follow ...	Sono appassionata/o di ...; Tifo per ...
Who's your favourite ... ?	Chi/Qual è la /il tua/o ... preferita/o?
player	giocatrice/giocatore
sportsperson	sportiva/o
athlete	atleta
team	squadra

GOING TO THE MATCH

Would you like to go to a ... game?	Ti piacerebbe andare a una partita di ...?
Where is it being held?	Dove viene giocata/o?
What time does it start?	A che ora comincia?
Who is playing?	Chi gioca?
Who's winning?	Chi vince?
Who do you think will win?	Chi pensi che vincerà?
What's the (final) score?	Qual è il punteggio (finale)?
It's three goals to one.	È tre a uno.

It was a draw.	Hanno pareggiato; C'è stato un pareggio.
Who are you supporting?	Per chi fai il tifo?
I'm supporting ...	Tifo per ...
That was a really good game!	Che bella partita!; Che partitona!
What a bad game!	Che partitaccia!

SOCCER

Although many sports are popular in Italy, soccer is undoubtedly the country's favourite. Italy's Serie A is regarded as one of the best leagues in the world with clubs such as AC Milan and Juventus having much success in European and world club competitions. The national team, the Azzurri, has won the World Cup three times. Famous players include Dino Zoff, Paolo Rossi, Roberto Baggio and Gianfranco Zola.

corner	l'angolo
cup	la coppa
fans/supporters	i tifosi; i sostenitori
foul	un fallo
goalkeeper	il portiere

ACTIVITIES

THEY MAY SAY ...

Forza!; Dài	Come on!
Gol!; Rete!	Goal!
Che ...!	What a ...!
gol; rete	gaol
colpo	hit
calcio	kick
passaggio	pass
esecuzione	performance

league	la serie
offside	fuori gioco
penalty	un rigore
to score	segnare; marcare
to shoot	tirare

THEY MAY SAY ...

You'll often hear fans shouting **Alé!** or **Forza ragazzi!** at soccer matches.

ACTIVITIES

Some Italian Soccer Clubs

AC Milan	Lazio
Atalanta	Lecce
Bari	Napoli
Bologna	Parma
Brescia	Piacenza
Empoli	Roma
Fiorentina	Sampdoria
Genoa	Torino
Internazionale di Milano (Inter)	Udinese
Juventus	Vicenza

IMPORTANT SOCCER TOURNAMENTS

Serie A	1st Division - Top National League
Serie B	2nd Division
Coppa Italia	Italian Cup
Coppa UEFA	UEFA Cup
Coppa Delle Coppe	Cup-winner's Cup
Champions League	Champions' League
Campionato Europeo	European Cup
Mondiali	World Cup

CYCLING

If you're serious about cycling in Italy, a mountain bike is a good idea as so much of the country is hilly. There are also plenty of marked trails and guided bike rides. It is quite cheap to take bikes on planes, trains and ferries in Italy.

Is this road OK for bikes?	Si può percorrere in bici questa strada?
Is there a cycling track?	C'è una pista per le biciclette?
Excuse me, I'm looking for a bike shop.	Scusi, sto cercando un negozio di biciclette.

ACTIVITIES

bicycle	una bicicletta; una bici
cycle race	una gara ciclistica
mountain bike	una bici da montagna; una mountain bike; un rampichino
racing bike	una bici da corsa

See also Bicycle, page 72.

SWEARING

Damn (...)!	Accidenti (a ...)!; Maledizione!
Shit!	Merda!
Fucking hell!	Cazzo (fottuto)!
Fuck!	Cazzo!
Bloody ...!	Maledetto ...!; Dannato ...!; ... fottuto!
Blast!/ ... Hell!	Boia (di ...)!
God!	Dio!
Christ!	Cristo!
Jesus!	Gesú!
Goodness!	Madonna!

These last four interjections are often creatively combined with other swear words for a much stronger effect.

ACTIVITIES

SKIING

Ski season in Italy is generally from December to late March but some areas have year-round skiing. There are a number of ski resorts in the Dolomites which offer the most dramatic scenery.

WATCH IT!

Don't ever point at anyone with your little finger and index finger. It is considered a great insult in Italy.

Is it possible to go cross-country skiing at ...?	Si può fare lo sci di fondo a ...?
How much is a pass for these slopes?	Quant'è il pass per queste piste?
What are the skiing conditions like at ...?	In quali condizioni sono le piste a ...?
What is the snow like on the different slopes?	Di quale consistenza è la neve sulle varie piste?
Which are the hardest/easiest slopes?	Quali sono le piste piu facili/ piu difficili?
Is it possible to snowboard on this slope?	Si può praticare il surf da neve su questa pista?

cable car	la funivia
instructor	una/un maestra di sci
skis	gli sci
ski-poles	i bastoncini
ski-pass	lo ski-pass
ski-boots	gli scarponi da sci
ski-lift	la seggiovia; la sciovia
ski resort	la località sciistica
ski-suit	la tuta da sci
slope	una pista
skiing lesson	una lezione di sci
sleet	il nevischio
sunblock	la crema solare
snowboard	una tavola da neve;un snowboard

QUATIC SPORTS

dyboard/boogieboard	una tavola corta (da surf)
nghy/boat	un canotto; una barchetta
ving	il tuffo; l'immersione
ggles	gli occhiali sub
ebelt/lifebuoy	un salvagente;
	una cintura di salvataggio
otorboat	un motoscafo
iling	andare a vela
iling boat/yacht	una banca a vela; lo yacht
uba diving/skin diving	l'immersione subacquea
nblock	la crema solare
rf	il cavallone
surf	surfare
rfboard	una tavola da surf
rfer	una/un surfista
vimmer	una nuotatrice/un nuotatore
vimming pool	una piscina
aterskiing	lo sci acquatico
vindsurfing	il windsurf

ACTIVITIES

ee also At the Beach, page 195.

DID YOU KNOW ...

Every year in Sanremo, on the Italian Riviera, there is a contest for the best song of the year. The Festival Nazionale della Canzone di Sanremo features the best (or worst) of Italy's singers and songwriters and is watched on TV by more than 20 million people

ACTIVITIES

KEEPING FIT

Where is the nearest ...?	Dov'è la/il più vicina/o ...?
gym	palestra
swimming pool	piscina
tennis court	campo da tennis
What is the charge per ...?	Qual è il prezzo richiesto ...?
day	per la giornata
game	per una partita
hour	all'ora
Can I hire ...?	Posso noleggiare ...?
a bicycle	una bicicletta
a racquet	una racchetta
skis	degli sci
a surfboard	una tavola da surf
a wetsuit	una muta; una tuta sub
Do I have to be a member?	È necessario essere soci?
Where can I do aerobics/yoga?	Dove si fa/pratica l'aerobica/lo yoga?
Where can we go jogging?	Dove possiamo praticare il footing/jogging?

HORSE RACING

In Italy, horseracing is not as celebrated as it is in Anglo-Celtic countries, but there is a loyal and sizeable following. The largest and most established racecourses are San Siro in Milan, Capannelle in Rome and Agnano in Naples. Betting on the horses through bookmakers or the totalizer (TOTIP) is popular on Sundays.

I'd like to have a bet on number (twelve).	Vorrei scommettere/puntare sul numero (dodici).

bookmaker	l'allibratore
dividend	il dividendo
each-way bet	l'accoppiata invertibile/reversibile
form guide	il programma delle corse
jockey	la/il fantina/o
odds	la posta; la quota
racecourse/racetrack	l'ippodromo
totalizer	il totalizzatore
trifecta	il trio

USEFUL WORDS

ball	la palla
basket	il canestro
bat	la mazza; il bastone
court; field	il campo
goalpost	il palo (della porta)
loser	la/il perdente
net	la rete
point	il punto
racquet	la racchetta
referee	l'arbitro
rules	le regole
scoreboard	il tabellone
tie/draw	un pareggio; i pari punti
tournament	un torneo
winner	la vincitrice/il vincitore

ACTIVITIES

DID YOU KNOW ...

When Italians have skiing holidays, their time off is referred to as **la settimana bianca**, literally 'the white week'.

ACTIVITIES

GAMES

Do you play ...?	Giochi ...?
billiards/pool	a (biliardo a) buca
bingo	a tombola
cards	a carte
chess	a scacchi
computer games	ai videogiochi
dominoes	a domino
draughts	a dama
ludo	al gioco dell'oca
monopoly	a monopoli
pinball machine	a flipper
roulette	alla roulette
scrabble	a scarabeo
snooker	a snooker
table football	a calcetto
trivial pursuit	a trivial pursuit

How do you play ...?	Come si gioca a ...?
What are the rules?	Quali sono le regole?
Shall we have a bet?	Facciamo una scommessa?
How much do you want to bet?	Quanto vuoi scommettere/ puntare?

THEY MAY SAY ...

A chi tocca/sta adesso?	Whose turn is it?
È il mio turno; Tocca a me; Sta a me.	It's my turn.
Sto vincendo/perdendo (io).	I'm winning/losing.
Smettila di imbrogliare/bararel	Stop cheating!
Cinquinal	Line!
Tombolal	Bingo!

Cards

The games, **scopa, briscola** and **scopone** are Italian card games played with Neapolitan cards which feature swords, clubs, coins and cups instead of the traditional spades, clubs, hearts and diamonds.

ACTIVITIES

Do you want to play ...?	**Vuoi** (sg)/**Volete** (pl) **giocare a ...?**
cards	**carte**
bridge	**bridge**
poker	**poker**

ace	**asso**	hearts	**cuori**
joker	**jolly**	diamonds	**quadri**
king	**re**	clubs	**fiori**
queen	**regina**	spades	**picche**
jack	**fante; gobbo**		

Chess

chess	**gli scacchi**	pawn	**il pedone**
chessboard	**lo scacchiere**	move	**una mossa**
queen	**la regina**	checkmate	**lo scaccomatto**
king	**il re**	stalemate	**lo stallo**
bishop	**l'alfiere**	white	**bianco**
knight	**il cavallo**	black	**nero**
rook/castle	**il torre**		

THEY MAY SAY ...

Ho scalogna.	I'm jinxed.
Che sfortuna!	Hard/Bad luck!
La mia solita fortuna!	Just my luck!
Che culo!	You're lucky!

ACTIVITIES

TV

There are as many as 600 TV stations in Italy, from magnate
owned networks to provincial studios.

Do you have a TV guide?	**Hai una guida-TV?**
What's on TV today?	**Che c'è/dànno alla tivù oggi?**
There's ... on today.	**Oggi c'è/dànno ...**
What channel is it on?	**Su quale canale è?**
Do you mind if I turn the volume up/down?	**Ti dispiace se alzo/abbasso il volume?**
May I change the channel?	**Posso cambiare canale?**
Which channel do you want to watch?	**Quale canale vuoi guardare?**
I want to watch the film on channel ...	**Voglio guardare il film sul canale ...**
Why don't we watch ...?	**Perché non guardiamo ...?**

WHAT'S ON THE BOX?

film	un film
current affairs	attualità
game show	gioco televisivo; quiz
variety program	un varietà; variety
the news	il telegiornale
the sports news	il notiziario sportivo
series	una serie; un telefilm
soap opera	una telenovela
documentary	un documentario
kids' program	varietà/programma per ragazzi/bambini
cartoons	disegni animati
sports program	una trasmissione sportiva
music show	un programma musicale
infotainment	varietà informazioni
TV sales program	televendita
talk show	un talk show

ACTIVITIES

Useful Words

cable TV	TV via cavo
channel	il canale
pay-TV	TV a pagamento; pay TV
remote control	telecomando
television	televisione
TV	TV; tivù; tivvù
TV addict/junkie	la/il teledipendente
TV commentator	la/il telecronista
TV host	la/il presentatrice/ presentatore
TV program	una trasmissione televisiva; un programma televisivo
TV reporter/correspondent	l'/la/il inviata/o/cronista

ACTIVITIES

VIDEOS

Where is the video shop?	Dov'è la videoteca?
Do you loan videos here?	Noleggiate video qui?
No, we only sell them.	No, li vendiamo soltanto.
Do I have to be a member to borrow videos?	Devo essere socio per prendere in prestito i video
How can I become a member?	Come posso diventare/farmi socia/o?
How much does it cost to hire a video?	Quanto costa prendere a noleggio questo video?
Is this film for daily or weekly hire?	Questo film è a noleggio giornaliero o settimanale?
How long can I borrow this for?	Per quanto tempo posso averlo in prestito?
Do you have ...?	Avete ...?

FESTIVALS & HOLIDAYS

PUBLIC HOLIDAYS

January	Epiphany
March/April	Easter Monday
5 April	Liberation Day
May	Labour Day
5 August	Feast of the Assumption (Ferragosto)
November	All Saints' Day
December	Feast of the Immaculate Conception
5 December	Christmas Day
6 December	Feast of Santo Stefano

FESTIVALS

Carnevale

During the period before Ash Wednesday many towns stage carnivals and enjoy their last opportunity to indulge before Lent. The carnival held in Venice during the 10 days before Ash Wednesday is the most famous, but the more traditional and popular carnival celebrations are held at Viareggio on the north coast of Tuscany and at Ivrea, near Turin.

DID YOU KNOW ...

Most Italians take their annual holidays in August which means that many businesses and shops close for at least part of the month, particularly during the week around Ferragosto (15 August).

Le Feste di Pasqua

Holy Week in Italy is marked by solemn processions and passion plays. At Taranto in Apulia on Holy Thursday there is the Procession of the Addolorata and on Good Friday the Procession of the Mysteries, when statues representing the Passion of Christ are carried around the town. One of Italy's oldest and most evocative Good Friday processions is held at Chieti in Abruzzo. The week is marked in Sicily by numerous events, including a Procession of the Mysteries at Trapani and the celebration of Easter according to Byzantine rites at Piana degli Albanesi, near Palermo. Women in colourful 15th-century costume give out Easter eggs to the public.

Corsa dei Ceri (Race of the Candles), May

This exciting and intensely traditional event is held at Gubbio in Umbria on 15 May. Groups of men carrying huge wooden shrines race uphill to the town's basilica, dedicated to the patron saint, Ubaldo.

Maggio Musicale Fiorentino, May & June

A music festival held in Florence.

Festival dei Due Mondi (Festival of Two Worlds), June

This major festival of the arts is held in June and July at Spoleto, a beautiful hill town in Umbria. Created by Gian Carlo Menotti, the festival features music, theatre, dance and art exhibitions.

Il Palio, July

The pride and joy of Siena, this famous traditional event is held twice a year – on 2 July and 16 August – in the town's beautiful Piazza del Campo. It involves a dangerous bareback horse race around the piazza, preceded by a parade of supporters in traditional costume.

esta del Redentore (Feast of the Redeemer), July
Fireworks and a procession over the bridge to the Church
of the Redeemer on Giudecca Island in Venice.

mbria Jazz, July
Held at Perugia in Umbria in July, this week-long festival
features performers from around the world.

iving Chess Game, September
The townspeople of Marostica in the Veneto dress as chess
figues and participate in a match on a chessboard marked
out in the town square. Games are held in even years on
the first weekend in September.

hristmas
During the weeks preceding Christmas there are numerous processions, religious events etc. Many churches set up
elaborate cribs or nativity scenes known as **presepi**.

BIRTHDAYS & NAME DAYS

Your name day – onomastico – is the feast day of the saint with the same name as you. To some Italians it is more important and is therefore celebrated more, than a birthday.

When is your birthday/name day?
Quand'è il tuo compleanno/onomastico?

Happy birthday!
Buon compleanno!

Happy name day!
Buon onomastico!

Best wishes!
Tanti auguri!

Many happy returns!
Cento di questi giorni!

THEY MAY SING ...

Tanti Auguri a Te
Tanti Auguri a Te
Tanti Auguri a ...
Tanti Auguri a Te

(Happy Birthday to You)

CHRISTMAS & NEW YEAR

Christmas Eve	Vigilia di Natale
Christmas Day	Natale
New Year's Eve	San Silvestro; Fine (d')Anno
New Year's Day	Capodanno
Epiphany/Twelfth Night	Epifania; Befana
Happy Christmas Eve!	Buona Vigilia di Natale!
Merry Christmas!	Buon Natale!
Happy New Year's Eve!	Buona Fine (d') Anno!
Happy New Year!	Felice Capodanno!; Felice Anno Nuovo!
Happy Epiphany!	Buona Epifania!; Buona Befana!

FESTIVALS & HOLIDAYS

CRISTMAS & NEW YEAR GOODIES

panettone	a large spongy Christmas cake with sultanas and candied fruit
pandoro	large, light, fluffy cake topped with castor sugar
panforte	flat, hard cake with candied fruit, spices, almonds, cocoa and honey, toppedwith icing sugar
ricciarelli	large, soft biscuits made with almond paste and honey and topped with castor sugar
cavallucci	large, soft biscuits made with walnut paste, honey and pepper
brutti & buoni	butter biscuits with almonds, hazelnuts, cinnamon and vanilla
torrone	marzipan
carbon dolce	dark, rock-like sugar candy for bad girls and boys. (Good kids get real presents from the good old witch, Befana.)
tacchino	turkey
zaleti	Venetian cornflour biscuits eaten with an **ombrina** (glass of wine) for morning teain winter
torta di marroni al cioccolato	chestnut torte with chocolate
pabassinas	Sardinian shortbread biscuits with dry figs and sultanas dipped in grape juice

FESTIVALS & HOLIDAYS

EASTER

In Sicily and Abruzzi villagers observe La Squilla on Holy Thursday, when bells are tolled for a long time as a sign of peace. A metal dove, hurtled through the Easter Mass crowd in Florence crashes into a cart laden with firewords culminating in the Scoppio del Carro, an imposing pyrotechnical display. Spring cleaning in Italy is an Easter affair and on Pasquetta, the day after Easter, the custom is to go for a picnic (la merendina).

Shrove Tuesday	Martedì Grasso
Holy Thursday	Giovedì Santo
Good Friday	Venerdì Santo
Holy Saturday	Sabato Santo; Sabato Grasso
Easter Sunday	Domenica di Pasqua
Easter Monday	Pasquetta
Happy Easter!	Buona Pasqua!
Holy Week	Settimana Santa
religious procession	processione religiosa

Easter Goodies

uova al cioccolato	eggs made of all types of chocolate, usually with a present inside
uova sode	hard boiled eggs as an entree, either plain or with variations on the theme
colomba	dove-shaped cake; much like the panettone but with almonds

DID YOU KNOW ... The term felliniano, taken from the name of the great Italian film director, Federico Fellini, is used to mean 'over the top, extravagant, crazy' – much like the characters in Fellini's films.

CHRISTENINGS & WEDDINGS

baptism	un battesimo
engagement	un fidanzamento
wedding	uno sposalizio; le nozze
wedding ring	una fede nuziale
wedding anniversary	l'anniversario di matrimonio/ delle nozze
wedding breakfast/reception	il rinfresco/ricevimento nuziale
wedding cake	la torta nuziale
wedding presents	i regali di nozze
honeymoon	la luna di miele

YOU MAY SAY ...

Felice Luna di Miele!	Happy Honeymoon!
Congratulazioni!; Felicitazioni!; Auguri!	Congratulations!
Viva gli Sposi!	To the Bride and Groom!

TOASTS & CONDOLENCES

Good health!; Cheers!	Cin cin!; (Alla) Salute!; Prosit!
Bon appétit!	Buon appetito!
Same to you!	Altrettanto!

Sickness

Get well soon!	Rimettiti presto (in salute)!; Auguri di pronta guarigione!
Bless you!	Salute!

Death

I'm very sorry.	Sono molto addolorata/o; Condoglianze.
My deepest sympathy.	Le mie piu sentite condoglianze.
My thoughts are with you.	Sentei miei pensieri.

Travel

Bon voyage!	Buon viaggio!
Pleasant journey!	Buon proseguimento!

Goodbye & Good Luck

Good luck!	Buona fortuna!
Hope it goes well!	In gamba!; In bocca al lupo!

PLACES

Where is (the nearest) ...?	Dov'è ... (più vicina/o)?
doctor	la/il dottoressa/dottore; medico
hospital	l'ospedale
chemist	la/il farmacista
dentist	la/il dentista

SIGN

PRONTO SOCCORSO	CASUALTY

AT THE DOCTOR

I am sick.	Mi sento male.
My friend is sick.	La mia amica è malata. (f); Il mio amico è malato. (m)
I need a doctor (who speaks English).	Ho bisogno di un medico (che parli inglese).
Could the doctor come here?	Può venire qua il medico?
I'm ill.	Sto male; Non mi sento bene.
I've been vomiting.	Continuo a vomitare; Ho vomitato più volte.
I feel ...	Ho ...
dizzy	il capogiro
nauseous	la nausea
shivery	i brividi
weak	debolezza
I can't move my ...	Non riesco a muovere ...
It hurts here.	Mi fa male qui.

HEALTH

225

I have a ... pain here.

constant	continuo
dull	sordo
intense	intenso
irregular	sporadico
light	lieve
occasional	isolato
sharp	acuto
spasmodic	spasmodico
strong	forte
throbbing	martellante

THE DOCTOR MAY SAY ...

What's the matter?	Cosa sente?; Cos'ha?
Do you feel any pain?	Sente qualche dolore?
Where does it hurt?	Dove le fa male?
Do you have a temperature?	Ha la febbre?
How long have you been like this?	Da quanto (tempo) è che si sente così?
Have you had this before?	Si è mai sentita/o così prima?
Are you on medication?	Sta prendendo una medicina?
Do you smoke?	Fuma?
Do you drink?	Beve?
Do you take drugs?	Si droga?; Prende la droga?
Are you allergic to anything?	È allergica/o a una particolare medicina?
Do you have a medical condition?	Ha qualche problema medico?
Are you menstruating?	Ha le mestruazioni?
Are you pregnant?	È incinta?
Do you have any STDs?	Ha malattie veneree?

HEALTH

AILMENTS

suffer from ...	Soffro di/per ...
have ...	Ho ...
a bite	un morso
a blister	una vescica
bronchitis	la bronchite
a bruise	un livido
a burn	una scottatura; un'ustione
a cold	il raffreddore
constipation	la stitichezza
a cough	la tosse
diarrhoea	la diarrea
a fever	la febbre
glandular fever	la mononucleosi infettiva
hayfever	la febbre da fieno
a headache	il mal di testa
hepatitis	l'epatite
indigestion	l'indigestione
an infection	un'infezione
an inflammation	un'infiammazione
influenza	l'influenza
an itch	un prurito
lice	i pidocchi
a lump	un gonfiore
a migraine	un'emicrania
a rash	uno sfogo; un'eruzione
rheumatism	i reumatismi
a sore throat	il mal di gola
a sprain	uno strappo muscolare
a stomachache	il mal di stomaco
sunburn	una scottatura
travel/sea sickness	il mal d'auto; il mal di mare
a venereal disease	una malattia venerea
worms	i vermi

HEALTH

WOMEN'S HEALTH

Could I see a female doctor?	Posso vedere una dottoressa?
I'm on the pill.	Prendo la pillola.
I haven't had my period for ... months.	Sono ... mesi che non mi vengono le mestruazioni.
I'd like to have a pregnancy test.	Vorrei avere un test di gravidanza.
I'd like to get the morning after pill.	Vorrei la pillola del mattino dopo.
I'd like to terminate my pregnancy.	Vorrei interrompere la gravidanza.
I have morning sickness.	Soffro di nausee mattutine.
I'm pregnant.	Sono incinta.

abortion	un aborto
breast cancer	il cancro al seno
cervical cancer	il cancro cervicale
cystitis	la cistite
diaphragm	una diaframma
endometriosis	l'endometriosi; l'endometrite
IUD	il DIU
mamogram	una mamografia
miscarriage	l'aborto naturale
pap smear	il paptest
period	le mestruazioni
period pain	i dolori mestruali
premenstrual syndrome	la sindrome premestruale
the pill	la pillola (contraccettiva)
thrush/candida	la candida

HEALTH

DID YOU KNOW ...   The film studios in Rome (Cinecittà) were also used for many great foreign productions, including *Ben Hur* and *Cleopatra*.

MEN'S HEALTH

I'd like to see a male doctor.	Vorrei vedere un dottore (uomo).
It's been ... months/years since my last medical visit.	Sono passati ... mesi/anni dalla mia ultima visita medica.
Could I have a thorough examination?	Mi fa un controllo completo?
I have a weak/strong heart.	Sono di cuore debole/forte.

bald	calvo
baldness	la calvizie
circumcision	la circoincisione
(un)circumcised	(non) circoinciso
impotence	l'impotenza
premature ejaculation	l'eiaculazione prematura
prostate cancer	il cancro alla prostata
testicular cancer	il cancro testicolare
vasectomy	la vasectomia

SPECIAL HEALTH NEEDS

I'm ...	Sono ...
anaemic	anemico/a
asthmatic	asmatica/o
blind	cieca/o; non vedente
deaf and dumb	sordomuta/o
diabetic	diabetica/o
disabled	disabile
epileptic	epilettica/o
HIV negative	sieronegativa/o
HIV positive	sieropositiva/o

I have a pacemaker.	Ho uno stimolatore cardiaco.
I have a weak heart.	Ho il cuore debole
I have low/high blood pressure.	Ho la pressione bassa/alta.

HEALTH

Allergies

I have a skin allergy.	Ho una allergia alla pelle.
I'm allergic to ...	Sono allergica/o ...
antibiotics	agli antibiotici
aspirin	all'aspirina
bees	alle api
codeine	alla codeina
dairy products	ai latticini
lactose	al lattosio
legumes	ai legumi
penicillin	alla penicillina
pollen	al polline
sugars	agli zuccheri
ventolin	al Ventolin
wasps	alle vespe
wheat	ai cereali
yeasts	ai lieviti;
	alle sostanze fermentanti

See Disabled Travellers, page 235, for more special health needs.

ALTERNATIVE TREATMENTS

acupuncture	l'agopuntura
aromatherapy	l'aromaterapia
herbalist	l'erborista
homeopath/y	l'omeopata;
	l'omeopatia
massage	il massaggio
meditation	la meditazione
naturopath/y	il naturopata;
	la naturopatia
physiotherapy	la fisioterapia
reflexology	la riflessologia
yoga	lo yoga

IL/LO

The masculine definite article **il** becomes **lo** before nouns beginning with **st, z, gn, ps, x** and **y**.

HEALTH

PARTS OF THE BODY

ankle	la caviglia	finger	il dito (pl: le dita)
arm	il braccio	foot	il piede
	(pl: le braccia)	hand	la mano
back	la schiena;	head	la testa
	il dorso	hip	l'anca
breast	la mammella;	knee	il ginocchio
	il seno;	leg	la gamba
	il petto	mouth	la bocca
buttocks	le natiche	neck	il collo
chest	il torace; il petto	nose	il naso
ear	l'orecchio	shoulder	la spalla
elbow	il gomito	stomach	lo stomaco
eyes	gli occhi	throat	la gola

AT THE CHEMIST

Where is the nearest (all-night) chemist?	Dov'è la piu vicina farmacia (di turno)?
I need something for ...	Ho bisogno di qualcosa per ...
I have a prescription.	Ho una ricetta/prescrizione?
Do I need a prescription?	C'è bisogno di prescrizione?
How many times a day?	Quante volte al giorno?
Take ... tablets ... times a day before/after meals.	Prenda ... compresse/ pasticche ... volte al giorno prima/dopo i pasti.
Could I please (not) have ...	Potrebbe (non) darmi ... per favore?

antibiotics	degli antibiotici
aspirins	delle aspirine
contraceptives	dei contraccettivi
cough syrup/lozenges	uno sciroppo; delle pastiglie contro la tosse
laxatives	dei lassativi
painkillers	un analgesico; un calmante
sleeping pills	dei sonniferi

See page 160 for a list of toiletries.

See page 160 for a list of toiletries.

DID YOU KNOW ... Pasta was not always the cheap and readily available food that it is today. Until about the 18th century it was considered a luxury food and was even eaten as dessert. This was because it had to be imported from Sicily or Puglia and so it was expensive and eaten only by the wealthier classes.

HEALTH

AT THE DENTIST

I have a toothache.	Ho mal di denti.
I have a cavity.	Ho una cavità.
I have tooth decay.	Ho la carie.
I've lost a filling.	Ho perso un'otturazione.
I've broken a tooth.	Mi si è rotto un dente.
My gums hurt.	Mi fanno male le gengive.
I don't want it extracted.	Non voglio che mi venga tolto.
Please give me an anaesthetic.	Mi dia un anestetico, per favore.
tooth enamel	il smalto dei denti
tooth nerve	il nervo dei denti

USEFUL WORDS & PHRASES

I can't sleep.	Non riesco a dormire.
I have been vaccinated.	Sono stata/o vaccinata/o.
I have my own syringe.	Ho con me la mia siringa.
I feel better/worse.	Mi sento meglio/peggio.
I don't want a blood tranfusion.	Non voglio una trasfusione di sangue.
I don't want an operation.	Non voglio un intervento.
This is my usual medicine.	Questa è la mia medicina consueta.
May I have a receipt for my health insurance?	Potrebbe darmi una ricevuta per l'assicurazione?
I wear contact lenses/glasses.	Porto le lenti a contatto/gli occhiali.
accident	un incidente
antibiotics	gli antibiotici
antiseptic	l'antisettico
appendix	l'appendice
bacteria	i batteri

HEALTH

bandage	una benda; una fascia
blood group	il gruppo sanguigno
blood pressure	la pressione (del sangue)
blood test	l'analisi del sangue
body	il corpo
bone	l'osso
cure	la cura
drugs	le droghe; gli stupefacenti
heart	il cuore
injection	un'iniezione; una puntura
medicine	la medicina
muscle	il muscolo
oxygen	l'ossigeno
skin	la pelle
virus	un virus
vitamins	le vitamine
a wound	una ferita

HEALTH

SPECIFIC NEEDS

DISABLED TRAVELLERS

Holidays & Travel Abroad: A Guide for Disabled People, published each year by the Royal Association for Disability & Rehabilitation, gives a good overview of facilities available to disabled travellers throughout Europe.

SIGN	
RISERVATO AI DISABILI	**RESERVED FOR DISABLED**

I'm disabled/handicapped.	Sono disabile/handicappata/o.
I need assistance.	Ho bisogno di assistenza.
What services do you have for disabled people?	Di quali servizi disponete per i disabili?
Is there wheelchair access?	C'è un'entrata per sedie a rotelle?
I'm deaf. Speak more loudly, please.	Sono sorda/o. Parli più forte, per favore.
I can lipread.	So leggere le labbra.
I have a hearing aid.	Ho un apparecchio acustico.
Does anyone here know sign language?	C'è qualcuno qua che conosce il linguaggio visivo?
Are guide dogs permitted?	Sono ammessi i cani guida?
braille library	una biblioteca braille
disabled person	la/il disabile
disabled ex-servicemen	gli ex militari disabili
guide dog	un cane guida
paraplegic	la/il paraplegica/o
quadriplegic	la/il quadriplegica/o
wheelchair	una sedia a rotelle
wheelchair access	l'accesso per sedie a rotelle

GAY TRAVELLERS

Babilɔnia, published monthly, is the national gay magazine. *Guida Gay Italia* is an annual publication. Specifically for women there is *Lesbo Mese* and *Lesbo Italia. Spartacus*, the international guide, covers in detail the gay scene in several Italian cities.

Where are the gay hangouts?	**Dove si trovano i locali gay di punta?**
Is there a (predominantly) gay street/district?	**C'è una strada/un quartiere (prevalentemente) gay?**
Are we/Am I likely to be harassed (here)?	**Ci/Mi daranno noia (qui)?**
Are people generally cool/ relaxed about gays here?	**È abbastanza disinvolta qua la gente con i diversi?**
Is there a gay bookshop around here?	**C'è una libreria gay da queste parti?**
Is there a local gay guide?	**C'è una guida gay locale?**
Where can I buy some gay/ lesbian magazines?	**Dove posso comprare riviste gay/lesbiche?**
Is there a gay telephone hotline?	**C'è una linea telefonica d'informazioni gay?**

TRAVELLING WITH THE FAMILY

I'm travelling with my family.	**Sono in viaggio con la famiglia.**
Are there facilities for babies?	**Ci sono i servizi per i bebè?**
Are there other families in the hotel/group?	**Ci sono altre famiglie nell'albergo/nel gruppo?**
Do you have a child minding service?	**Disponete di un servizio di babysitter?**
Where can I find a (English-speaking) babysitter?	**Dove posso trovare un babysitter/una bambinaia che parla inglese?**

SPECIFIC NEEDS

Can you put an (extra) bed/cot in the room?	È possibile avere un (altro) lettino/una (altra) culla in camera?
I need a car with a child seat.	Avrei bisogno di un'auto munita di un seggiolino per bambini.
Is it safe for babies/children?	È sicura/o per i bambini?
Is it suitable for children?	È adatto ai bambini?; Va bene per i bambini?
Are there any activities for children?	Quali attività ricreative/divertimenti ci sono per i bambini?
Is there a family discount?	Esistono riduzioni/sconti per la famiglia?
Are children allowed?	I bambini sono ammessi?
Do you have a children's menu?	Avete un menu per i bambini?
Is there a playground around here?	C'è un parco giochi da queste parti?

For phrases on shopping for the baby, see page 161.

DID YOU KNOW ...

When you want to say that you miss something in Italian you must literally say that something is missed to you. When you use the verb **mancare** ('to miss') the thing that is missed becomes the subject and the person doing the missing becomes the object:

Mi manca Andrea.
I miss Andrea.
(lit: to me is missed Andrea)

SPECIFIC NEEDS

LOOKING FOR A JOB

Non-EÚ citizens must have a work permit to work in Italy. Although EU citizens are allowed to work in Italy, they still need a **permesso di soggiorno** from the main police station of the town in which they intend to work.

Where can I find local job advertisements?	Dove posso trovare le offerte locali di impiego/lavoro?
By what date do I have to apply?	Entro quale giorno devo fare domanda?
Do I need a work permit?	Ho bisogno di un permesso di lavoro?
What qualifications do I need?	Che qualifiche devo avere?
What experience do I need?	Di che tipo di esperienza ho bisogno?
I've had experience.	Ho esperienza in questo.
I haven't had experience.	Non ho esperienza in questo.
I've come about the position advertised.	Sono qui/Mi presento per il posto offerto.
I'm ringing about the position advertised.	Desidero presentare domanda per l'impiego/il lavoro offerto.
What are the job requirements?	Quali sono le competenze richieste?
What sort of training do you offer?	Quale tipo di addestramento viene offerto?
What is the wage?	Quant'è la paga?
How often will I be paid?	Ogni quanto tempo si è pagati?
Do I have to pay tax?	Devo pagare le tasse?
When can I start?	Quando posso iniziare?

I can start ...	Io posso cominciare ...
today	oggi
tomorrow	domani
next week	la prossima settimana

(job) application	una domanda (d'impiego)
casual	occasionale; saltuario
certificate	il certificato
degree/diploma	la laurea; il diploma
employee	l'impiegata/o
employer	la/il datrice/datore di lavoro; la/il principale
full-time	tempo pieno
interview	il colloquio (selettivo)
job	un lavoro; un impiego
occupation/trade	un'occupazione; un mestiere
part-time	tempo ridotto/parziale
qualifications	le qualifiche
references	le referenze
resume/cv	il curriculum vitae; il curricolo
skills	le abilità
traineeship	l'apprendistato
union	il sindacato
voluntary (work)	(lavoro) volontario
work experience	l'esperienza lavorativa

For more phrases about occupations see Meeting People, page 52.

ON BUSINESS

Like English, Italian has a business jargon derived from the world of economics, marketing and computers, and is difficult to understand for the uninitiated. The following will be of help for anyone dealing casually with the business community.

JUST MAKE ME

When the verb **fare** ('to do/make') is used with an infinitive it means 'to make/have someone do something':

Me l'hanno fatto mangiare.
   They made me eat it.

SPECIFIC NEEDS

I need to send a fax/an email.	Dovrei mandare un fax/ un Email.
I'm on a course.	Sto facendo/frequentando un corso.
We're attending a ...	Stiamo assistendo ad una ...
conference	conferenza
meeting	riunione
trade fair	fiera commerciale
Here's my business card.	Ecco il mio biglietto da visita.
I have an appointment with ...	Ho un appuntamento con ...
I need an interpreter.	Ho bisogno di un'/un interprete.
I need to use a computer.	Avrei bisogno di usare un computer.

ballpark figure	il calcolo presuntivo; il preventivo
branch office	la filiale; la succursale
cellular/mobile phone	il cellulare; il telefonino
client	la/il cliente
colleague	una/un collega
distributor	una/un fornitrice/fornitore
exhibition	un'esposizione
exhibitor	un'espositrice/un espositore
fax	un fax
loss	la perdita; il deficit
manager	la direttrice/il direttore; la gestrice/il gestore
modem	il modem
overhead projector	una lavagna luminosa
presentation	una presentazione
profit	il profitto; l'utile
profitability	la redditività
proposal	una proposta; un'offerta
sales department	il reparto vendite

Technology

May I use the computer here?	Potrei usare il computer qui?
I'd like to access/surf the Internet.	Vorrei accedere all'Internet.
I'd like to print out from this disk.	Vorrei stampare da questo dischetto.
Where's the nearest computer shop?	Dove si trova il negozio d'informatica più vicino?
I'd like a box of 10 high-density disks.	Vorrei una scatola da dieci dischetti ad alta densità.
Is there an Internet/cyber café around here?	L'Internet/il cyber caffè è da queste parti?

application window	la barra delle applicazioni
CD ROM	il CD rom
cursor	il cursore
disk	un dischetto; un disco
email	la posta elettronica; la Email
file	un file
hard disk	lo hard disk
hardware/software	lo hardware/il software
hypertext	l'ipertesto
keyboard	la tastiera
layout	l'impostazione
monitor	il monitor
mouse	il mouse
multimedia	i multimedia; la multimedialità
printer	la stampante
programme	il programma; il sistema operativo
scanner	lo scanner
screen	lo schermo
to surf the net	surfare il net
videogames	i videogiochi
virtual reality	la realtà virtuale
window	una finestra

SPECIFIC NEEDS

ON TOUR

We're part of a group.	Siamo membri di un gruppo.
We're on tour.	Stiamo facendo un tour.

I'm with the ...
  group
  band
  team

Sono con ...
  il gruppo
  la band
  la squadra

Please speak with our manager.	Si rivolga al nostro manager, per favore.
We've lost our equipment.	Abbiamo perduto la nostra attrezzatura.

We sent equipment on this ...

  flight
  train
  bus

Abbiamo fatto venire la nostra attrezzatura su questo ...
  volo
  treno
  autobus

I'm staying with a host family.	Sono ospite di una famiglia.
We're taking a break of ... days.	Facciamo una sosta di ... giorni.
We're playing on ...	Suoniamo/Ci esibiamo/ Teniamo un concerto il ...
I'm still a groupie after all these years.	Sono ancora una/un fan accanita/o dopo tutti questi anni.

DID YOU KNOW ... Some names in Italian sound like they should be for women but are in fact, men's names. For example, Luca, Nicola and Andrea – and sometimes even Maria – are men's names.

FILM & TV

We're on location.
  Siamo sul posto.
We're filming!
  Si gira!
May we film here?
  Possiamo filmare qui?

THEY MAY SAY ...	
Azione!	Action!
Si filma!	Rolling!
Alt!	Cut!

We're making a ...   Stiamo girando ...
  film   un film
  documentary   un documentario
  TV series   una serie televisiva

See page 130 for useful words on film.

INSULTS

You're such a ...!   Sei proprio una/un ...!
Don't be a ...!   Non essere una/un ...!

son of a bitch	figlio di puttana
bastard	bastarda/o; stronza/o
dickhead	testa di cazzo
shit	merdaiola/o
boor; oaf	cafona/e; buzzurra/o
wretch	carogna
idiot; ass; fool	idiota
stupid	stupida/o
pig	porca/o; maiala/o
moron; jerk; creep	cogliona/e
dick; dropkick	sega (wank)
fool	scema/o; fessa/o
loser	fallita/o
halfwit	tonta/o
wanker	montata/o; segaiola/o
pain in the neck/arse	rompiscatole; rompipalle; rompicoglioni

SPECIFIC NEEDS

PILGRIMAGE & RELIGION

SIGN	
MESSA IN CORSO	SERVICE IN PROGRESS

Can I attend this service/ mass?	Posso partecipare a questa funzione religiosa/messa?
Can I pray here?	Si può pregare qui?
Where can I pray/worship?	Dove posso pregare?
Where can I make confession (in English)?	Dove posso confessarmi (in inglese)?
Can I receive communion here?	Posso ricevere la comunione qui?

baptism/christening	il battesimo
cemetery	un cimitero; un camposanto
church	la chiesa
communion	la comunione
confession	la confessione
confirmation	la cresima
cross	la croce
crucifix	il crocifisso
funeral	un funerale
holy water	l'acqua santa
prayer	la preghiera
priest	il prete
relic	un reliquiario
religious procession	una processione religiosa
sabbath	il sabato
sacraments	i sacramenti
saint	una/un santa/o
shrine	il santuario; il tempio
wedding	lo sposalizio; le nozze; il matrimonio

For a list of religions, see page 54.

RACING ROOTS & HISTORY

I think) my ancestors came from this area.	Credo che i miei antenati provenissero da questa zona.
m looking for my relatives.	Sono alla ricerca dei miei parenti.
s there anyone here by the name of ...?	C'è nessuno qui dal nome di ...?
have/had a relative who was n the ...	Ho/Avevo un parente che era ...
army	nell'Esercito
navy	nella Marina
airforce	nell'Aviazione
think he fought/died near here.	Credo che abbia combattuto/ sia morto qui.
My (father) fought/died here in WWI/II.	Mio (padre) combatté qui nella Prima/Seconda Guerra Mondiale.
My (grandmother) nursed here in WWI/II.	Mia (nonna) fu infermiera qui nella Prima/Seconda Guerra Mondiale.

ee Family, page 110, for names of family members.

n which cemetery would I find ...'s grave?	In quale cimitero è la tomba di ...
Vhere would I find the remains of ...?	Dove riposano le spoglie di ...?

CROSSWORD – SPECIFIC NEEDS

Across

1. If you have a confession, you may want one
2. You join to see the world
4. Keeps the boss in order
7. Better than not to have

Down

3. If you have one you might get a better job
5. Put a few suits together and you've got one
6. Rome has more than a few
8. Without one, a screen is helpless

Answers on page 324

TELLING THE TIME

The 24-hour clock is commonly used in Italy, ie 1 pm is 13.00, 2 pm is 14.00, etc.

What time is it?	Che ora è? (sg); Che ore sono? (pl)
It's one o'clock.	È l'una.
It's (two o'clock).	Sono le (due).
It's five past six.	Sono le sei e cinque.
It's a quarter to four.	Sono le quattro meno un quarto;
	Sono le tre e quarantacinque.
It's half past eight.	Sono le otto e mezza/o.
It's about eleven.	Sono le undici circa;
	Sono quasi le undici.
It's early.	È presto.
It's late.	È tardi.
in the morning	di mattina
in the afternoon	di pomeriggio
in the evening	di sera
in the night	di notte
clock/watch	un orologio

DAYS

Days of the week are not capitalised in Italian.

Monday	(il) lunedì
Tuesday	(il) martedì
Wednesday	(il) mercoledì
Thursday	(il) giovedì
Friday	(il) venerdì
Saturday	(il) sabato
Sunday	(la) domenica

To express a repeated event on a particular day we use the wor 'every'. In Italian, the definite article is used instead.

Every Tuesday I have yoga   **Il martedì ho lezioni di yoga.**
class.

However, to express a single event, the definite article is left out.

On Thursday I'm going to   **Giovedì vado da mio zio.**
my uncle's.

MONTHS

January	**gennaio**
February	**febbraio**
March	**marzo**
April	**aprile**
May	**maggio**
June	**giugno**
July	**luglio**
August	**agosto**
September	**settembre**
October	**ottobre**
November	**novembre**
December	**dicembre**

LEI

The word **lei** means 'she/it'. When it has a capital (**Lei**) it is the formal and polite pronoun 'you' for either gender. See page 23.

DATES

What date is it today?	**Che giorno è oggi?**
It's 26 April	**È il ventisei (d') aprile**
It's 4 September	**È il quattro (di) settembre**
It's 1 February	**È il primo (di) febbraio ***

* Note that only the first day of the month is indicated by cardinal number.

calendar	**il calendario**
diary	**un'agenda; un diario**

Centuries

There is a particular way of naming centuries in Italian. You will hear the following terms mainly in reference to periods of history and art:

Cinquecento (lit: the 500s)	16th century
Quattrocento (lit: the 400s)	15th century
Trecento (lit: the 300s)	14th century
Duecento (lit: the 200s)	13th century
(sometimes referred to as **Dugento**)	

PRESENT

today	oggi
this morning	stamattina; stamani
this afternoon	questo pomeriggio
tonight	stasera
this week	questa settimana
this month	questo mese
this year	quest'anno
now	adesso; ora
right now/at this moment	in questo momento/istante

TIME & DATES

DID YOU KNOW ... Tarantism, a ritual that had its roots in the mass manias that swept Europe during the Middle Ages, survives in the small town of Galatina in Apulia. The folk dance known as the tarantella, developed from the dance ritual performed by people known as **tarantolati** victims of a spider bite.

TIME & DATES

PAST

yesterday	ieri
day before yesterday	l'altro ieri; avant'ieri
yesterday morning	ier(i) mattina
yesterday afternoon	ieri pomeriggio
last night	ieri sera; ieri notte
last week	la settimana scorsa/passata
last month	il mese scorso/passato
last year	l'anno scorso/passato
twenty minutes ago	venti minuti fa
days ago	giorni fa
years ago	anni fa
a while ago	tempo fa
since May	da maggio

FUTURE

tomorrow	domani
day after tomorrow	dopodomani; doman(i) l'altro
tomorrow morning	domani mattina
tomorrow afternoon	domani pomeriggio
tomorrow evening/night	domani sera/notte
next week	la settimana prossima/ventura

next month
    il mese prossimo/venturo
next year
    l'anno prossimo/venturo
in (five) minutes
    fra/tra cinque minuti
in (six) days
    fra/tra (sei) giorni
within (two) years
    entro (due) anni
until June
    fino a giugno

NY

The combination **gn** is pronounced as the 'ny' in the word 'canyon' So, the word **gnocchi** is pronounced *nyocki;* and **bagno** ('bath') is pronounced *banyo.*

DURING THE DAY

afternoon	il pomeriggio
day	il giorno
dinner/tea/supper time	l'ora di cena
evening	la sera
lunchtime	l'ora di pranzo
midnight	la mezzanotte
midday/noon	il mezzogiorno
morning	la mattina; il mattino
night	la notte
snack time	l'ora di merenda/dello spuntino
sundown/sunset	il tramonto
sunrise/dawn	l'alba

USEFUL WORDS

ahead	avanti
after	dopo
almost	quasi
already	già
always	sempre
annual	annuale
before	prima
behind	dietro
ever	mai
every day	tutti i giorni
from ... to ...	da ... a ...
forever	per sempre
fortnight	quindici giorni
future	futuro; avvenire
minute	un minuto
never	non ... mai
not yet	non ancora
often	spesso
in time	in tempo
on the dot/exactly	in punto; esattamente

TIME & DATES

TIME & DATES

past	passato
present	presente
recently	recentemente; di recente
a second	un secondo
still	ancora; tuttora
then	allora (in that time)/poi (after)
sometimes	talvolta; a volte
soon	fra/tra poco

NUMBERS & AMOUNTS

CARDINAL NUMBERS

0	zero	16	sedici
1	uno	17	diciassette
2	due	18	diciotto
3	tre	19	diciannove
4	quattro	20	venti
5	cinque	21	ventuno
6	sei	22	ventidue
7	sette	30	trenta
8	otto	40	quaranta
9	nove	50	cinquanta
10	dieci	60	sessanta
11	undici	70	settanta
12	dodici	80	ottanta
13	tredici	90	novanta
14	quattordici	100	cento
15	quindici	101	cento uno

158	centocinquantotto
1000	mille
2000	duemila (note the plural form of mille)
1241	milleduecentoquarantuno
10000	diecimila
14863	quattordicimilaottocentosessantatré
100000	centomila
one million	un milione
one billion	un miliardo

ORDINAL NUMBERS

first	prima/o
second	seconda/o
third	terza/o
fourth	quarta/o
fifth	quinta/o
sixth	sesta/o
seventh	settima/o
eighth	ottava/o
ninth	nona/o
tenth	decima/o
eleventh	undicesima/o
twelfth	dodicesima/o
...nth	...esima/o (from 11th onwards)

NUMBERS & AMOUNTS

DID YOU KNOW ...
In Italy, as in most of Europe, decimals are indicated with commas, and thousands with points. So you'll see prices written as L100.000 and decimals as 10,25.

FRACTIONS

1/4	un quarto
1/3	un terzo
1/2	un mezzo; la metà
3/4	tre quarti

USEFUL WORDS

little (amount)	(un) poco, un po'
all	tutta/o
couple	una coppia
double	doppia/o
dozen	una dozzina
enough!	Basta!
few	poche; pochi
less	meno
many	tante/i
more	più
none	niente; nulla
once	una volta
pair	un paio
per cent	percento
some	qualche; alcune/i
too much	troppo
twice	due volte
three times	tre volte

CROSSWORD – NUMBERS AND AMOUNTS

NUMBERS & AMOUNTS

Across

1. The age of majority
2. A group of 12
5. Garibaldi needed this many men
6. A large number
7. Count your change or you might get this

Down

2. Trouble comes in pairs
3. Equal division
4. Beethoven's most famous work

Answers on page 324.

When Italy became a politically unified country in 1861, Standard Italian was a highly sophisticated written language, but was spoken only by about 2.5% of the total population. Dialects were not only used by the 75% of Italian people who were illiterate, but those who could read and write, used dialects when they spoke. Dialects are local varieties which have evolved from spoken Latin and have been affected over the centuries by contact with the peoples who invaded and ruled various parts of Italy after the fall of the Roman Empire.

In some parts of Italy, a number of other separate languages or dialects are spoken. Other than standard Italian there are 13 languages and many dialects spoken in Italy. Provençal is used in north-west Italy, near the French border and in a small area in Calabria. Ladin is used in parts of north-east Italy, mainly in the

DIALECTS

Dolomites. A southern variety of German is used in South Tyrol (the region known as Alto-Adige in Italy), near the Austrian border. Slovenian is used at the border with the former Yugoslavia. Some Greek- and Albanian-speaking areas are found in Southern Italy and Sicily.

In the 1990s, thanks to widespread education and the influence of the media, Standard Italian is spoken and understood throughout the country. However, dialects are still in widespread use. Most Italians still show their regional origins in their accent, and occasionally in their vocabulary and use of verb tenses. In 1995 less than 50% of Italians spoke only Italian at home and with their friends, just under 25% spoke only dialect, and just over 25% alternated between Italian and dialect. Dialects do not generally have a homogenous written form and as a consequence the same word can be pronounced and written differently in a relatively small area. For example the Standard Italian **oggi** (today) is quite different in three cities in Veneto:

Venice	**ancuo**
Padua	**incò**
Vicenza	**oncò**

The dialects of Italy can be roughly divided into three major groups:

Northern Dialects (**dialetti settentrionali**)
Central Dialects (**dialetti centrali**)
Southern Dialects (**dialetti meridionali**)

A basic division of the areas where these groups of dialects are spoken can be made by drawing two imaginary lines across the country (see map). The first one, between la Spezia and Rimini separates Northern from Central dialects. The second one, between Rome and Ancona, separates Central from Southern dialects.

DIALECTS

THE NORTH

(Piedmont, Lombardy, Emilia-Romagna, Liguria, Veneto, Valle d'Aosta, Trentino, Friuli Venezia-Giulia.) This group of dialects has the following characteristics:

- Most vowels at the end of words (except **a**) disappear:

	Standard Italian	Northern Dialects
bread	**pane**	**pan**
train	**treno**	**tren**

- The vowels **o** and **u** are often pronounced as the French *u* and the German *ü* (this is not the case, however, with Venetian dialects):

	Standard	Northern
ugly	**brutto**	**brüt**
bedsheet	**lenzuolo**	**lensú**

- The consonants **t**, **f** and **c** between two vowels are pronounced *d*, *v* and *g* respectively:

	Standard	Northern
brother	**fratello**	**fradel**
not at all	**mica**	**miga**

- The consonants **c** and **g** before **e** and **i** are often pronounced as *s* and *z* respectively:

	Standard	Northern
the 1500s	**cinquecento**	**sinsent**
people	**gente**	**zent**

- All double consonants are pronounced weakly:

	Standard	Northern
feather	**penna**	**pena**
tax	**tassa**	**tasa**

• There is a tendency to double the pronouns:

	Standard	Veneto	Emiliano (Bologna)
you say	tu dici	ti te dizi	ti t di

• In Venetian dialects, many consonants between two vowels disappear:

	Standard	Venetian
wheel	ruota	roa
polenta	polenta	poenta

Some Words From The North

	Standard	Northern
I	io	mi
uncle	zio	barba
girl/boy	ragazza/ragazzo	tosa/toso
baker	fornaio	prestiné (Piedmont, Lombardy)
chair	sedia	carega (Veneto)

THE CENTRE

Tuscany, Marche, Umbria and northern Lazio),

These dialects are very similar to Standard Italian since they derive from the Tuscan dialect which is also the basis of Standard Italian. Tuscan, however, can't be considered Standard Italian as Standard Italian is derived from the Tuscan spoken around 1300. As a consequence, Tuscan and its dialects have many characteristics which are quite different from Standard Italian:

WORD ORDER

Remember that word order in Italian is the same as in English, ie subject-verb-object:

We are eating beef.
(Noi) mangiamo il manzo.
(lit: (we) we are eating the beef)

DIALECTS

- A typical feature found only in Tuscany is the tendency for c between two vowels to be pronounced as *h*, or to disappear altogether:

	Standard	Tuscan
Coca-Cola	Coca-Cola	Hoha-Hola; Oha-Oha
house	casa	hasa; asa
few	poco	poho

- Throughout Central Italy, c before e and i is pronounced as *sh*:

	Standard	Central
kiss	bacio	basho
ten	dieci	dieshi

- Often, where Standard Italian has -nd-, -mb- or -ld-, Central dialects have -nn-, -mm- or -ll-:

	Standard	Central
when	quando	quanno
world	mondo	monno
hot	caldo	callo

Some Words From The Centre

	Standard	Central
rascal	mascalzone	birbaccione
lamb	agnello	abbacchio (Rome)
broken	rotto	scassato
rip-off	fregatura	bidone (Rome)

DIALECTS

DID YOU KNOW ...	In Standard Italian the word **ennesima** means 'umpteenth': **l'ennesima volta** the umpteenth time

THE SOUTH

(Abruzzo, Calabria, Campania, Molise, Puglia, Sicily and south-ern Lazio.) The linguistic overview of Southern dialects is more complex than elsewhere because there is less linguistic uniformity:

- There is a tendency (except in parts of Calabria and Sicily) for **p**, **t**, **c** and **s** to be pronounced as *b*, *d*, *g* and *z* after **m** and **n**:

	Standard	Southern
to buy	comprare	combrare
happy	contento	condendo
still; yet	ancora	angora
salad	insalata	inzalata

- In most of Southern Italy (except parts of Calabria and Sicily) vowels at the end of words (except **a**) and most unstressed vowels within words are pronounced as an indistinct sound similar to the first vowel sound of 'career' in English:

	Standard	Southern
wine	vino	vin
night	notte	nott
females	femmine	femmn

- Where standard Italian has -**ll**-, dialects have -**dd**-, especially in Calabria and Sicily:

	Standard	Southern
hair	capelli	capiddi
knife	coltello	cuteddu; cutieddu

- Southern dialects of the South often use the simple past to refer to past events instead of the perfect – passato prossimo – especially when speaking (see Grammar, page 28, for an ex planation of the past tenses):

	Standard	Southern
I ate/have eaten	ho mangiato	mangiai

DIALECTS

Some Words From The South

	Standard	Southern
on top of	sopra	ngopp
boy	ragazzo	guaglion; quatrar; carusu
then	allora	tann; tannu
poor man	poveretto	mischinu (Sicilian)

ITALIANS ABROAD

Italians who have emigrated tend to maintain the use of their dialect. Therefore Central and Southern dialects dominate for Italo-Americans, dialects from the Centre and North dominate for South American Italian emigrants while in Australia dialects from the Centre and the South are more common among Italian immigrants.

EMERGENCIES

SIGNS

POLIZIA; CARABINIERI	POLICE
QUESTURA; CASERMA	POLICE STATION
PRONTO SOCCORSO	CASUALTY

Help!	Aiuto!
Officer!	Guardia!; Agente!; Carabiniere!
Look out!	Attenzione!
Fire!	Al fuoco!
Go away!	Va' via!; Lasciami in pace!
Thief!	Al ladro!

There's been an accident!	C'è stato un incidente!
It's an emergency!	È un'emergenza!
Call the police!	Chiami la polizia!
Call a doctor!	Chiami un medico/dottore!
Call an ambulance!	Chiami un'ambulanza!
Where is the police station?	Dov'è la questura?

I am ill.	Sono malata/o.
My friend is ill.	La mia amica è malata. (f)
	Il mio amico è malato. (m)
I have medical insurance.	Ho l'assicurazione medica.
I've been robbed!	Mi hanno derubata/o!
This woman/man has been robbed.	Questa/o signora/e è stato/a derubata/o.
I've been raped.	Sono stata/o violentata/o.
Could you help me please?	Mi può aiutare?
Could I please use the telephone?	Posso fare una telefonata?

EMERGENCIES

I want to report an offence.	Voglio sporgere una denuncia/querela.
I'm lost.	Mi sono persa/o.
I've lost my friend.	Ho perso la/il mia/o amica/o.

I've lost ... Ho perso ...

my backpack	il mio zaino
my handbag	la mia borsetta
my luggage	i miei bagagli
my money	i miei soldi; il mio denaro
my papers	i miei documenti
my passport	il mio passaporto
my travellers' cheques	i miei travellers cheques; assegni turistici
my wallet	il mio portafogli

My possessions are insured.	La mia roba è assicurata.
Where are the toilets, please?	Dove sono i gabinetti, per favore?

DEALING WITH THE POLICE

The polizia are a civil police force and operate under the Ministry of the Interior. They wear blue-grey uniforms. The carabinieri are the military police and fall under the Ministry of Defence. They wear black and red uniforms. Both forces are responsible for public order and security.

I'm sorry. I apologise.	Mi scusi. Mi dispiace.
I didn't realise I was doing anything wrong.	Non sapevo che facevo qualcosa di male.
I'm innocent.	Sono innocente.
I didn't do it.	Non l'ho fatto io.
I'm a foreigner.	Sono straniera/o.
I'm a tourist.	Sono una/un turista.
I (don't) understand.	(Non) capisco.

CHARGES (IMPUTAZIONE)

theft	**furto**
possession (drugs/ weapons)	**detenzione di stupefacenti/ armi**
rape	**stupro**
murder	**omidicio; assassinio**
aiding & abetting	**fiancheggiamento**
disturbing the peace	**disturbo della quiete pubblica**
drunk & disorderly	**ubriachezza molesta**

speak English.	Parlo inglese.
May I speak with someone in English?	Posso parlare con qualcuno in inglese?
'm sorry I don't speak Italian.	Mi dispiace, ma non parlo italiano.
What am/was I accused of?	Di che mi si accusa?; Di che sono stata/o accusata/o?
Do I have the right to make a call?	Ho il diritto di fare una telefonata?
May I call someone?	Posso chiamare qualcuno?
I wish to contact my embassy/ consulate.	Vorrei contattare la mia ambasciata/il mio consolato.
May I call my lawyer?	Posso chiamare il mio avvocato?
I'd like to see my duty solicitor.	Vorrei parlare con il mio procuratore legale?
I'll only make a statement in the presence of my lawyer.	Darò una deposizione solo in presenza del mio avvocato.
I want to see a female/male police officer.	Desidero parlare con una/ un poliziotta/o.

EMERGENCIES

arrested	arrestata/o
police car	la pantera; la macchina della polizia
prison/jail	la prigione; il carcere; la galera
cell	la cella
lawyer	l'avvocato
police court	la corte di giustizia
judge	il giudice
identity card	la carta d'identità

THEY MAY SAY ...

Quali sono i suoi dati personali/di stato civile?	What is your name and address?
Mi faccia vedere ... il suo passaporto i suoi documenti la sua patente	Show me your ... passport identity papers driver's licence
Mi mostri il suo permesso di lavoro.	Show me your work permit.
Lei è in arresto.	You have been arrested.
Le diamo una multa (stradale).	We're giving you a traffic fine.
Ci accompagni in questura.	You must come with us to the police station.
Non è tenuta/o a dire niente finché non è presente un avvocato.	You don't have to say anything until you are in the presence of a lawyer.
Adesso sarà accompagnata/o alla corte di giustizia.	Now you will be taken to the police court.
Le è stata/o assegnata/o un procuratore legale.	We have assigned you a duty solicitor.

A

In this dictionary we have included the definite article (**la**, **il**, **l'** or **lo** corresponding to 'the' in English) or the indefinite article (**una**, **un'** or **un**, corresponding to 'a' in English) with each noun. We have chosen either the definite or indefinite article according to the way the word is most likely to be used.

However, note that in most cases the articles are interchangeable. Thus **un cane**, 'a dog' may also be **il cane**, 'the dog'; **la casa**, 'the house' may also be **una casa**, 'a house'. See Grammar, page 19 for an explanation of articles.

Past participles of some verbs have been given in brackets. See Grammar, page 28, for an explanation of verbs and past participles.

A

able (to be; can)		**potere**
Can you take us?		
Ci può portare? (pol)		
We can go (tomorrow).		
Possiamo andare (domani)		
abortion	un	**aborto**
above		**su; sopra**
abroad		**all'estero**
Absolutely!		**Assolutamente!**
to accept		**accettare**
I accept.		
Accetto.		
Do you accept?		
Accetti? (inf)		
accident	un	**incidente**
accommodation	l'	**alloggio** (m)
account (bank)	il	**conto**
accountant	una/un	**ragioniere**
across		**attraverso;**
		dall'altro lato di
to act		**recitare**
action	un'	**azione**
actor	una/un	**attrice/attore**
adaptor	l'	**adattatore** (m);
		una spina intermedia
addiction	la	**dipendenza**

address	l'	**indirizzo**
administration	l'	**amministrazione** (f)
adventure	l'	**avventura** (f)
advice	un	**consiglio**
to advise		**raccomandare**
aerogram	un'	**aerogramma**
aeroplane	l'	**aereo** (m)
affair (love)	una	**relazione**
to be afraid		**aver paura**
after		**dopo**
afternoon	il	**pomeriggio**
aftershave	il	**dopobarba**
again		**ancora;**
		un'altra volta
against		**contro**
age	l'	**età** (f)
to agree		**essere d'accordo**
I agree.		
Sono d'accordo.		
I disagree.		
Non sono d'accordo;		
Non la vedo così.		
aggressive		**aggressiva/o**
agriculture	l'	**agricoltura** (f)
ahead		**avanti**

air	l'	aria (f)
airmail		via aerea
air-conditioning	l'	aria condizionata
(air)plane	l'	aereo (m)
airport	l'	aeroporto (m)
alarm clock	la	sveglia
alcohol	l'	alcole
all		tutta/o
allow		permettere
It's allowed.		
(È) Permesso.		
It's not allowed.		
(È) Vietato.		
almost		quasi
alone		da sola/o
already		già
also		anche
alternative	un'	alternativa
always		sempre
amateur	una/un	dilettante
amazing		incredibile
ambassador	l'	ambasciatrice/
	l'	ambasciatore
ambitious		ambiziosa/o
among		fra; tra
ancient		antica/o
and		e
angry		arrabbiata/o
animal	un	animale
ankle	la	caviglia
annual		annuale
another	un	altro
answer	una	risposta
to answer		rispondere
ant	una	formica
antibiotics	gli	antibiotici
antique		antica/o
any		ogni
anything		ogni cosa
anytime		ogni volta
anywhere		da qualche parte;
		in qualche luogo

(job) application	una	domanda
		(d'impiego)
appointment	un	appuntamento
April		aprile
approximate		approssimata/o
archaeological		archeologica/o
architecture	l'	architettura (f)
to argue		litigare
argument	un	argomento
arm	il	braccio (s)/
	le	braccia (pl)
arrivals		arrivi
to arrive		arrivare
art	l'	arte (f)
art gallery	una	galleria d'arte;
		pinacoteca
artist	una/un	artista
arts (humanities)	le	Lettere
as ... as		(tanto) ...quanto;
		(così) ... come
as soon as		appena
ask		chiedere
ashtray	un	portacenere
aspirin	l'	aspirina (f)
at		a
athlete	una/un	atleta
athletics	l'	atletica (f)
ATM	il	Bancomat;
	la	cassa automatica
audience	il	pubblico;
	gli	spettatori
August		agosto (m)
aunt	la	zia
automatic		automatica/o
autumn	l'	autunno (m)
avenue	il	viale
awful		terribile

B

B&W (film)		bianco e nero
baby	la/il	bimba/o; bebé
baby chair	il	seggiolino

English	Italian
baby buggy	una carrozzina
baby powder	il borotalco
babysitter	la/il baby-sitter
back	la schiena;
	il dorso
backpack	lo zaino
bacteria	i batteri
bad	male
badger	il tasso
bag	la borsa
baggage	il bagaglio
baggage claim	il reclamo bagagli
bakery	il fornaio;
	la panetteria
balcony	il balcone
ball (sports)	la palla
ball (dancing)	il ballo
ballpark figure	un calcolo
	presuntivo;
	preventivo
band (music)	un gruppo
bandage	una fascia
bank (money)	la banca
banker	una/un banchiere
baptism	il battesimo
basket	il canestro
basketball	la pallacanestro
bat (sports)	la mazza;
	il bastone
bather	una/un bagnante
bathroom	il bagno
batteries	le pile
battery (for car)	la batteria
to be	essere
beach	la spiaggia
bear	un orso
beautiful	bella/o
because	perché; siccome
bed	un letto
before	prima
beggar	una/un mendicante
to begin	cominciare
beginner	una/un principiante
behind	dietro
belt	una cintura
below	sotto
beside	accanto
the best	la/il migliore
better	migliore
between	fra; tra
bib	il bavaglino
bicycle	la bicicletta
big	grande;
	grossa/o
bike	la bicicletta; bici
bill (account)	il conto
billion	un miliardo
binoculars	il binocolo
bird	un uccello
birthday	il compleanno
biscuits	i biscotti
bite	un morso
bitter	amara/o
black	nera/o
black comedy	un tragicomico
blanket	una coperta
to bless	benedire;
	santificare;
	consacrare
blind	cieca/o
blood group	il gruppo
	sanguigno
blood test	l' analisi (f) del
	sangue
blown glass	il vetro soffiato
blue (dark)	blu
blue (light)	azzurra/o;
	celeste
boarding pass	una carta d'imbarco
boat	la barca; nave
body	il corpo
to boil	bollire
boiling	bollente
bomb	una bomba

English		Italian
bone	l'	osso (m)
book	un	libro
to book		prenotare; riservare
bookmaker	l'	allibratrice/ allibratore
bookshop	la	libreria
boots	gli	stivali
bored		annoiata/o
boring		noiosa/o
to borrow		prestare
boss	il	capo; padrone
both		tutti e due
bottle	una	bottiglia
bottle opener	un	apribottiglie
bowl	un	piatto fondo
box	la	scatola
boxing	il	pugilato;
	la	boxe
boy	il	bambino
(my) boyfriend	il	(mio) ragazzo
bracelet	un	braccialetto
brakes	i	freni
branch office	la	filiale;
	la	succursale
brass		ottone
brave		coraggiosa/o
bread	il	pane
to break (s'thing)		rompere
breakfast	la	(prima) colazione
breast	la	mammella;
	il	seno; il petto
bribe	una	tangente;
	una	bustarella
to bribe		corrompere
bridge	il	ponte
bright		luminosa/o
to bring		portare
broadcast	la	trasmissione
broken		rotta/o
bronze		bronzo
brooch	una	spilla
brother	il	fratello

English		Italian
brother-in-law	il	cognato
brown		marrone
brushstroke	la	pennellata
budgerigar	una	cocorita
budget hotel	l'	albergo (m)
building	l'	edificio (m)
to burn		bruciare
bus	l'	autobus (m)
business	gli	affari
business person	una/un	donna/uomo d'affari
busker	una/un	musicista ambulante
busy		occupata/o
but		ma; però
butter	il	burro
butterfly	una	farfalla
to buy		comprare
by (beside)		da (accanto)

C

cable car	la	funivia
café	un	caffè; un bar
calendar	un	calendario
calm		calma/o
camera	la	macchina fotografica
camera shop	il	fotografo
to go camping		accamparsi; piantare la tenda
camping ground	il	camping; campeggio
can (tin)	una	scatola
can (to be able)		potere
can opener	l'	apriscatole (m)
to cancel		cancellare
candle	una	candela
canvas	la	tela
capitalism	il	capitalismo
to care (about s'thing)		interessarsi (di)
	She/He doesn't care.	
	Non le/gli interessa di ...	

I don't care (mind). Non m'importa.	
to take care of	avere cura di
Take care! Mi raccomando!; Attenzione!	
careful	attenta/o
car racing	l' automobilismo (m)
to carry	portare
carton	un cartone
cartoons	i disegni animati
cashier	la cassa
cassette	una cassetta
castle	il castello
casualty (dept)	il pronto soccorso
cat	un gatto
cathedral	la cattedrale; il duomo
caves	le grotte
CD	un cidì
cellular phone	il cellulare; il telefonino
cemetery	il cimitero; il camposanto
centimetre	un centimetro
ceramic	la ceramica
cereal	i cereali
to be certain	essere sicura/o; certa/o
chain	una catena
chair	una sedia
challenging	provocante
championship	il campionato
chance	la fortuna
change (coins)	gli spiccioli
to change	cambiare
charcoal	il carboncino
cheap	a basso prezzo; economica/o; buon mercato
check in	poto; banco di controllo
checkmate	lo scaccomatto
cheese	il formaggio

chess	gli scacchi
chest	il torace; petto
chicken	il pollo
children	i figli; bambini
chocolate	il cioccolato
to choose	scegliere
Christmas Day	il Natale
Christmas Eve	la Vigilia di Natale
church	la chiesa
cigar	il sigaro; toscano
cigarette papers	le cartine (per sigarette)
cigarettes	le sigarette
cinema	il cinema
cinema critic	una/un critica/o; recensore
citizenship	la cittadinanza
city	la città
city centre	il centro (città)
city walls	le mura
class system	il sistema delle classi sociali
clean	pulita/o
clerk	un'/un impiegata/o
client	una/un cliente
cliff	la scogliera; il dirupo
to climb	scalare
clock	l' orologio
close (adj)	vicino
to close	chiudere
clothing	gli abiti; i vestiti l' abbigliamento (m)
clothing store	un negozio di abbigliamento
cloudy	nuvoloso
clown	la/il pagliaccio
clutch (car)	la frizione
coast	la costa
coat	il cappotto
coffee	il caffè
coin change	gli spiccioli; le monetine
cold (illness)	un raffreddore

cold (temperature)	fredda/o
cold water	l' acqua (f) fredda
colleague	una/un collega
college	il collegio universitario;
	la residenza universitaria
colour	il colore
comb	il pettine
to come	venire
Come off it!	
Vien via!	
comedy	una commedia;
	un film brillante
comfortable	comoda/o
comics	i fumetti
communion	la comunione
communist	una/un comunista
companion	una/un compagna/o
compass	la bussola
competition	la gara;
	l' attività sportiva
computer	il computer
conceptt	un concetto
concert	un concerto
concert hall	la sala per concerti;
	il teatro comunale
conditioner	il balsamo per i capelli
condoms	i preservativi
confession	la confessione
to confirm	confermare
Congratulations!	Congratulazioni!
confirmation (Catholic)	la cresima
conservative	conservatore
constitution	la costituzione
consulate	il consolato
contact lens	la lente a contatto
contagious	contagiosa/o
contraceptives	i contraccettivi

convent	il convento
conversation	una conversazione;
	un discorso
to cook	cucinare
corner	l' angolo (m)
corrupt	corrotta/o
corruption	la corruzione
to cost	costare
costume	il costume
costume designer	una/un costumista
cotton	il cotone
cough syrup	lo sciroppo;
to count	contare
country (nation)	il paese
countryside	la campagna
couple (people)	una coppia
courtyard	un cortile
cousin	una/un cugina/o
cow	la mucca; vacca
craft shop	la bottega d'artigianato
crampons	i ramponi
crayon	il gessetto
crazy	matta/o; pazza/o
credit card	la carta di credito
creek	il ruscello;
	la baia;
	l' insenatura
crime novels	i gialli
crops	il raccolto
cross	la croce
crowded	affollata/o
crucifix	il crocifisso
cup	una coppa; tazza
cupboard	una credenza
cure	la cura
current affairs	le attualità
customs	la dogana
to cut	tagliere
cycle race	
cycling	il ciclismo

D

ad	il	papà
aily	il	quotidiano
amp		umida/o
dance		ballare
ance	un	ballo
angerous		pericolosa/o
ark		scura/o
ate (time)	la	data
ate of birth	la	data di nascita
aughter	la	figlia
aughter-in-law	la	nuora
awn	l'	alba (f)
ay	un	giorno
ay after tomorrow		dopodomani
ay before yesterday	l'	altro ieri
ead		morta/o
eaf		sorda/o
ealer (drugs)	una/un	spacciatrice/ spacciatore
eath	la	morte
ecember	il	dicembre
decide		decidere
ecision	una	decisione
eer	un	cervo
efence	la	difesa
eforestation	la	deforestazione
egree	la	laurea
	il	diploma
elicatessen	la	pizzicheria;
	la	salumeria
elicious		deliziosa/o
elirious		delirante
emocracy	la	democrazia
emocratic		democratica/o
emonstration	una	manifestazione;
(protest)	una	dimostrazione
ental floss	il	filo interdentale
entist	la/il	dentista
deny		negare
eodorant	il	deodorante
depart		partire
epartment store	un	grande magazzino

departures	le	partenze
deposit	un	deposito;
	un	acconto
desert	il	deserto
dessert	un	dolce
destination	la	destinazione
to destroy		distruggere
detail (n)	un	dettaglio
development	uno	sviluppo
dial tone	il	segnale (acustico)
diary	l'	agenda (f);
	il	diario
dictatorship	una	dittatura
dictionary	il	dizionario; vocabolario
diesel	il	diesel
different		diversa/o
difficult		difficile
dining car	la	carrozza ristorante
dinner	la	cena
dinner time	l'	ora di cena
diploma	il	diploma;
	la	laurea
diposable nappies	i	pannolini usa e getta
direct		diretto
direction	la	direzione
director (films)	il	regista
dirty		sporca/o
disadvantage	uno	svantaggio
discount	lo	sconto
to discover		scoprire
discrimination	la	discriminazione
dishwashing liquid	il	detergente per piatti
disinfectant	il	disinfettante
disintoxication	la	disintossicazione
disk	il	dischetto; disco
distant		lontana/o
diving	il	tuffo
divorced		divorziata/o
dizzy		stordita/o

D I C T I O N A R y

to do	fare
doctor	una/un dottoressa/ dottore;
	un medico
documentary	un documentario
dog	un cane
dole	il sussidio di disoccupazione
doll	una bambola
dolphin	un delfino
domestic flights	i voli domestici
donkey	un asino
dope	l' erba (f);
	l' insalata (f)
double	doppia/o
double bed	un letto matrimoniale
down (there)	giù; laggiù
downtown	il centro(città)
dozen	una dozzina
drama	una dramma
dramatic	drammatica/o
to draw	disegnare
drawing	un disegno
dream	un sogno
dried	secca; essiccata/o
drink	una bevanda
to drink	bere (pp bevuto)
drinkable (water)	(acqua) potabile
driver	l' autista (f/m)
driver's licence	la patente (di guida)
drug addict	una/un drogata/o; tossicomane; tossicodipendente
drug addiction	la tossicomania
drugs	la droga; gli stupefacenti
drugstore	una bottega; un negozio
dry	secca/o
duck	un' anatra
dummy	il ciucciotto

during	durante
dust	la polvere

E

ear	l' orecchio
early	presto
to earn	guadagnare
earnings	i guadagni
earrings	gli orecchini
Earth	la Terra
earthquake	un terremoto
east	est (m)
Easter Sunday	la Domenica di Pasqua
easy	facile
to eat	mangiare
Have you eaten yet?	
Hai già mangiata/o?	
economical	a buon mercato
economy	l' economia (f)
education	l' istruzione (f)
eggs	le uova
eight	otto
eighteen	diciotto
eighth	ottava/o
eighty	ottanta
either ... or ...	o ... o ...
elbow	il gomito
elder	la/il più grande
elections	le elezioni
electorate	l' elettorato (m)
electrician	una/un elettricista
electricity	l' elettricità (f)
elevator	l' ascensore (m)
eleven	undici
eleventh	undicesima/o
email	la posta elettronica; un messaggio elettronico
to embarrass	imbarazzare
... embassy	l' ambasciata (f) ...
employee	l' impiegata/o

F

employer	la/il datrice/datore di lavoro;
	la/il principale
empty	vuota/o
end (n)	la fine
energy	l' energia (f)
engagement	il fidanzamento
engine	il motore
engineer	un'/un ingegnere
engineering	la ingegneria
English	inglese
engrossing	avvincente
to enjoy (oneself)	divertirsi
enough	abbastanza
enough!	Basta!
to enter	entrare
entertaining	divertente
entry	l' entrata (f)
envelope	una busta
environment	l' ambiente (m)
epiphany	l' Epifania;
	la Befana
equal	uguale
equality	l' eguaglianza (f)
equestrian sport	l' equitazione (f)
espionage	lo spionaggio
estate agent	l' agente immobiliare
European	l' europa (f)
euthanasia	l' eutanasia (f);
even so ...	Eppure è ...;
	Comunque ...
evening	la sera
event	un avvenimento
ever	mai
every day	tutti i giorni
everyone	tutte/i
everything	tutto
exactly!	Esattamente!
excellent	brillante; magnifica/o
exchange	il cambio
exciting	eccitante
excluded	esclusa/o

Excuse me.	Mi scusi; Permesso.
exhibition	l' esposizione (f)
exhibitor	una/un espositrice/espositore
exile	l' esilo (m)
exotic	esotica/o
expensive	cara/o
experience	l' esperienza (f)
to export	esportare
express	l' espresso;
	il rapido
expressive	espressiva/o
extraterrestrials	gli extraterrestri
eyes	gli occhi

F

factory	una fabbrica
faint	sfumata/o
false	falsa/o
family	la famiglia
fan	il ventilatore
fans	i tifosi; sostenitori
fantasy	fantastica/o
far	lontano da
farm	una fattoria
farmer	un agricoltore
fascinating	affascinante
fast (not eat)	digiunare
fast (quick)	veloce; rapida/o
fat	grassa/o
father	il padre
father-in-law	il suocero
fault	la colpa
my fault	colpa mia
fax	un fax
fear	la paura
February	febbraio
fee	la tassa;
	i diritti
feeding bottle	il biberon
to feel (emotion)	sentire
feeling	un sentimento

female		femmina	
fence	il	recinto	
fencing (sport)	la	scherma	
ferry	il	traghetto	
festival	una	festa	
fever	la	febbre	
few		poca/o; poche; pochi	
fiancée/fiancé	una/un	fidanzata/o	
fiction	la	narrativa; novellistica	
field	il	campo	
fifteen		quindici	
fifth		quinta/o	
fifty		cinquanta	
fight	un	incontro	
film (movies)	un	film	
film (for camera)	la	pellicola	
film speed	la	sensibilità	
filtered		con filtro	
fine (penalty)	una	multa	
finger	il	dito	
	le	dita (pl)	
fire (outside)	un	incendio	
fire (general)	il	fuoco	
firewood	la	legna da ardere	
first	la/il	prima/o	
first aid kit	una	cassetta di pronto soccorso	
fish shop	una	pescheria	
fish merchant	un	pescivendolo	
fishing	la	pesca	
five		cinque	
flag	la	bandiera	
flash	il	flash	
flashlight (torch)	la	torcia elettrica;	
	la	pila tascabile	
flight	il	volo	
flood	l'	alluvione (f)	
floor	il	pavimento	
flour	la	farina	
flower	un	fiore	
flower seller	una/un	fioraia/o	

fly	una	mosca	
flying saucers	i	dischi volanti	
foggy		nebbioso	
to follow		seguire	
food	il	cibo;	
	l'	alimento (m)	
food poisoning	l'	intossicazione (f) alimentare	
foot	il	piede	
for		per	
foreigner	una/un	straniera/e	
forest	una	foresta	
forever		per sempre	
to forget		dimenticare	
I forgot.			
Ho dimenticato.			
to forgive		perdonare	
fork	una	forchetta	
formal		formale	
fortnight	una	quindicina	
fortune teller	una/un	indovina/o	
forty		quaranta	
four		quattro	
fourteen		quattordici	
fourth		quarta/o	
fox	un	volpe	
frame	un	telaio	
fragile		fragile	
free (of charge)		gratis	
free (not boun)		libera/o	
fresh		fresca/o	
Friday		venerdì	
fried		fritta/o	
friend	un'/un	amica/o	
friendly		simpatica/o	
frog	una	rana	
from ... to ...		da ... a ...	
in front of		davanti a	
frozen foods	i	surgelati	
fruit	la	frutta	
fruit juice	il	succo di frutta	
full		piena/o; completa/o	
fun	il	divertimento	

...eral	il	funerale	
...ny		divertente; comico; buffa/o	
...ure	il	futuro	

...

...mbler	una/un	giocatrice/ giocatore d'azzardo
...me	un	gioco
...me (sport)	una	partita
...me show	un	gioco televisivo; quiz
...rage	un	garage;
	un'	autorimessa
...rbage	i	rifiuti
	le	immondizie
...rdening	i	(lavori di) giardinaggio
...rdens	i	giardini
...s (petrol)	la	benzina
...s cylinder	una	bombola a gas
...te	il	cancello
...y		gay
...eneral		generale
...enerous		generosa/o
...osts	gli	spiriti
...rl	una	ragazza
...y) girlfriend	la	(mia) ragazza
give		dare

...ive me ... (inf)
Mi dài ...; Dammi ...
I'll give it to you.
Te lo do.

...ass	il	vetro
...ass (drinking)	un	bicchiere
...asses	gli	occhiali
...oves	i	guanti
...go		andare

I'm going to ...
Vado a ...

Go straight ahead.
Si va sempre diritto.
Let's go!
Andiamo.
I'm going out.
Esco.

goalkeeper	una/un	portiere
goat	una	capra
goddess/god		dea/dio
gold		oro
goldfish	un	pesciolino rosso
golf	il	golf
to go out		uscire
good		buona/o

Good evening. Buonasera.
Good Friday Venerdí Santo
Good day. Buongiorno.
Goodbye. Arrivederci; Ciao.
Goodnight. Buonanotte.

government	il	governo
gram	un	grammo
grandfather	il	nonno
grandmother	la	nonna
graphic art	l'	arte (f) grafica
great		ottima/o
greedy		avida/o
green		verde
greengrocer	il	fruttivendolo
grey		grigia/o
grocery store	un	negozio di alimentari;
	una	drogheria
to grow		crescere
to grow up		crescere
to guess		indovinare
guesthouse	una	pensione
guide	una/un	guida
guidebook	un	libro di viaggio
guilty		colpevole
guitar	una	chitarra
gym	la	palestra
gymnastics	la	ginnastica

H

hail	la	grandine
It's hailing.		
Grandina		
hairbrush	una	spazzola (per i capelli)
haircut	un	taglio
hairdresser	una/un	parrucchiera/e
hairstyle	la	pettinatura
half	il	mezzo; la metà
to hallucinate		allucinare
hallucinogen	l'	allucinogeno (m)
hammock	l'	amaca (f)
hand	la	mano/
	le	mani (pl)
handbag	una	borsa; borsetta
handball	la	pallamano
handicrafts	il	lavoro artigianale
handsome		bello
happy		felice
Happy Easter!		Buona Pasqua!
hard		difficile
hard boiled eggs	le	uova sode
hardware shop	la	ferramenta
hare	una	lepre
harvest	la	vendemmia;
	la	raccolta
hat	il	cappello
to hate		odiare
to have		avere
I have ...		
Ho ...		
You have ...		
Hai ...		
Have you (got) ...?		
... ce l'hai?		
head	la	testa
headlights	i	fari
health	la	salute
health shop	l'	erboristeria (f)

to hear		sentire; udire
heart	il	cuore
heat	il	caldo
heater	la	stufa
heavy		pesante
Hello.		Buongiorno; Ciao.
helmet	il	casco
to help		aiutare
Help!		Aiuto!
here		qui; qua
heroin addict	l'	eroinomane
heron	l'	airone (f)
high		alta/o
high school	l'	istituto (m) superiore;
	la	scuola superiore
hiking	l'	escursionismo (m)
hill	una	collina
to hire		noleggiare
I want to hire it.		
Vorrei noleggiarlo.		
to hitchhike		fare l'autostop
hobbies	i	passatempi
holiday (public)	una	feria
holidays (vacation)	le	vacanze; ferie
holy		santa/o
holy water	l'	acqua (f) santa
home	la	casa
homeless people	i	senzatetto
to be homesick		avere nostalgia
homosexual		omosessuale
honest		onesta/o
honesty	l'	onestà (f)
honey	il	miele
honeymoon	la	luna di miele
honour	l'	onore (m)
hope	la	speranza
horror	l'	orrore (m)
horse	un	cavallo
horseracing	l'	ippica (f)
hospital	l'	ospedale (m)
hospitality	l'	ospitalità (f)
hot		caldo

280

t water	l' acqua (f) calda	illegal	illegale
tel	un albergo	imagination	la fantasia
use	la casa	to be imaginative	avere fantasia; fantasiosa/o
usework	le pulizie	immediately	mmediatemente; subito
w	come		
ow are you?	Come sta? (pol); Come stai? (inf)	immigration	l' immigrazione (f)
How come?	Come mai?	in	in; nel
How much? (amount)	Quanto?	in a hurry	in; di fretta
How much? (cost)	Quanto costa?	In any case ...	In ogni caso ...; Ad ogni modo
wever	però; comunque	in front of	davanti a
man being	un essere umano	included	inclusa/o; compresa/o
man rights	i diritti umani	indicator	le frecce; i lampeggiatori
mour	l' umorismo	industrial art	l' arte (f) industriale
ndred	cento	inequality	l' ineguaglianza (f)
nger	la fame	inflation	l' inflazione (f)
be hungry	avere fame	information	le informazioni
I'm hungry. Ho fame.		infotainment	il varietà informazioni
be in a hurry	essere in fretta	injection	un iniezione; una puntura
be hurt	farsi male; ferita/o	ink	l' inchiostro (m)
He's hurt. Si è fatto male; È ferito.		inline skating	il pattinaggio in linea
sband	il marito	innovative	una innovatrice/ un innovatore
droplane	l' idrovolante (m)	insect	un insetto
pertext	l' ipertesto (m)	installation	l' installazione (f)
	io	to insure	assicurare
ex	il stambecco	I'm insured. Ho l'assicurazione.	
e-axe	il ghiaccio / una piccozza	intelligent	intelligente
cream	un gelato	interested	interessata/o
ea	un' idea	interesting	interessante
entification	il documento d'identità	international	internazionale
card	la carta d'identità	international flights	i voli internazionali
se	malata/o	interview	il colloquio (selettivo)

I

to invite		invitare
Italian		italiano
itch	un	prurito

J

jacket	una	giacca
jail (gaol)	la	galera;
		prigione;
	il	carcere
jam	la	marmellata;
		confettura di
		frutta
January	il	gennaio
jealous		gelosa/o
jewellery	i	gioielli
job	un	lavoro;
	un	impiego;
	un	mestiere
jockey	il	fantino
joke	uno	scherzo
I'm joking.		
Scherzo		
journalist	una/un	giornalista
judo	il	judo
July		luglio
jumper	un	maglione;
		pullover
June		giugno
junkie	una/un	drogata/o;
		rimbata/o
justice	la	giustizia

K

knee	il	ginocchio
key	la	chiave
to kill		ammazzare;
		uccidere
kilogram	un	chilo(grammo)
kilometre	un	chilometro;
		kilometro
kind		gentile
king	il	re

kiss	un	bacio
kitten	un	gattino; micino
knapsack	lo	zaino
knife	un	coltello
to know (a person)		conoscere
to know (how to)		sapere

L

labourer	una	lavoratrice/
	un	lavoratore
lace	il	merletto
land	la	terra
landslide	una	frana
lake	il	lago
language	la	lingua
last	l'	ultima/o (m)
last month	il	mese scorso/
		passato
last night		ieri sera
last week	la	settimana
		scorsa/
		passata
last year	l'	anno (m)
		scorso/
		passato
late		in ritardo; tard
It's late.		
È tardi.		
launderette	la	lavanderia
law	la	legge;
	la	giurisprudenz
lawyer	una/un	avvocata/
laxatives	i	lassativi
lay-by	il	pagamento a
		rate
lazy		pigra/o
lead	la	grafite;
	il	piombo
leaded		con piombo
to learn		imparare
I'm learning Italian.		
Sto imparando l'italiano.		
to lease (from)		locare; affitta

...ather	la	pelle; cuoio	local	il	locale

English		Italian
...ather	la	pelle; cuoio
...ft (not right)	la	sinistra
Turn left ...		
Gira a sinistra ...		
...ft (behind)		lasciato; dimenticato
...ft(-wing)		(di) sinistra
...ft luggage		deposito bagagli
...ft over		rimasta/o
...g	la	gamba
...gal		legale
...galisation	la	legalizzazione
...gislation	la	legislazione
...ns	l'	obiettivo (m)
...sbian	una	lesbica
...ss		(di) meno
...tter	una	lettera
...ar	una/un	bugiarda/o
...eral		liberale
...rary	la	biblioteca
...e	la	vita
...t	l'	ascensore (m)
...ght		chiara/o
...ght (not heavy)		leggera/o
...ght (not dark)		luminosa/o
...ghtbulb	la	lampadina
...ght meter	l'	esposimetro
...ghter	l'	accendino (m); accendisigari (m)
...e (similar)		come
...like		piacere
I like ...		
Mi piace ...		
...e	la	linea
... balm	il	burro per le labbra
...listen		ascoltare
...re	un	litro
...tle		piccola/o
...little (amount)	un	po'; poco
...zard	una	lucertola;
	un	ramarro
...live		vivere

English		Italian
local	il	locale
lock	la	serratura
long		lunga/o
long ago		molto tempo fa
to look at		guardare
to look for		cercare
I'm looking for ...		
Sto cercando ...		
loose		larga/o
loose change	gli	spiccioli
to lose		perdere
loss	una	perdita;
	un	deficit
a lot		molta/o; tanta/o
loud		alta/o
to love		amare; volere bene
I love it.		
Mi piace molto.		
I love you.		
Ti amo; Ti voglio bene.		
lover	una/un	amante
loyal		leale; fedele
lucky		fortunata/o
lunch	il	pranzo;
	la	colazione
lunchtime	l'	ora (f) di ranzo

M

English		Italian
machine	una	macchina
mad (crazy)		matta/o; pazza/o
Madam; Mrs; Ms		Signora
made of ...		fatto di ...
magician	una/un	maga/o
mailbox	una	cassetta postale
main road	la	strada principale
main square	la	piazza principale
majority	la	maggioranza
to make		fare
many		tante/i; molte/i

map (road/city)	una	pianta; carta
marble	il	marmo
March	il	marzo
margarine	la	margarina
market	il	mercato
marriage	il	matrimonio;
(ceremony)	le	nozze
to be married		essere sposati
to marry		sposare
match (sport)	una	partita; gioco
matches	i	fiammiferi; cerini
mattress	il	materasso
May		maggio
maybe		forse; può darsi
mechanic	un	meccanico (f/m)
medal	una	medaglia
medicine	la	medicina
to meet		incontrare

I'll meet you there.
Ci vediamo lì.
Let's meet up.
Facciamo un appuntamento!
Pleased to meet you.
Piacere.

menthol		alla menta
menu	il	menu
	la	lista
message	un	messaggio
metal	il	metallo
meter	il	metro
midday	il	mezzogiorno
midnight	la	mezzanotte
migrants	gli	immigrati
military service	il	servizio militare
milk	il	latte
milk bar	una	bottega;
	un	negozio
millimetre	un	millimetro
million	un	milione
mind	la	mente
to mind		importarsi
Never mind.		Non importa;
		Non fa niente.
mineral water	l'	acqua minerale

minorities	le	minoranze
minute (time)	un	minuto
mirror	lo	specchio
to miss		mancare
(feel absence)		
to miss (the bus)		perdere
mistake	uno	sbaglio
to mix		mescolare
modem	un	modem
modern		moderna/o
moisturising cream	la	crema idratante
monarchy	la	monarchia
monastery	il	monastero
Monday	il	lunedì
money	i	soldi;
	il	denaro
money (change)	gli	spiccioli
month	il	mese
monument	il	monumento
more		(di) più
morning	la	mattina
this morning		stamattina;
		stamani
mosque	una	moschea
mother	la	madre
mother-in-law	la	suocera
motorboat	il	motoscafo
motor scooter	un	motorino
motorway	l'	autostrada (f)
mountain lodge	il	rifugio alpino
mountains	le	montagne
mouth	la	bocca
movie	un	film
movie camera	la	cinepresa
mule	un	mulo
mum	la	mamma
murder (n)	un	omicidio
to murder		assassinare
muscle	il	muscolo
museum	il	museo
music	la	musica
music show	un	musicale
musician	una/un	musicista
my	la/il	mia/o

lclippers	un	tagliaunghie
me	il	nome
What's your name? (pol)		
Come si chiama?		
My name is ...		
Mi chiamo ...		
rcotic	il	narcotico
tional		nazionale
ure	la	natura
usea	la	nausea
ar		vicino a
cessary		necessario
ck	il	collo
cklace	una	collana
need		avere bisogno; bisognare
ther ... nor ...		né ... né
ofascist	una/un	neofascista
ohew	il	nipote
	una	rete
ver		(non ...) mai
w		nuova/o
w Year's Day		Capodanno
w Year's Eve		San Silvestro; Fine (d')Anno
w Year's gifts	le	strenne;
	i	doni
ws	le	notizie
ws (on TV)	il	telegiornale
wsagency	l'	edicola;
	il	cartolaio
wspaper	il	giornale
xt	il	prossimo
xt month	il	mese prossimo;/ venturo
xt to		accanto a
xt week	la	settimana prossima;/ ventura
xt year	l'	anno (m) prossimo/ venturo

niece	la	nipote
night	la	notte
nightclub	un	nightclub
nine		nove
nineteen		diciannove
ninety		novanta
ninth		nona/o
No.		No
No way!		Per nulla/niente; Neanche per sogno!
noise	un	rumore
noisy		rumorosa/o
none		niente; nulla
non-fiction	la	saggistica
north	il	nord
nose	il	naso
not yet		non ancora
novel	il	romanzo
November		novembre
now		adesso; ora
nuclear energy	l'	energia nucleare
nuclear testing	gli	esperimenti nucleari
nurse	una/un	infermiera/e
nylon	il	nailon

O

obvious		ovvio; chiaro
ocean	l'	oceano
occupation	un	lavoro;
	un	impiego;
	un	mestiere
October	l'	ottobre (m)
Of course!		Certamente!; (Di) Certo!
off (appliance)		spenta/o
off (food)		guasta/o
to offend		offendere
to offer		offrire
office	l'	ufficio (m)
office worker	una/un	impiegata/o

often		spesso
oil	l'	olio (m)
oil painting	un	dipinto a olio
OK		passabile
old		vecchia/o; antica/o
old city	la	cittadella
Olympic Games	le	Olimpiadi;
	i	Giochi Olimpici
on		su
on (appliance)		accesa/o
on sale		in svendita; saldo
on time		in tempo
once	una	volta
one		uno
only		solo; solamente
to open		aprire

What time does it open?
A che ora apre?

opera house	il	teatro dell'opera
opinion	l'	opinione (f)
opportunity	l'	opportunità (f)
opposite		di fronte a
opposition	l'	opposizione (f)
optician	l'	ottico (m)
optometrist	la/il	optometrista
or		o; oppure
orange	un'	arancia
orchestra	l'	orchestra (f)
order	l'	ordine (m)
ordinarily		di solito
ordinary		solito
organisation	l'	organizzazione (f)
to organise		organizzare
original		originale
other		altra/o
otherwise		altrimenti
outside		fuori
out of focus		sfuocata/o
outgoing		estroversa/o
over (above)		su; sopra

overdose	un'	overdose;
	un	iperdosaggio;
	l'	abuso (m) di stupefacenti
to owe		dovere

I owe you. (inf)
Ti devo.
You owe me
Mi dovete.

owner	la/il	proprietaria/o
ox	il	bue
oxygen	l'	ossigeno (m)

P

packet	il	pacchetto
packet of cigarettes	un	pacchetto di sigarette
pad	un	pannolino
padlock	il	lucchetto
pain	il	dolore
painful		dolorosa/o
painkillers	un	analgesico;
	un	calmante
to paint		dipingere; pitturare
paintbrush	il	pennello
painter	una/un	pittrice/pitto
painting	un	quadro; dipinto
pair	un	paio
palace	il	palazzo
paper	la	carta
parcel	un	pacchetto
park	un	parco
parliament	il	parlamento
part	la	parte
party	una	festa
passenger	la/il	passeggera/o
passport	il	passaporto
passport control	il	controllo di passaporto
past	il	passato

stry shop	la	pasticceria
th	il	sentiero
pay		pagare
ace	la	pace
ak	il	picco;
	la	vetta
n (ballpoint)	una	penna (a sfera)
ncil	una	matita
nknife	un	temperino
nsioners	i	pensionati
ople	la	gente
pper	il	pepe
rcent	la	percentuale
rfect		perfetto
rformance	l'	esecuzione (f);
		esibizione (f)
		musicale
rformance art	l'	arte
		d'esibizione
rfume	il	profumo
rmanent		permanente
rmission	il	permesso
permit		permettere
rsecution	la	persecuzione
rson	una	persona
rsonal		personale
rsonality	la	personalità
trol station	la	stazione di
		servizio
armacy	la	farmacia
one booth	una	cabina
		telefonica
onebook	l'	elenco (m)
		telefonico
onecard	una	carta telefonica
otograph	una	fotografia
photograph		fotografare
ece	un	pezzo
g	un	maiale
llow	il	cuscino
nk		rosa
pe	una	pipa
ace	un	posto
ane	l'	aereo (m)

plant	una	pianta
plastic	la	plastica
plate	un	piatto
platform	il	binario
play (theatre)	il	teatro
to play (a game)		giocare
to play (music)		suonare
player	una/un	giocatrice/
		giocatore
Please.		Per favore;
		Per piacere;
		Per cortesia.
plenty (inf)	un	mucchio; sacco
poetry	la	poesia
point	il	punto
police	la	polizia
policy	la	politica
politics	la	politica
pollution	l'	inquinamento (m)
pond	lo	stagno;
pool (swimming)	una	piscina
poor		povera/o
port	il	porto
post-modernism	il	postmoderno
postcard	una	cartolina
postcode	la	codice postale
poste restante	il	fermo posta
post office	la	posta;
	l'	ufficio postale
pottery	gli	oggetti in
		ceramica
potty	il	vasino
power	il	potere
pram	una	carrozzina
prayer	la	preghiera
to prefer		preferire
pregnant		incinta; gravida
prepare		preparare
present (time)	il	presente
present (gift)	un	regalo
presentation	una	presentazione
president	la/il	presidente
pretty		carina/o;
		bellina/o

price	il	prezzo

Can you lower the price?
Può farmi lo sconto?

priest	il	prete
prime minister	la/il	primo ministro
prison	la	galera; prigione
	il	carcere
prisoner	una/un	prigionera/o
private		privata/o
privatisation	la	privatizzazione
problem	il	problema
producer	il	direttore di produzione
profit	il	profitto;
	l'	utile (m)
profitability	la	redditività
promise	una	promessa
proposal	una	proposta;
	un'	offerta
prostitute	una/un	prostituta/o
to protect		proteggere
protest	una	manifestazione
public	il	pubblico
public relations	le	relazioni pubbliche
public toilet	un	gabinetto;
	un	bagno;
	i	servizi igienici
pure		pura/o
purple		viola
to push		spingere
pusher (baby)	il	passeggino

qualifications	le	qualifiche
quality	la	qualità
quarter	un	quarto
question	una	domanda
quick		veloce; rapida/o
quiet		silenziosa/o; tranquilla/o

rabbit	un	coniglio
race (contest)	una	corsa; gara
racecourse (cars)	una	pista
racecourse (horses)	l'	ippodromo (m)
racism	il	razzismo
racquet	la	racchetta
radiator	il	radiatore
radical		radicale
radio	la	radio
radio announcer	un'	annunciatrice;
	un	annunciatore
rain	la	pioggia

It's raining.
Piove

raincoat	l'	impermeabile (r
rape (n)	la	violazione;
	lo	stupro
to be raped		essere violentata/o; essere stuprata/
rare		rara/o
raw		cruda/o
razor (electric)	un	rasoio (elettrico
razor blades	le	lamette
to read		leggere
to be ready		essere pronta/

Really!
Davvero!

reason	la	ragione
receipt	una	ricetta
recently		recentemente; di recente
to recommend		raccomandare
record (lp)	un	disco
recycling	il	riciclaggio
red		rossa/o
references	le	referenze
refugees	i	rifugiati
refund	un	rimborso
to refuse		rifiutare
region	la	regione
registered mail	la	(posta) raccomanda

registration	la	registrazione	
regulation	una	regola	
rehearsal	una	prova	
relation	un	parente	
relationship	il	rapporto	
to relax		rilassarsi	
religion	la	religione	
to remember		ricordare	
remote		remoto; lontano	
rendition	l'	interpretazione (f)	
rent	l'	affitto (m)	
to rent		prendere in affitto	
repairs		riparazioni	
representative	una/un	deputata/o	
republic	la	repubblica	
republican	una/un	repubblicana/o	
reservation	una	prenotazione	
to reserve		fare una prenotazione	
respect	il	rispetto	
responsibility	la	responsabilità	
to rest		rilassare	
rest	il	resto	
restaurant	un	ristorante	
to return		ritornare	
review	una	critica	
revolution	la	rivoluzione	
rich		ricca/o	
right (not left)		destra	
Turn right ...			
Gira a destra ...			
right (correct)		giusto	
right(-wing)		(di) destra	
right now		in questo momento; quest'istante	
ring	un	anello	
risk	il	rischio	
river	il	fiume	
road	la	strada	
road map	una	carta stradale	
robber	un	ladro	
robbery	un	furto	

rock climbing	l'	alpinismo (m)	
roof	il	tetto	
room	una	camera	
rope	una	corda	
round		rotonda/o	
rubbish	i	rifiuti;	
	le	immondizie	
rug	il	tappeto	
ruins	le	rovine	
rules	le	regole	

S

sachet	un	sacchettino	
sacraments	i	sacramenti	
sad		triste	
safe (n)	una	cassaforte	
safe (secure)		sicura/o	
safe (not dangerous)		fuori pericolo	
safety	la	sicurezza	
sailing	la	vela	
saint	la/il	santa/o	
salary	lo	stipendio	
salt	il	sale	
salty		salata/o	
same	la/lo	stessa/o	
sand	la	sabbia	
sandals	i	sandali	
sanitary napkins	gli	assorbenti igienici	
satin		raso	
Saturday	il	sabato	
to save		salvare	
to say		dire	
scene	la	scena	
scenery	il	paesaggio	
sceptical		scettica/o	
school (primary)	la	scuola (elementare)	
science	la	scienza	
science fiction	la	fantascienza	
scientific		scientifica/o	
scientist	una/un	scienziata/o	

scissors	le	forbici
screen	lo	schermo
scuba diving	l'	immersione (f) subacquea
to sculpt		scolpire
sculptor	una/un	scultrice/ scultore
sculpture	la	scultura
sea	il	mare
seat (place)	un	posto
seat (chair)	una	sedia
	un	sedile
seatbelt	la	cintura di sicurezza
second		seconda/o
second (time)	un	secondo
secret	un	segreto
secretary	una/un	segretaria/o
selfish		presuntuosa/o
to sell		vendere
to send		mandare
separated		separata/o
September		settembre
series	una	serie; un telefilm
serious		seria/o; grave

Are you serious?
Fai sul serio?

seven		sette
seventeen		diciassette
seventh		settima/o
seventy		settanta
several		diverse/i
to sew		cucire
sexism	il	sessismo
shade	l'	ombra (f)
shampoo	lo	shampoo
shape	una	forma
to share		dividere
shaving cream	la	crema da barba
sheep	una	pecora
sheet	il	lenzuolo/
	le	lenzuola (pl)
shirt	la	camicia

shoes	le	scarpe
shoeshop	un	negozio di scarpe
to go shopping		fare lo shopping
shopping centre	un	centro commerciale
short (time)		breve
short (length)		corta/o
short (height)		bassa/o
shorts	i	pantaloni corti; pantaloncini
shoulder	la	spalla
to shout		urlare
show	uno	spettacolo
	una	mostra
to show		mostrare

Could you show me?
Mi può far vedere?

shower	la	doccia
shrine	il	reliquiario;
	il	santuario;
	il	tempio
Shrove Tuesday		Martedí Grasso
shut		chiusa/o
to shut		chiudere

Shut up!
Sta' zitto! (inf); Stia zitto (pol)

shy		timida/o
to be sick		essere malata/o
sickness	una	malattia
side	il	lato
sign	un	segno
signature	la	firma
silk	la	seta
silly		sciocca/o; stupida/o
silver	l'	argento (m)
similar		similare; simile
since		da

since May
da maggio

| since (because) | | siccome |
| singer | una/un | cantante |

ingle (unmarried)	nubile (f/m); celibe (m); scapolo (m)
ingle room	una camera singola
ir; Mr	Signore
ister	la sorella
ister-in-law	la cognata
o sit	sedere
ituation	la situazione
ix	sei
ixteen	sedici
ixth	sesta/o
ixty	sessanta
ize (general)	le dimensioni
ize (clothes)	la taglia; misura
ki resort	la località sciistica
kiing	lo sci
kill	l' abilità (f)
kin	la pelle
kirt	una gonna; sottana
o sleep	dormire
leeping bag	un sacco a pelo
leeping car	il vagone letto
leeping pills	i sonniferi
leepy	il sonno
I'm sleepy.	
Ho sonno.	
leet	il nevischio
ides	le diapositive
lope	la pista
low	lenta/o
lowly	lentamente
mall	piccola/o
mell	un odore
nack time	l' ora (f) di merenda; dello spuntino
nake	il serpente
now	la neve
It's snowing.	
Nevica	
o; therefore	dunque; quindi
o that	in modo che
oap	il sapone

soap opera	una telenovela
soccer	il calcio
social security	la previdenza sociale
social welfare	l' assistenza (f) sociale
socialist	una/o socialista
sociology	la sociologia
socks	i calzini
solid	solida/o
some	qualche; alcune/i
somebody	qualcuna/o
someone	qualcuno
something	qualcosa
sometimes	talvolta; a volte
son	il figlio
son-in-law	il genero
song	una canzone
soon	presto; fra/tra poco
Sorry. (Excuse me/Forgive me)	
Mi dispiace; Mi scusi; Mi perdoni.	
south	il sud
souvenir shop	il negozio di souvenir
to speak	parlare
I (can't) speak Italian.	
Non parlo italiano.	
Do you speak English?	
Parla inglese?	
special	speciale
specialist	una/uno specialista
species	una specie
speed limit	il limite di velocità
spicy	piccante
spider	un ragno
spokes	i raggi
spoon	un cucchiaio
sport	lo sport
sports program	una trasmissione sportiva
sportsperson	una/un sportiva/o

S

D
I
C
T
I
O
N
A
R
Y

spring	la	primavera
square	la	piazza
squash	la	pallaelastica
stadium	lo	stadio
stage	il	palcoscenico
stamps	i	francobolli
to start		cominciare
station	la	stazione
statues	le	statue
to stay (behind)		stare; rimanere
to stay (hotel, etc)		fermarsi
to steal		rubare
stick	una	stecca
still		ancora; tuttora
stockings	le	calze
stomach	lo	stomaco
stone	la	pietra
to stop		fermare
Stop here, please.		
Ferma qui, per favore.		
storey	il	piano
story (tale)	una	storia; favola
stove (portable)	il	fornellino;
	la	stufa (a gas)
straight		diritta/o
Go straight ahead.		
Si va sempre diritto.		
strange		strana/o
stranger	una/o	sconosciuta/o
street	la	strada
street march	una	manifestazione
		demonstration
street kids	i	ragazzi di
		strada
street-seller	la/il	venditrice/
		venditore
		ambulante
strike	uno	sciopero
strong		forte
stubborn		ostinata/o
student	una/uno	
		studentessa/
		studente

students	gli	studenti
studio	lo	studio
stuff (things)	la	roba
stupid		stupida/o
style	lo	stile
subtitles	i	sottotitoli
suburb	la	periferia;
	il	quartiere
suddenly		all'improvviso
sugar	lo	zucchero
suitcase	una	valigia
sultry		afosa/o
summer	l'	estate (f)
sun	il	sole
sunblock		crema solare
Sunday	la	domenica
sunglasses	gli	occhiali da sole
sunny		soleggiata/o
sunrise	l'	alba (f)
sunset	il	tramonto
supermarket	il	supermercato
superstitious		superstiziosa/o
supporters	i	sostenitori
to be sure		essere sicura/o
surf	il	cavallone; surf
surface mail	la	posta non-
		aerea;
		ordinaria;
		via marittima
surfer	una/un	surfista
surfing	il	surf
surname	il	cognome
surprise	una	sorpresa
to survive		sopravvivere
		(pp sopravvisuta/o)
sweet		dolce
to swim		nuotare
swimming	il	nuoto
swimming pool	la	piscina
swimsuit	il	costume da
		bagno
synagogue	la	sinagoga
syringe	una	siringa

T

t-shirt	una	maglietta
table	la	tavola
tail lights	i	fanalini di coda
to talk		parlare
talcum powder	il	borotalco
talk show	un	talk show
tall		alta/o
to take		portare
tampons	i	tamponi
tape (music)	il	nastro
tasty		buon sapore; gustosa/o
tax	la	tassa
tea	il	tè
teacher	una/un	insegnante; professoressa/ professore
team	la	squadra
teaspoon	il	cucchiaino
technique	la	tecnica
teenage		di adolescenti
telephone	il	telefono
telephone number	il	numero di telefono
telephone office	il	centro telefonico
telephone token	il	gettone
telephoto lens	il	teleobiettivo
television	la	televisione; televisore
temperature	la	temperatura
temple	un	tempio
ten		dieci
tenant	l'	inquilina/o; la/il locataria/o
tennis	il	tennis
tennis court	il	campo da tennis
tent	la	tenda
tent pegs	i	picchetti (per la tenda)
tenth		decima/o

test	una	prova
to thank		ringraziare
Thankyou.		Grazie.
that		quella/o
That's fine; You're welcome.		Prego.
That's not true!		Non è affatto vero!
that is ...		cioè ...
theatre	il	teatro
theft	un	furto
then		allora (in that time); poi (after)
there		lì; là
thin		magra/o
to think		pensare
third		terza/o
a third	un	terzo
thirst	la	sete
I'm thirsty.		Ho sete.
thirteen		tredici
thirty		trenta
this afternoon		questo pomeriggio
this month		questo mese
this morning		stamattina; stamani
this week		questa settimana
this year		quest'anno
thoroughbred	il	purosangue
thousand		mille
three		tre
three-quarters		tre quarti
thriller	un	giallo
throat	la	gola
Thursday	il	giovedì
ticket	un	biglietto
ticket collector	il	controllore; bigliettaia/o
ticket office	la	biglietteria
tight		aderente; stretta/o

DICTIONARY

time	il	tempo
on time		in orario
What's the time?		Che ora è; Che ore sono?
three times		tre volte
timetable	l'	orario
tin (can)	il	scatoletta
tip (gratuity)	la	mancia
tired		stanca/o
tissues	i	fazzolettini di carta
tobacco (pipe)	il	tabacco (da pipa) ...
tobacconist	la	tabaccheria
today		oggi
together		insieme
toilet	il	gabinetto
toilet paper	la	carta igienica
tomorrow		domani
tonight		stasera
too		anche
too much/too many		troppa/o/e/i
toothbrush	il	spazzolino da denti
toothpaste	il	dentifricio;
	la	pasta dentifricia
toothpicks	gli	stuzzicadenti
torch (flashlight)	la	torcia elettrica
to touch		toccare
tour	un	giro;
	una	gita
tourist	una/un	turista
tourist information office	l'	Ente (m) del turismo; ufficio informazioni
tournament	il	torneo
towards		verso
towel	l'	asciugamano (m)
toy	un	giocattolo
tracks/slopes	la	pista
trade union	il	sindacato; unione
traffic lights	il	semaforo
trail	il	sentiero

train	il	treno
traineeship	l'	apprendistato (m)
to translate		tradurre
travel agency	l'	agenzia (f) di viaggi
travel writing	i	libri di viaggio
to travel		viaggiare
to trek	lo	fare il trekking; scialpinismo
trousers	i	pantaloni
true		vero
truth	la	verità
trust	la	fiducia
to try		provare
Tuesday	il	martedì
turned on (appliance)		accesa/o
turtle	una	tartaruga
TV	il	TV; tivú
tweezers	il	depilatore
twelfth		dodicesima/o
twelve		dodici
twenty		venti
twenty-one		ventuno
twice		due volte
two		due
tyre/s	la/le	gomma/e

U

umbrella	l'	ombrello
uncomfortable		scomoda/o
under		sotto
underwear	la	biancheria intima
to understand		capire
Do you understand?		Hai capito?; Capisci?
I (don't) understand.		(Non) Ho capito.
unemployment benefit	il	sussidio di disoccupazione
unemployed		disoccupata/o
university	l'	università
ugly		brutta/o

uncle	lo	zio
unemployment	la	disoccupazione
union	il	sindacato
unsafe		pericolosa/o
until		finché
until (June)		fino a (giugno)
up		su
useful		utile

V

vacation	le	vacanze; ferie
vaccination	una	vaccinazione
valuable		preziosa/o
value (price)	il	valore
variety	la	varietà
vase	il	vaso
venue	un	locale
very		molta/o
video shop	la	videoteca
videotape	il	videonastro
view	la	vista
village	un	villaggio; paese
vine	le	vite
vinegar	l'	aceto
virus	un	virus
visa	il	visto
to visit		visitare; andare a vedere
vitamins	le	vitamine
voice	la	voce
volleyball	la	pallavolo
voluntary (work)	il	(lavoro) volontario
vote	il	voto
vote counting	lo	scrutinio
voter	la/il	votante

W

to wait		aspettare
waiter	una/un	cameriera/e
waiting room	la	sala d'aspetto
to walk		camminare

to want		volere
I want ...		
Vorrei ... (pol); Voglio ... (inf)		
Do you want ...?		
Vorrebbe (pol); Vuoi ...? (inf)		
war	la	guerra
wardrobe	l'	armadio (m)
warm		tiepida/o
wash (oneself)		lavarsi
wash (clothes, etc)		lavare
washing powder	il	detersivo
watch		guardare
(wrist) watch	l'	orologio (m) (da polso)
water	l'	acqua (f)
water bottle/flask	la	borraccia
watercolour	un	acquarello
waterfall	la	cascata
waterpolo	la	pallanuoto
waterskiing	lo	sci acquatico
wave	l'	onda (f)
way	la	via
Which way?		
Quale direzione?		
weakness	la	debolezza
wealthy		ricca/o
weather	il	tempo
wedding	le	nozze;
	il	matrimonio;
	lo	sposalizio
Wednesday	il	mercoledì
week	la	settimana
weightlifting	il	sollevamento pesi
weight training	il	culturismo
welcome		benvenuto
well (state)		bene
well (for water)	il	pozzo
Well then ...		Allora ...
west	l'	ovest (m)
wet		bagnata/o
what		(che) cosa
What's this?		
Che cos'è?		

wheel | la ruota
wheel hub | il mozzo
when | quando
  When will the bus leave?
  Quando parte l'autobus?
where | dove
  Where is the ...?
  Dov'è ...?
  Where are the toilets?
  Dove sono i gabinetti?
while | mentre
white | bianca/o
who | chi
  Who is it?
  Chi è?
whole | intera/o; tutta/o
why | perche
wide | larga/o
widow/er | una/un vedova/o
wife | la moglie
wild | selvaggia/o; selvatica/o
wild boar | un cinghiale
to win | vincere (pp vinto)
wind | il vento
  It's windy.
  Tira vento; È ventoso.
window (house) | la finestra
window (shop) | la vetrina
windscreen | un parabrezza
wine tasting | la degustazione; delibazione (del vino)
winner | la/il vincitrice/vincitore
winter | l' inverno (m)
wire | il filo
wise | saggia/o
with | con
within (two) hours | entro (due) ore
without | senza
wolf | il lupo

wood | il legno
wool (pure, new) | la (pura) lana (vergine)
work | il lavoro
work (of art, etc) | l' opera (f)
worried | preoccupata/o
worse | peggiore
wound | una ferita
to write | scrivere (pp avere scritto)
to be wrong | avere torto; sbagliare
to write | scrivere
writer | una/uno scrittrice/scrittore
wrong | sbagliata/o
  I'm wrong.
  Ho torto.

Y

year | l' anno (m)
last year | l' anno scorso
this year | quest'anno
years ago | anni fa
yellow | gialla/o
yes | sì
yesterday | ieri
yesterday morning | ier(i) mattina
yet | ancora
yoghurt | l' yogurt (m)
you | tu (inf); La (pol); voi (pl)
young | giovane
youth hostel | l' ostello (m) della gioventù

Z

zero | zero
zoo | lo zoo; il giardino zoologico

In this dictionary we have included the definite article (la, il, l' or lo corresponding to 'the' in English) or the indefinite article (una, un' or un, corresponding to 'a' in English) with each noun. We have chosen either the definite or indefinite article according to the way the word is most likely to be used.

However, note that in most cases the articles are interchangeable. Thus un cane, 'a dog' may also be il cane, 'the dog'; la casa, 'the house' may also be una casa, 'a house'. See Grammar, page 9 for an explanation of articles.

Past participles of some verbs have been given in brackets. See Grammar, page 28, for an explanation of verbs and past participles.

A

a	at
li abbaglianti	headlights (high beam)
abbastanza	enough
abbigliamento (m)	clothes
li abiti	clothing
n aborto	abortion
accamparsi	to go camping
accanto	beside
accanto a	next to
accendino (m);	lighter
accendisigari (m)	
accesa/o	on (appliance)
accettare	to accept
Accetti? (inf)	
Do you accept?	
Accetto.	
I accept.	
n acconto	deposit
n accordo	agreement
ssere d'accordo	to agree
(Non) Sono d'accordo.	
I (dis)agree.	

l' aceto (m)	vinegar
l' acqua (f)	water
l' acqua calda	hot water
l' acqua fredda	cold water
l' acqua potabile	drinkable (water)
l' acqua santa	holy water
l' acqua bollente	boiled water
l' acqua gassata	water with gas
un acquarello	watercolour
l' adattatore (m);	adaptor
aderente	tight
adesso; ora	now
i adolescenti	teenagers
l' aereo (m)	aeroplane
alcune/i	some
gli affari	business
affittare	to lease (from)
affascinante	fascinating
l' affitto (m)	rental (n)
affollata/o	crowded
afosa/o	sultry
l' agenda (f)	diary
l' agente	estate agent
immobiliare (f/m)	

l'	agenzia di viaggi (f)	travel agency	un'/un	amica/o	friend

l' **agenzia** travel agency
di viaggi (f)
aggressiva/o aggressive
agosto (m) August
una/un **agricoltore** farmer
l' **airone** (m) heron
aiutare to help
Aiuto!
Help!

l' **alba** (f) dawn; sunrise
un **albergo** hotel
alcune/i some; a few
all'estero abroad
all'improvviso suddenly
alla menta menthol
l' **allibratrice** (f) bookmaker
l' **allibratore** (m)
l' **alimento** (m) food
l' **alloggio** accommodation
allora in that time
allucinare to hallucinate
l' **allucinogeno** hallucinogen
l' **alluvione** (f) flood
l' **alpinismo** rock climbing
alta/o high; loud; tall
altra/o other
un'altra volta again
altrimenti otherwise
l' **altro ieri** day before
yesterday

l' **amaca** (f) hammock
una/un **amante** lover
amara/o bitter
amare to love
Ti amo;
I love you.
l' **ambasciata** (f) embassy
l' **ambasciatrice** (f) ambassador
l' **ambasciatore** (m)
l' **ambiente** (m) environment
ambiziosa/o ambitious

un'/un **amica/o** friend
ammazzare to kill
l' **amministrazione** (f) administration
ammirare to admire
gli **anabbaglianti** headlights (low
beam)

un **analgesico** painkillers
l' **analisi** (f) **del** blood test
sangue
un'**anatra** duck (n)
anche also; too
ancora still (up to now,
yet)

ancora again
andare to go
(pp essere andata/o)
Vado a ...
I'm going to ...
Si va sempre diritto.
Go straight ahead.
Andiamo.
Let's go!
un **anello** ring
l' **angolo** corner
anni fa years ago
l' **anno** (m) year
l' **anno passato** last year
l' **anno prossimo** next year
l' **anno scorso** last year
l' **anno venturo** next year
annoiata/o bored
annua/o annual
gli **antibiotici** antibiotics
antica/o ancient; antique
appena as soon as
l' **apprendistato** traineeship
approssimativa/o approximate
un **appuntamento** appointment
un **apribottiglie** bottle opener
aprile April
aprire to open
(pp essere aperta/o)

apriscatole (m)	can opener
l'arancia	orange
arbitro (m)	referee
argento (m)	silver
l'argomento	topic
aria (f)	air
armadio (m)	wardrobe
arrabbiata/o	angry
arrivare	to arrive
(pp essere arrivata/o)	
Arrivederci.	Goodbye.
Arrivi	Arrivals
ascensore (m)	lift; elevator
asciugamano (m)	towel
ascoltare	to listen
l'asino	a donkey
aspettare	to wait
assassinare	to kill (murder)
assicurare	to insure
Ho l'assicurazione.	
I'm insured.	
assistenza (f)	social welfare
sociale	
i assorbenti igienici	sanitary napkins
na/un atleta	athlete
attenta/o	careful
Attenzione!	
Watch out!	
attraverso	across
na/un attrice/attore	actor
attualità	current affairs
autista (f/m)	driver
l'autorimessa	garage
automobilismo (m)	car racing
autostrada (f)	motorway
autunno (m)	autumn
avanti	ahead
avere	to have
Ho ...	
I have ...	
... ce l'hai?	
Do you have ...?	

avere bisogno di	to need
avere cura di	to care (to take care of)
avere nostalgia	to be homesick
aver paura	to be afraid
avere torto	to be wrong
avida/o	greedy
un avvenimento	event
l' avventura (f)	adventure
avvincente	engrossing
una/un avvocata/o	lawyer
un'azione	action
azzurra/o	blue (light)

B

il bacino	pond
un bacio	kiss
il bagaglio	baggage
una/un bagnante	bather
bagnata/o	wet
il bagno	bathroom; toilet
ballare	to dance
il ballo	ball (dancing)
un ballo	dance (n)
il balsamo per i capelli	conditioner
la/il bambina/o	girl/boy
i bambini	children
una bambola	doll
una/un banchiere	banker
il bancomat	ATM
la bandiera	flag
la barca	boat
bassa/o	low; short
a basso prezzo	cheap
Basta!	Enough!
il bastone	bat (sports)
i batteri	bacteria
la batteria	battery (for car)

B

D
I
C
T
I
O
N
A
R
Y

il battesimo	baptism
il bavaglino	bib
bella/o	beautiful/ handsome
bene	well (state)
benedire	to bless
benvenuto	welcome
la benzina	gas (petrol)
bere (pp avere bevuto)	to drink
una bevanda	drink
bianca/o	white
la biancheria intima	underwear
il bianco e nero	B&W (film)
il biberon	feeding bottle
la biblioteca	library
un bicchiere	glass (for drinking)
la/il bigliettaia/o	ticket collector
la biglietteria	ticket office
un biglietto	ticket
la/il bimba/o	baby
il binario	platform no.
i biscotti	biscuits
la bocca	mouth
bollente	boiling
bollire	to boil
una bombola a gas	gas cylinder
il borotalco	talcum powder
la borraccia	water bottle/ flask
una borsa; borsetta	bag; handbag
una borsa di cuoio	leather bag
una bottega	milk bar; drugstore
una bottega d'artigianato	craft shop
una bottiglia	bottle
un braccialetto	bracelet
il braccio	arm
breve	short (time)

i brividi	shivers
bronzo	bronze
bruciare	to burn
brutta/o	ugly
il bue	ox
buffa/o	funny
una/un bugiarda/o	liar
buona/o	good
a buon mercato	economical
Buonanotte.	Goodnight.
Buonasera.	Good evening.
Buongiorno.	Good morning; afternoon.
il burro	butter
il burro per le labbra	lip balm
la bussola	compass
una busta	envelope
una bustarella	bribe (n)

C

una cabina telefonica	phone booth
il caffé	coffee
un caffè; bar	a café
il calcio	soccer
calda/o	hot
il caldo	heat
le calze	stockings; pantyhose
un calmante	painkillers
i calzini	socks
cambiare	to change
il cambio	exchange
una camera	room
una/un cameriera/e	waiter
la camicia	shirt
camminare	to walk
la campagna	countryside
il campeggio	camping ground

C

campionato	championship
campo da tennis	tennis court
campo	field
camposanto	cemetery
cancellare	to cancel
cancello	gate
una candela	candle
un cane	dog
canestro	basket
una/un cantante	singer
una cantautrice	singer-song-writer
un cantautore	
una canzone	song
capire	to understand
Hai capito?; Capisci?	
Do you understand?	
(Non) Ho capito.	
I (don't) understand.	
capo	boss
Capodanno	New Year's Day
cappello	hat
cappotto	coat
una capra	goat
cara/o	expensive
carboncino	charcoal
carcere	prison; jail
una/un caricaturista	portrait sketcher
carina	pretty
carrozza ristorante	dining car
una/un carrozziere	panel beater
una carrozzina	pram/baby carriage
carta	paper; map
una carta d'imbarco	boarding pass
carta igienica	toilet paper
una carta stradale	road map
una carta telefonica	phonecard
cartine (per sigarette)	cigarette papers
cartolaio	newsagency; stationer's

una cartolina	a postcard
la casa	house; home
la cascata	waterfall
il casco	helmet
la cassa	cashier's window
la cassa automatica	ATM
una cassaforte	safe (for valuables)
una cassetta di pronto soccorso	first aid kit
una cassetta postale	mailbox
il castello	castle
una catena	chain
un cavallo	a horse
il cavallo da corsa	racehorse
il cavallone; surf	surf
la caviglia	ankle
celibe (m)	single (not married)
il cellulare; telefonino	cellular; mobile phone
la cena	dinner
cento	a hundred
il centro (città)	city centre; downtown
un centro commerciale	shopping centre
cercare	to look for
Sto cercando ...	
I'm looking for ...	
i cerini	matches
Certamente!; (Di) Certo!	Of course!
(essere) certa/o	to be sure; certain
un cervo	deer
che	what
Che cos'è?	
What's this?	
Che ora è?;	
Che ore sono?	
What's the time?	

**D
I
C
T
I
O
N
A
R
Y**

chi	who
Chi è?	
Who is it?	
chiara/o	light
chiaro; ovvio	obvious/clear
la chiave	key
chiedere	to ask
la chiesa	church
chiudere	to close
(pp avere chiuso)	
chiunque	anyone
chiusa/o	shut
ciascuna/o	each
il cibo	food
cieca/o	blind
il cimitero	cemetery
la cinepresa	movie camera
un cinghiale	wild boar
cinquanta	fifty
cinque	five
la cintura di sicurezza	seatbelt
una cintura	belt
cioè	that is
la città	city
la cittadella	old city
la cittadinanza	citizenship
il ciucciotto	dummy (for baby); pacifier
una/un cocainomane	cocaine addict
una cocorita	a budgerigar
il codice postale	postcode
la cognata	sister-in-law
il cognato	brother-in-law
il cognome	surname
una collana	necklace
una collina	hill
il collo	neck
il colloquio (selettivo)	interview
la colomba	dove-shaped cake

la colpa	fault
colpa mia	my fault
colpevole	guilty
un colpo	a hit/strike
un coltello	knife
coltivare	to grow
come	how
Come si chiama?	
What's your name? (pol)	
Come sta? (pol)	
Come stai? (Inf)	
How are you?	
come	like (similar)
cominciare	to begin; start
un comizio	rally
una commedia	comedy; play
comoda/o	comfortable
una/un compagna/o	companion
il compleanno	birthday
comprare	to buy
la comunione	communion
comunque	however; but
Comunque ...	Even so ...; All the same ...
con	with
con piombo	leaded (petrol)
la confettura di frutta	jam
un coniglio	rabbit
conoscere	know (a person
(pp avere conosciuto)	
consacrare	to bless
conservatore	conservative
il consiglio	advice
il consolato	consulate
contagiosa/o	contagious
contare	to count
il conto	bill (account); check
i contraccettivi	contraceptives
contro ...	against ...

Italian	English
/il controllore	ticket collector
a coperta (di lana)	blanket (wool)
a coppa	cup
a coppia	a couple (people)
coraggiosa/o	brave
a corda	rope
corpo	body
corriera	long-distance bus
corrotta/o	corrupt
a corsa	race (contest)
corta/o	short (height)
cortile	courtyard
costare	to cost
(pp essere costato)	
costume da bagno	swimsuit
a credenza	cupboard
crema da barba	shaving cream
crema idratante	moisturising cream
crema solare	sunblock
crescere	to grow up
(pp essere cresciuta/o)	
cresima	confirmation (religious)
a critica	review (n)
croce	cross
crocifisso	crucifix
cruda/o	raw
cucchiaino	teaspoon
cucchiaio	spoon
cucinare	to cook
cucire	sewing
a/un cugina/o	cousin
culturismo	weight training
cuoio	leather
cuore	heart
cura	cure
cuscino	pillow

D

Italian	English
da	since
da (accanto)	by (beside)
da ... a ...	from ... to ...
da qualche parte	anywhere
da sola/o	alone
dare	to give
Mi dai ...; Dammi ... (inf) Give me ...	
Te lo do. I'll give it to you.	
la data	date (time)
la data di nascita	date of birth
la/il datrice/datore di lavoro	employer
davanti a	in front of
Davvero!	Really!
debole	faint
la debolezza	weakness
decidere	to decide
(pp avere deciso)	
decima/o	tenth
il degustazione (del vino)	wine tasting
il delibazione (del vino)	wine tasting
un delfino	dolphin
delirante	delirious
il denaro	money
il dentifricio	toothpaste
una/un deputata/o	representative
il deserto	desert
destra	right (not left)
(di) destra	right(-wing)
il detersivo	washing powder
un dettaglio	detail (n)
di	of
di adolescenti	teenage

	di fronte a	opposite	la	disoccupazione	unemployment

di fronte a — opposite
le diapositive — slides
il dicembre — December
diciannove — nineteen
diciassette — seventeen
diciotto — eighteen
dieci — ten
dietro — behind
la difesa — defence
difficile — difficult; hard
digiunare — to fast (not eating)
una/un dilettante — amateur
dimenticare — to forget
Ho dimenticato. — I forgot.
dimenticato — left (behind)
dio — God
la dipendenza — addiction
dipingere — to paint
un dipinto — painting
un dipinto a olio — oil painting
dire — to say
(pp avere detto)
diretto — direct
il direttore di produzione — producer
diritta/o — straight
Si va sempre diritto. — Go straight ahead.
i diritti — rights
i diritti degli omosessuali — gay rights
i diritti umani — human rights
i dischi volanti — flying saucers
un disco — record (lp)
il disboscamento — deforestation
un discorso — conversation
disegnare — to draw
un disegno — drawing
disoccupata/o — unemployed

la disoccupazione — unemployment
dispiacere — to be sorry
(essere dispiaciuta/o)
Mi dispiace. — Sorry. (Excuse me/Forgive me)
distruggere — to destroy
il/le dito/dita (pl) — finger/s
una dittatura — dictatorship
diversa/o — different
diverse/i — several
divertente — entertaining
il divertimento — fun
divertirsi — to enjoy (onese
(pp essere divertita/o)
dividere una stanza — to share a roo
divorziata/o — divorced
la doccia — shower
dodicesima/o — twelfth
dodici — twelve
la dogana — Customs
dolce — sweet
un dolce — dessert
il dolore — pain
dolorosa/o — painful
una domanda — question (n)
una domanda — (job) applica-
(d'impiego) — tion
domani — tomorrow
domani mattina — tomorrow morning
domani pomeriggio — tomorrow afternoon
domani sera/notte — tomorrow evening/night
la domenica — Sunday
la Domenica di Pasqua — Easter Sunday
dopo — after
il dopobarba — aftershave
dopodomani — day after tomorrow

doppia/o	double
una doppia a due letti	double room with twin beds
una doppia matrimoniale	double room with double bed
dormire	to sleep
il dorso	back
una dottoressa (f)	doctor
un dottore (m)	doctor
dove	where
Dov'è ...?	
Where is the ...?	
Dove sono (i gabinetti)?	
Where are (the toilets)?	
dovere	to owe
Ti devo.	
I owe you. (inf)	
dovunque	wherever
una dozzina	a dozen
un dramma	drama
una/un drogata/o	junkie
una drogheria	grocery store
due	two
due giorni	two days
due volte	twice
dunque	so; therefore
il duomo	cathedral
durante	during

E

e	and
edicola (f);	newsagency; stationer's
edificio (m)	building
eguaglianza (f)	equality
elenco telefonico (m)	phonebook
elettorato (m)	electorate
una/un elettricista	electrician
l' elettricità (f)	electricity
le elezioni	elections
gli emigranti extracomunitari	(not EU) migrants
emozionante	exciting; moving
l' Ente (m) del Turismo	tourist information office
entrare (pp essere entrata/o)	to enter
l' entrata	entry
entro (due) ore	within (two) hours
Eppure ...	Even so ...; All the same ...
l' equitazione (f)	equestrian sports
l' erba (f)	grass; dope
l' erboristeria (f)	health shop
l' eroinomane (f/m)	heroin addict
un esame	test
esatta/o	exact
Esattamente!	Exactly!
esclusa/o	excluded
Esco.	I'm going out.
l' escursionismo (m)	hiking
l' esilio	exile
esportare	to export
l' esposimetro (m)	light meter
l' esposizione (f)	exhibition
espressiva/o	expressive
l' espresso (m);	express (fast)
essere (pp essere stata/o)	to be
l' est (E) (m)	east
l' estate (f)	summer
estroversa/o	outgoing
gli esuli politici	political exiles
l' età (f)	age

F

una **faccenda**	affair
le **faccende**	housework
facile	easy
la **fame**	hunger
Ho fame.	
I'm hungry.	
i **fanalini di coda**	tail lights
la **fantascienza**	science fiction
la **fantasia**	imagination
avere fantasia;	to be imaginative
fantasiosa/o	
fantastica/o	fantastic
la/il **fantina/o**	jockey
fare	to do; to make
fare l'autostop	to hitchhike
fare lo shopping	to go shopping
fare una	to go for a stroll
passeggiata	
fare una	to reserve
prenotazione	
una **farfalla**	butterfly
i **fari**	headlights
la **farina**	flour
la **farmacia**	pharmacy
farsi male	to be hurt
Si è fatto male.	
He's hurt.	
una **fascia**	bandage
fatto	made (to be made of)
una **fattoria**	farm
una **favola**	story (tale)
un **fax**	fax
i **fazzolettini**	tissues
(di carta)	
febbraio	February
una **febbre**	fever
la **fede nuziale**	wedding ring
fedele	loyal

felice	happy
femmina	female
le **ferie**	holidays
una **ferita**	a wound
ferita/o	to be hurt
È ferito.	
He's hurt.	
fermare	to stop
Stop here, please.	
Si fermi qui, per favore.	
fermarsi	to stay (hotel,
(pp si **essere fermata/o**)	etc)
il **fermo posta**	poste restante
la **ferramenta**	hardware shop
una **festa**	festival; party
i **fiammiferi**	matches
il **fidanzamento**	engagement
una/un **fidanzata/o**	fiancée/fiancé
la **fiducia**	trust
i **figli**	children
la **figlia**	daughter
la **figliastra**	stepdaughter
il **figliastro**	stepson
il **figlio**	son
il **filiale**	branch office
il **filo**	wire
il **filo interdentale**	dental floss
finché	until
la **fine**	end (n)
Fine (d')Anno	New Year's Eve
la **finestra**	window (house)
fino a (giugno)	until (June)
una/un **fioraia/o**	flower seller
un **fiore**	flower
la **firma**	signature
il **fiume**	river
una **foratura**	puncture
le **forbici**	scissors
una **forchetta**	fork
il **formaggio**	cheese
una **formica**	ant

fornaio; panetteria	bakery
fornellino;	stove (portable)
forse	maybe
forte	strong
fortuna	chance
fortunata/o	lucky
fotografo	photographer
fra	between
fra (sei) giorni	in (six) days
fra cinque minuti	in (five) minutes
fra poco	soon
una frana	landslide
francobolli	stamps
fratellastro	stepbrother
fratello	brother
freddo	cold (temperature)
freni	brakes
fresca/o	fresh
(avere) fretta	to be in a hurry
in fretta	in a hurry
fritta/o	fried
frizione	clutch
fruttivendolo	greengrocer
fumetti	comics
funivia	cable car
fuoco	fire (general)
fuori	outside
fuori gioco	offside
fuori pericolo	safe (not dangerous)
furto	robbery; theft

G

gabinetto;	toilet
galera carcere	prison; jail
una galleria d'arte	art gallery
gamba	leg

una gara	race (contest)
un gattino	a kitten
un gatto	cat
gelata/o	cold; icy
il genero	son-in-law
il gennaio	January
la gente	people
gentile	kind
il gessetto	crayon
il gettone	telephone token
il ghiaccio	ice
già	already
una giacca	jacket
gialla/o	yellow
i gialli	crime/detective novels
i giardini	gardens
i (lavori di) giardinaggio	gardening
il ginocchio	knee
giocare	to play (a game)
una giocatrice (f)/ un giocatore (m)	player
un giocatore d'azzardo	gambler
un giocattolo	toy
un gioco	game
i gioielli	jewellery
il giornale	newspaper
il giornale radio	radio news
una/un giornalista	journalist
una giornata festiva	holiday (public)
un giorno	(one) day
giovane	young
il giovedì	Thursday
il Giovedì Santo	Holy Thursday
girare	to turn
Gira a destra ...	Turn right ...
Gira a sinistra ...	Turn left ...

Italian	English
un/una giro; gita	tour
giù	down (there)
il giugno	June
la giurisprudenza	law
la giustizia	justice
giusto	right (correct)
la gola	throat
il gomito	elbow
la gomma	tyre
una gonna	skirt
il governo	government
la grafite	lead
un grammo	gram
un grande magazzino	department store
grande	big
la grandezza	size (general)
la grandine	hail
grassa/o	big; fat
grave	serious
Grazie.	Thankyou.
grigia/o	grey
le grotte	caves
il gruppo sanguigno	blood group
un gruppo	band (music)
guadagnare	to earn
i guadagni	earnings
i guanti	gloves
guardare	to look at; to watch
guasta/o	off (food)
la guerra	war
una guida	guide (n)
gustosa/o	tasty

I

Italian	English
l' idrovolante (m)	hydroplane
ieri	yesterday
ier(i) mattina	yesterday morning

Italian	English
ieri pomeriggio	yesterday afternoon
ieri sera	last night
imbarazzare	embarrass
immediatamente	immediately
l' immersione (f) subacquea	scuba diving
l' immondizia	rubbish
un impiego	job; occupation (trade)
imparare	to learn
Sto imparando l'italiano.	
I'm learning Italian.	
l' impermeabile (m)	raincoat
un'/un impiegata/o	clerk; employee; office worker
importarsi	to matter
Non importa.	
Never mind.	
in	in
in modo che	so that
In ogni caso ...	In any case ...
un incendio	fire (outside)
l' inchiostro (m)	ink
un incidente	accident
incinta	pregnant
inclusa/o	included
incontrare	to meet
un incontro	fight
l' indirizzo (m)	address
una/un indovina/o	fortune teller
indovinare	to guess
l' ineguaglianza (f)	inequality
una/un infermiera/e	nurse
l' inflazione (f)	inflation
un'/un ingegnere	engineer
l' ingegneria	engineering
inglese	English
un'iniezione	injection
la/il inquilina/o	tenant
l' inquinamento (m)	pollution

L

una/un insegnante	teacher
un insetto	insect
insieme	together
Insomma ...	To be brief ...
intera/o	whole
interessante	interesting
interessarsi (di)	to care (about something)
Non si interessa.	She doesn't care.
interessata/o	interested
l' interpretazione (f)	rendition/ performance
l' intossicazione (f) alimentare	food poisoning
l' inverno (m)	winter
invitare	to invite
io	I
l' ippica (f)	horseracing
l' ippodromo (m)	racecourse (horses)
l' istituto superiore (m)	high school
l' istruzione (f)	education

L

un ladro	robber (thief)
laggiù	down (there)
il lago	lake
le lamette	razor blades
la lampadina	light bulb
la lana	wool
la (pura) lana (vergine)	wool (pure, new)
larga/o	loose; wide
lasciato	left (behind)
i lassativi	laxatives
il lato	side
il latte	milk
la laurea	degree; diploma

la lavanderia	laundry/ launderette
lavare (pp avere lavato)	wash (clothes, etc)
lavarsi (pp si essere lavata/o)	wash (yourself)
un lavoratore (m)	labourer
una lavoratrice (f)	labourer
lavorare	to work
il lavoro	work
il lavoro artigianale	handicrafts
un lavoro	job; occupation (trade)
il lavoro volontario	voluntary (work)
leale	loyal
legale	legal
la legalizzazione	legalisation
la legge	law
leggera/o	light
leggere	to read
la legna da ardere	firewood
il legno	wood
lenta/o	slow
la lente a contatto	contact lens
lentamente	slowly
il lenzuolo	sheet
le lenzuola (pl)	
una lepre	hare
lesbica	lesbian
una lettera	a letter
le Lettere	arts/humanities
un letto matrimoniale	double bed
un letto	a bed
una lezione	lesson
lì; là	there
libera/o	free (not bound)
la libreria	bookshop
un libro di viaggio	guidebook
un libro	book (n)
il limite di velocità	speed limit
la linea	line

la lingua	language
litigare	argue
un litro	litre
un locale	venue
la località sciistica	ski resort
la/il locataria/o	tenant
lontana/o	distant
lontano da	far
il lucchetto	padlock
una lucertola	a lizard
le luci di direzione	indicator
luglio	July
luminosa/o	light; bright
la luna di miele	honeymoon
il lunedì	Monday
lunga/o	long
il lupo	wolf

M

ma	but
Ma scherzi!	
You're kidding!	
Ma va'!	
Come off it!	
una macchina	engine; car
la macchina fotografica	camera
la madre	mother
una/un maga/o	magician
maggio	May
la maggioranza	majority
una maglietta	T shirt
un maglione	jumper; sweater
magra/o	thin
mai	ever; never
un maiale	pig
la maionese	mayonnaise
malata/o	ill
la malattia	sickness
(essere) malata/o	(to be) sick

male	bad
la mamma	mum
la mammella	breast
mancare	miss (feel absence of)
la mancia	tip (gratuity)
mandare	to send
mangiare	to eat
Hai già mangiata/o?	
Have you eaten yet?	
una manifestazione	protest (n)
la mano	hand
le mani (pl)	
una/un manovale	manual worker
il mare	sea
il marito	husband
la marmellata	jam
il marmo	marble
marrone	brown
Martedì Grasso	Shrove Tuesday
il martedì	Tuesday
il marzo	March
il materasso	mattress
una matita	pencil
la matrigna	stepmother
il matrimonio;	marriage (ceremony)
matta/o	mad; crazy
la mattina	morning
la mazza;	bat (sports)
il bastone	
un mazzo di fiori	a bunch of flowers
una medaglia	medal
una/un mendicante	beggar
un medico	doctor
(di) meno	less
la mente	mind (n)
mentre	while
il mercato	market
il mercoledì	Wednesday

Italian	English
il merletto	lace
mescolare	to mix
il mese	month
questo mese	this month
il mese prossimo; venturo	next month
il mese scorso; passato	last month
un messaggio	message
un mestiere	job; occupation (trade)
la metà	half (n)
il metro	meter
la mezzanotte	midnight
il mezzo	half (n); half (adj)
il mezzogiorno	midday; noon
la/il mia/o	my
un micino	a kitten
il miele	honey
migliore	better
la/il migliore	the best
un miliardo	a billion
un milione	a million
mille	a thousand
le minoranze	minorities
la misura	size (clothes)
in modo che	so that
la moglie	wife
molta/o	very; a lot
molto tempo fa	long ago
le montagne	mountains
un morso	bite (n)
morta/o	dead
la morte	death
una mosca	fly
una moschea	mosque
una mostra	show
mostrare	to show
il motore	engine
un motorino	motor scooter
il motoscafo	motorboat

Italian	English
il mozzo	wheel hub
la mucca	cow
un mucchio	plenty (inf)
un mulo	mule
una multa	fine (penalty)
le mura	city walls
il muscolo	muscle
il museo	museum
un musicale	music show
una/un musicista ambulante	busker
una/un musicista	musician

N

Italian	English
il nailon	nylon
la narrativa	fiction
il naso	nose
il nastro	tape (music)
il Natale	Christmas Day
né ... né	neither ... nor ...
nebbioso	foggy
necessario	necessary
negare	to deny
un negozio	shop; store
un negozio di abbigliamento	clothing store
un negozio di alimentari	grocery store
un negozio di scarpe	shoeshop
nella/o	in
nera/o	black
nessuna/o	no-one
la neve	snow
Nevica. It's snowing.	
il nevischio	sleet
niente; nulla	none; nothing
Non fa niente. Never mind.	
la/il nipote	niece/nephew

	noiosa/o	boring
	noleggiare	to hire
	Vorrei noleggiarlo.	
	I want to hire it.	
il	nome	name
	non	not
	non ... ancora	not yet
	Non è affatto vero!	
	That's not true!	
	Non parlo italiano.	
	I can't speak Italian.	
	nona/o	ninth
la	nonna	grandmother
il	nonno	grandfather
il	nord (N)	north
le	notizie	news
la	notte	night
	novanta	ninety
	nove	nine
il	novembre	November
le	nozze	marriage (ceremony)
	nubile (f)	single (not married)
	nulla; niente	none; nothing
il	numero di camera	room number
il	numero di telefono	telephone number
la	nuora	daughter-in-law
	nuotare	to swim
il	nuoto	swimming
	nuova/o	new
	nuvoloso	cloudy

O

	o; oppure	or
	o ... o ...	either ... or ...
l'	obiettivo (m)	lens; objective
gli	occhi	eyes
gli	occhiali	glasses

gli	occhiali da sole	sunglasses
	(essere) occupata/o	to be busy
l'	oceano (m)	ocean
	odiare	to hate
un	odore	smell (n)
	offendere (pp avere offeso)	to offend
	offrire (pp avere offerto)	to offer
gli	oggetti in ceramica	pottery
	oggi	today
	ogni	any
	ogni cosa	anything
	ogni volta	anytime
	In ogni caso ...; Ad ogni modo ...	
	In any case ...	
	ognuna/o	everyone
l'	olio (m)	oil
l'	olio d'oliva	olive oil
l'	olio di girasole	sunflower oil
l'	ombra (f)	shade (n)
un	omicidio	murder (n)
l'	onda (f)	wave
l'	onestà (f)	honesty
l'	opera (f)	work (of art, etc)
un'/un	operaia/o	factory worker
	oppure; o	or
l'	ora (f)	hour
l'	ora di cena	dinner; tea/ supper time
l'	ora (f) di merenda; dello spuntino	snack time
l'	ora di pranzo	lunchtime
l'	orario (m)	timetable
	in orario	on time
l'	ordine (m)	order (n)
gli	orecchini	earrings
l'	orecchio (m)	ear
	organizzare	to organise

P

l' oro (m)	gold
l' orologio (m)	clock
l' orologio (da polso) (m)	watch
l' orrore (m)	horror
un orso	bear
l' ospedale (m)	hospital
l' ospitalità (f)	hospitality
l' ossigeno (m)	oxygen
l' osso (m)	bone
Ostello (m) della Gioventù	Youth Hostel
ostinata/o	stubborn
ottanta	eighty
ottava/o	eighth
l' ottico (m)	optician
ottima/o	great
otto	eight
l' ottobre (m)	October
ottone	brass
l' ovest (O) (m)	west
ovvio	obvious; clear

P

un pacchetto	a packet; parcel
un pacchetto di sigarette	packet of cigarettes
la pace	peace
il padre	father
il padrone	boss
il paesaggio	scenery
il paese	country (nation);
pagamento a rate	lay-by
pagare	to pay
il pagliaccio	clown
un paio	a pair
il palazzo	palace
il palcoscenico	stage
la palestra	gym
la palla	ball (sports)

la pallacanestro	basketball
la pallaelastica	squash
la pallamano	handball
la pallanuoto	waterpolo
la pallavolo	volleyball
il pane	bread
la panetteria	bakery
i pannolini usa e getta	diposable nappies
un pannolino	pad
i pantaloni corti; pantaloncini	shorts
i pantaloni	trousers
il papa	the Pope
il papà	dad
un parabrezza	windscreen
un parco	park
un parente	relation
parlare	to speak
Parla inglese?	
Do you speak English?	
una/un parrucchiera/e	hairdresser
la parte	part
partenze	departures
partire (pp essere partita/o)	to depart
una partita	game (sport)
passabile	OK
il controllo dei passaporti	passport control
i passatempi	hobbies
il passato	past
la/il passeggera/o	passenger
fare una passeggiata	to go for a stroll
il passeggino	pusher/stroller
la pasta dentifricia	toothpaste
la pasticceria	pastry shop
la patente (di guida)	driver's licence
il patrigno	stepfather
il pattinaggio in linea	inline skating

S

la	paura	fear	
il	pavimento	floor	
	pazza/o	mad; crazy	
una	pecora	sheep	
	peggior	worse	
la	pelle	skin; leather	
la	pellicola	film (for camera)	
una	penna (a sfera)	pen (ballpoint)	
una	pennellata	brushstroke	
il	pennello	paintbrush	
	pensare	to think	
i	pensionati	pensioners	
una	pensione	guesthouse	
il	pepe	pepper	
	per ...	for ...	

Per favore;
Per piacere;
Per cortesia.
Please.

	percentuale	percent
	perché	because
	perdere	to lose; miss (the
	(pp avere perduto; perso)	bus, etc)
una	perdita	loss
	perdonare	to forgive
	perfetto	perfect
	pericolosa/o	dangerous; unsafe
la	periferia;	suburb
il	quartiere	
il	periodo in carica	term of office
	permanente	permanent
il	permesso	permission
	permettere	to permit; allow
	(pp avere permesso)	
	(È permesso.)	

It's allowed.

	però	however; but
la	persecuzione	persecution
una	persona	person
	pesante	heavy

la	pesca	fishing
una	pescheria	fish shop
un	pesce	fish
il	pescecane	shark
un	pesciolino rosso	a goldfish
un	pescivendolo	fish merchant
	pessima/o	really bad
la	pettinatura	hairstyle
il	pettine	comb
il	petto	breast; chest
un	pezzo	piece
	piacere	to like

Mi piace ... (sg)
Mi piacciono ... (pl)
I like ...
Piacere.
Pleased to meet you.
Mi piace molto.
I love it.

una	pianta	plant
una	pianta; carta	map (road/city)
un	piatto	plate
un	piatto fondo	bowl
la	piazza principale	main square
la	piazza	square
	piccante	spicy
i	picchetti (per la tenda)	tent pegs
il	picco	peak (mountain)
	piccola/o	little; small
il	piede	foot
	piena/o; completa/o	full
una	pietra	stone
	pigra/o	lazy
la	pila	torch (flashlight)
la	pila elettrica	battery
una	pinacoteca	art gallery
la	pioggia	rain

Piove.
It's raining.

314

È piovigginoso.
It's drizzly.

il **piombo** lead
con/senza **piombo**
leaded/unleaded petrol

la **piscina** swimming pool

una **pista** racecourse (cars)

la **pista** tracks

una/un **pittrice/pittore** painter

pitturare to paint

(di) **più** more

la/il **più grande** elder

la **pizzicheria** delicatessen

un **po'; poco** a little (amount)

poca/o (sg) few

poche/i (pl)

la **poesia** poetry

poi after; then

la **politica** policy; politics

la **polizia** police

il **pollo** chicken

la **polvere** dust

il **pomeriggio** afternoon

la **ponte** bridge

un **portacenere** ashtray

portare to bring; to take; to carry

una/un **portiere** goalkeeper

il **porto** port

la **posta elettronica** email

la **posta ordinaria** surface mail

la **(posta) raccomandata** registered mail

un **posto** place; seat (place)

potere can; to be able
Ci può portare? (pol)
Can you take us?

il **potere** power

povera/o poor

il **pozzo** well (for water)

pragmatica/o pragmatic

il **pranzo; colazione** lunch

preferire prefer

la **preghiera** prayer
Prego.
That's fine; You're welcome.

prendere to take

prendere in affitto to rent

prendere in prestito to borrow

prenotare to book (make a booking)

una **prenotazione** reservation (tickets, etc)

preoccupata/o worried

preparare prepare

il **presente** present (time)

i **preservativi** condoms

la **pressione (del sangue)** blood pressure

presto early

presto soon

presuntuosa/o selfish

il **prete** priest

la **previdenza sociale** social security

preziosa/o valuable

il **prezzo** price

la **prigione** prison; jail

una/un **prigioniera/o** prisoner

prima before

prima/o first

la **(prima) colazione** breakfast

la **primavera** spring

la/il **primo ministro** prime minister

la/il **principale** employer

una/un **principiante** beginner

probabilmente probably

un **professore** (m) teacher
una **professoressa** (f)

il **profumo** perfume

una **promessa** promise

Q

(essere) pronta/o	to be ready
il pronto soccorso	casualty (dept)
la propaganda	propaganda
una proposta	proposal
la/il proprietaria/o	owner
il prossimo	next
proteggere	to protect
una prova	rehearsal; trial
provare	to try
provocante	challenging
un prurito	itch
il pubblico	public
il pubblico	audience
il pugilato	boxing
pulita/o	clean
il punto	point
una puntura	injection
può darsi	maybe
pura/o	pure
un purosangue	thoroughbred

Q

qua	here
un quadro	painting
qualche	some
da qualche parte;	anywhere
in qualche luogo	
qualcosa	something; anything
qualcuna/o	somebody; someone
Quale direzione?	
Which way?	
la qualità	quality
qualsiasi;	any; whichever
qualunque	
quando	when
Quando parte l'autobus?	
When will the bus leave?	
quanto	how much

Quanto ?	
How much? (amount)	
Quanto costa?	
How much? (cost)	
quaranta	forty
il quartiere	suburb
quarta/o	fourth
un quarto	a quarter
quasi	almost
quattordici	fourteen
quattro	four
quella/o	that
questa/o	this
qui	here
quindi	so; therefore
quindici	fifteen
una quindicina	fortnight
la quinta/o	fifth
il quotidiano	daily (paper)

R

la raccolta	harvest
il raccolto	crops
raccomandare	to advise; to recommend
Ti raccomando!	
Watch out!	
i racconti	short stories
radicale	radical
un raduno	rally
un raffreddore	cold (illness)
una/un ragazza/o	girl/boy
la (mia) ragazza	(my) girlfriend
il (mio) ragazzo	(my) boyfriend
i ragazzi di strada	street kids
i raggi	spokes
la ragione	reason
una/un ragioniere	accountant
un ragno	spider
un ramarro	a lizard

i **ramponi**	crampons
una **rana**	a frog
il **rapido**	express (fast)
i **rapporti**	relationship
rara/o	rare
raso	satin
un **rasoio (elettrico)**	razor (electric)
(Ras)somiglia (a) ...	It's similar to ...; Looks like ...
il **razzismo**	racism
il **re**	king
recentemente	recently
recitare	to act
una/un **recensore**	reviewer
la **redditività**	profitability
le **referenze**	references
i **regali di nozze**	wedding presents
un **regalo**	present (gift)
il **regista**	director/film-maker
una **regola**	regulation; rule
una **relazione**	affair (of the heart)
le **relazioni pubbliche**	public relations
il **reliquiario**	shrine
remoto	remote
il **reparto vendite**	sales department
il **resto**	rest (remainder)
una **rete**	net
ricca/o	rich; wealthy
una **ricetta**	receipt
il **ricevimento nuziale**	wedding reception
il **riciclaggio**	recycling
ricordare	to remember
rifiutare	to refuse
i **rifiuti**	garbage
i **rifugiati**	refugees
il **rifugio alpino**	mountain lodge

rilassare	to rest
rilassarsi	to relax
(pp si essere rilassata/o)	(oneself)
rimasta/o	left over
un **rimborso**	refund
il **rinfresco nuziale**	wedding reception
ringraziare	to thank
i **riparazioni**	repairs
il **rischio**	risk
il **rispetto**	respect (n)
rispondere	to answer
una **risposta**	answer (n)
ritornare	to return
(pp essere ritornata/o)	
una/un **ritrattista**	portrait sketcher
la **rivoluzione**	revolution
la **roba**	stuff (things)
i **romanzi**	novels
un **romanzo in inglese**	novel in English
rompersi	to break (itself)
(pp si essere rotta/o)	
rosa	pink
rossa/o	red
rotonda/o	round
rotta/o	broken
le **rovine**	ruins
rubare	to steal
un **rumore**	noise
rumorosa/o	noisy
la **ruota**	wheel
il **ruscello**	creek

S

il **sabato**	Saturday
Sabato Santo	Holy Saturday
la **sabbia**	sand
un **sacchettino**	sachet; bag
un **sacco**	plenty (inf)
un **sacco a pelo**	sleeping bag

S

DICTIONARY

Italian	English
i sacramenti	sacraments
saggia/o	wise
la saggistica	non-fiction
la sala d'aspetto	waiting room
la sala per concerti;	concert hall
salata/o	salty
in saldo	on sale
il sale	salt
la salumeria	delicatessen
la salute	health
salvare	to save
San Silvestro	New Year's Eve
i sandali	sandals
il santa/o	holy
la/il santa/o	saint
santificare	to bless
il santuario	shrine
sapere	know (how to)
il sapone	soap
sbagliare	to be wrong
sbagliata/o	wrong
uno sbaglio	mistake
gli scacchi	chess
lo scaccomatto	checkmate
scalare	to climb
scapolo (m)	single (not married)
le scarpe	shoes
una scatola	box; can (tin)
uno scatolone	carton
scegliere (pp avere scelto)	to choose
la scena	scene
scettica/o	sceptical
la scherma	fencing
lo schermo	screen
uno scherzo	joke
Scherzo.	I'm joking.
la schiena	back
lo sci	skiing

Italian	English
lo scialpinismo	to trek
la scienza	science
una/un scienziata/o	scientist
sciocca/o	silly
uno sciopero	strike
lo sciroppo	cough syrup
la scogliera	cliff
scolpire	to sculpt
scomoda/o	uncomfortable
una/o sconosciuta/o	stranger
sconsacrare	deconsecrate
lo sconto	discount
scoprire (pp avere scoperto)	to discover
una scrittore (m)	writer
uno scrittrice (f)	
scrivere (pp avere scritto)	to write
lo scrutinio	vote counting
la scultura	sculpture
la scuola (elementare)	school (primary)
la scuola superiore	high school
scura/o	dark
scusare	to excuse
Mi scusi.	Excuse me.
se	if
secca/o	dry
seconda/o	second (place)
un secondo	(a) second
sedere	to sit
una sedia	seat (chair)
sedici	sixteen
il seggiolino	baby chair
il segnale (acustico)	dial tone
un segno	sign
una/un segretaria/o	secretary
un segreto	secret
seguire	to follow
sei	six

selvaggia/o; selvatica/o	wild (feral)	
il semaforo	traffic lights	
sempre	always	
per sempre	forever	
il seno	breast	
la sensibilità	film speed	
il sentiero	path; trail	
un sentimento	feeling	
sentire	to feel (emotion)	
sentire; udire	to hear	
senza	without	
senza piombo	unleaded (petrol)	
senzatetti	homeless people	
separata/o	separated	
sera	evening	
seria/o	serious	
Fai sul serio?		
Are you serious?		
una serie	series	
la serratura	lock	
il servizio militare	military service	
servizi igienici	a public toilet	
sessanta	sixty	
sessismo	sexism	
sesta/o	sixth	
la seta	silk	
la sete	thirst	
Ho sete.		
I'm thirsty.		
settanta	seventy	
sette	seven	
settembre	September	
settima/o	seventh	
la settimana	week	
la settimana prossima; ventura	next week	
la Settimana Santa	Holy Week	

la settimana scorsa; passata	last week	
sfuocata/o	out of focus	
sì	yes	
siccome	because; since	
sicura/o	safe (secure)	
(essere) sicura/o	to be sure; certain	
la sicurezza	safety	
il sigaro; toscano	cigar	
Signora	Madam/Mrs/Ms	
Signore	Sir/Mr	
silenziosa	quiet	
simpatica/o	friendly (nice)	
il sindacato	trade union	
la sinistra	left (not right)	
(di) sinistra	left(-wing)	
un sogno	dream (n)	
da sola/o	alone	
solamente	only	
i soldi	money	
il sole	sun	
soleggiata/o	sunny	
solida/o	solid	
solito	ordinary	
di solito	ordinarily	
il sollevamento pesi	weight lifting	
solo	only	
i sondaggi	polls	
i sonniferi	sleeping pills	
il sonno	sleep	
Ho sonno.		
I'm sleepy.		
sopravvivere (pp essere sopravvissuta/o)	to survive	
sorda/o	deaf	
la sorella	sister	
la sorellastra	stepsister	
una sorpresa	surprise.	
una sottana	skirt	

S

DICTIONARY

	sotto	below; under	
i	sottotitoli	subtitles	
uno	spacciatore (m)	dealer (drugs)	
una	spacciatrice (f)		
la	spalla	shoulder	
una	spazzola (per i capelli)	hairbrush	
lo	spazzolino da denti	toothbrush	
lo	specchio	mirror	
le	specie in via d'estinzione	endangered species	
una	specie	species	
	spenta/o	off (turned)	
la	speranza	hope	
	spesso	often	
uno	spettacolo	show	
gli	spettatori	audience	
la	spiaggia	beach	
gli	spiccioli	change (coins)	
una	spilla	brooch	
	spingere (pp avere spinto)	push	
lo	spionaggio	espionage	
gli	spiriti	ghosts	
	sporca/o	dirty	
lo	sport	sport	
una/un	sportiva/o	sportsperson	
	sposare	to marry	
	essere sposati	to be married	
la	squadra	team	
lo	squalo	shark	
lo	stadio	stadium	
lo	stagno	pond	
	stamattina; stamani	this morning	
lo	stambecco	ibex	
	stanca/o	tired	
	stare (pp esssere stata/o)	to be; to stay	
	stasera	tonight	

la	stazione di servizio	petrol station	
una	stecca	stick	
la/lo	stessa/o	same	
lo	stile	style	
lo	stipendio	salary	
gli	stivali	boots	
lo	stomaco	stomach	
	stordita/o	dizzy	
una	storia	story (tale)	
la	strada	road; street	
la	strada principale	main road	
	strana/o	strange	
una/uno	straniera/o	foreigner	
	stretta/o	tight	
uno	studente (m)	student	
una	studentessa (f)	student	
gli	studi magistrali	teaching studies	
la	stufa	heater	
gli	stupefacenti	drugs	
lo	stupro	rape (n)	
gli	stuzzicadenti	toothpicks	
	su	on; up	
	su; sopra	above; over	
	subito	immediately	
il	succo di frutta	fruit juice	
il	sud (S)	south	
la	suocera	mother-in-law	
il	suocero	father-in-law	
	suonare	to play (music)	
il	supermercato	supermarket	
	superstiziosa/o	superstitious	
il	surf	surfing	
una/un	surfista	surfer	
i	surgelati	frozen foods	
il	sussidio di disoccupazione	unemployment benefit	
uno	svantaggio	disadvantage	
la	sveglia	alarm clock	
	in svendita	on sale	
uno	sviluppo	development	

320

T

Italian	English
la tabaccheria	tobacconist
la taglia	size (clothes)
un tagliaunghie	nailclippers
tagliare	to cut
un taglio dei capelli	haircut
talvolta; a volte	sometimes
i tamponi	tampons
tante/i	many; a lot
tanto ... quanto	as ... as
una tangente	bribe (n)
il tappeto	rug
una tartaruga	turtle
la tassa	tax; fee
la tavola	table
una tazza	cup
il tè	tea
il teatro comunale	concert hall
il teatro dell'opera	opera house
la tela	canvas
un telaio	frame
il telegiornale	news (on TV)
una telenovela	soap opera
il teleobiettivo	telephoto lens
la televendita	telemarketing
un temperino	penknife
un tempio	temple
il tempo	time; weather
in tempo	on time
la tenda	tent
il tennis	tennis
la Terra	Earth
la terra	land
un terremoto	earthquake
terribile	awful
terza/o	third
un terzo	a third
la testa	head
il tetto	roof
i tifosi	fans/supporters
timida/o	shy
tirare	pull
i titoli di studio	qualifications
toccare	to touch
il torace	chest
la torcia elettrica	torch (flashlight)
il torneo	tournament
la torta nuziale	wedding cake
avere torto	to be wrong
il toscano	cigar
una/un tossica/o	junkie
la tossicomania	drug addiction
tra	among
tradurre	to translate
il traghetto	ferry
un tragicomico	black comedy
il tramonto	sundown/sunset
una trasmissione sportiva	sports program
tre	three
tre quarti	three quarters
tre volte	three times
tredici	thirteen
il treno	train
trenta	thirty
triste	sad
troppa/o	too much
troppe/i	too many
il tuffo	diving
tutta/o	all; everything
Tuttavia ...	Even so ...; All the same ...
tutte/i	everyone; everybody
tutti e due	both
tutti i giorni	every day
tutto	everything
tuttora	still (up to now/ yet)

U

un uccello	a bird
uccidere	to kill
udire	to hear
(pp avere ucciso)	
l' ufficio (m)	office
uguale	equal
ultima/o	last
un essere umano	human being
umida/o	damp
l' umorismo (m)	humour
undicesima/o	eleventh
undici	eleven
uno	one
una/o	one
le uova	eggs
le uova al cioccolato	chocolate eggs
le uova sode	hard boiled eggs
urlare	to shout
uscire	to go out
(pp essere uscita/o)	
utile	useful
le uva	grapes

V

le vacanze	holidays
la vacca	cow
una vaccinazione	vaccination
il vagone letto	sleeping car
una valigia	suitcase
il valore	value (price)
il varietà informazioni	infotainment
il vasino	potty
il vaso	vase
vecchia/o	old
una/un vedova/o	widow/er
la vela	sailing

veloce	quick; fast
la vendemmia	harvest
vendere	to sell
il venerdì	Friday
Venerdì Santo	Good Friday
venire	to come
(pp essere venuta/o)	
venti	twenty
il ventilatore	fan
il vento	wind
Tira vento; È ventoso.	
It's windy.	
ventuno	twenty-one
verde	green
la verità	truth
vero	true
verso	towards
la vetrina	window (shop)
il vetro	glass
il vetro soffiato	blown glass
la vetta	peak
via aerea	airmail
via	way
viaggiare	to travel
il viale	avenue
vicino	close (adj)
vicino a	near
il videonastro	videotape
la videoteca	video shop
(È) Vietato.	
It's not allowed.	
la Vigilia di Natale	Christmas Eve
un villaggio	village
vincere (pp avere vinto)	to win
il vincitore (m)	winner
la vincitrice (f)	winner
viola	purple
la violenza sessuale	rape (n)
(essere) violentata/o	to be raped
la vista	view
il visto	visa

la **vita**	life	i **voli internazionali**	international flights
la **vite**	vines	il **volo**	flight
vivere	to live	una **volpe**	fox
(pp avere vissuto)		una **volta**	once
il **vocabolario**	dictionary	a **volte**	sometimes
la **voce**	voice	la/il **votante**	voter
volere	to want	il **voto**	vote
Vorrei ... (pol)		**vuota/o**	empty
Voglio ... (inf)			
I want ...			
Vuoi ...?			
Do you want ...?		## Z	
volere bene	to love		
Ti voglio bene.		lo **zaino**	knapsack
I love you.		la **zia**	aunt
i **voli domestici**	domestic flights	lo **zio**	uncle
		lo **zucchero**	sugar

CROSSWORD ANSWERS

AROUND TOWN

Across	Down
1. segreteria	2. grotte
3. consolato	5. strada
4. mendicante	7. pagliaccio
6. cambio	8. centro

FAMILY

Across	Down
1. cognata	3. incrocio
2. figli	5. marito
4. nonna	6. bambina
7. mulo	8. fratello

SOCIAL ISSUES

Across	Down
1. senzatetto	3. nero
2. specia	5. cittadinanza
4. economia	7. tassa
6. destra	8. corrotta

SHOPPING

Across	Down
1. negozio	2. scure
2. svendita	3. mio
3. merletto	5. giallo
4. sconti	6. pantaloni

IN THE COUNTRY

Across	Down
1. apriscatole	2. percorso
2. palude	4. piove
3. domani	5. tenda
4. ponti	6. alpinismo

SPECIFIC NEEDS

Across	Down
1. prete	3. laurea
2. marina	5. riunione
4. sindicato	6. chiesa
7. avere	8. tastiera

NUMBERS & AMOUNTS

Across	Down
1. diciotto	2. doppia
2. dozzina	3. mezzo
5. mille	4. nona
6. tanti	
7. meno	

NOTES

LONELY PLANET PHRASEBOOKS

Complete your travel experience with a Lonely Planet phrasebook. Developed for the independent traveller, the phrasebooks enable you to communicate confidently in any practical situation – and get to know the local people and their culture.

Skipping lengthy details on where to get your drycleaning ironed, information in the phrasebooks covers bargaining, customs and protocol, how to address people and introduce yourself, explanations of local ways of telling the time, dealing with bureaucracy and bargaining, plus plenty of ways to share your interests and learn from locals.

Arabic (Egyptian)
Arabic (Moroccan)
Australian
  *Introduction to Australian English,
  Aboriginal and Torres Strait languages*
Baltic States
  *Covers Estonian, Latvian and
  Lithuanian*
Bengali
Brazilian
Burmese
Cantonese
Central Asia
Central Europe
  *Covers Czech, French, German,
  Hungarian, Italian and Slovak*
Eastern Europe
  *Covers Bulgarian, Czech, Hungarian,
  Polish, Romanian and Slovak.*
Ethiopian (Amharic)
Fijian
French
German
Greek
Hindi/Urdu
Indonesian
Italian
Japanese
Korean
Lao
Malay
Mandarin
Mediterranean Europe
  *Covers Albanian, Croatian, Greek,
  Italian, Macedonian, Maltese, Serbian
  and Slovene*

Mongolian
Nepali
Papua New Guinea (Pidgin)
Pilipino (Tagalog)
Quechua
Russian
Scandinavian Europe
  *Covers Danish, Finnish, Icelandic,
  Norwegian and Swedish*
South-East Asia
  *Covers Burmese, Indonesian, Khmer,
  Lao, Malay, Tagalog (Pilipino), Thai and
  Vietnamese*
Spanish (Castilian)
  *Also includes Basque, Catalan and-
  Galician*
Spanish (Latin American)
Sri Lanka
Swahili
Thai
Thai Hill Tribes
Tibetan
Turkish
Ukrainian
USA
  *Introduction to US English,
  Vernacular, Native American
  languages and Hawaiian*
Vietnamese
Western Europe
  *Useful words and phrases in Basque,
  Catalan, Dutch, French, German,
  Greek, Irish, Italian, Portuguese,
  Scottish Gaelic, Spanish (Castilian) and
  Welsh*

COMPLETE LIST OF LONELY PLANET BOOKS

AFRICA
Africa - the South • Africa on a shoestring • Arabic (Moroccan) phrasebook • Cape Town • Central Africa • East Africa • Egypt • Egypt travel atlas • Ethiopian (Amharic) phrasebook • Kenya • Kenya travel atlas • Malawi, Mozambique & Zambia • Morocco • North Africa • South Africa, Lesotho & Swaziland • South Africa, Lesotho & Swaziland travel atlas • Swahili phrasebook • Trekking in East Africa• West Africa • Zimbabwe, Botswana & Namibia • Zimbabwe, Botswana & Namibia travel atlas

Travel Literature: The Rainbird: A Central African Journey • Songs to an African Sunset: A Zimbabwean Story

ANTARCTICA
Antarctica

AUSTRALIA & THE PACIFIC
Australia • Australian phrasebook • Bushwalking in Australia • Bushwalking in Papua New Guinea • Fiji • Fijian phrasebook • Islands of Australia's Great Barrier Reef • Melbourne • Micronesia • New Caledonia • New South Wales • New Zealand • Northern Territory • Outback Australia • Papua New Guinea • Papua New Guinea phrasebook • Queensland • Rarotonga & the Cook Islands • Samoa • Solomon Islands • South Australia • Sydney • Tahiti & French Polynesia • Tasmania • Tonga • Tramping in New Zealand • Vanuatu • Victoria • Western Australia

Travel Literature: Islands in the Clouds • Sean & David's Long Drive

CENTRAL AMERICA & THE CARIBBEAN
Bermuda • Central America on a shoestring • Costa Rica • Cuba • Eastern Caribbean • Guatemala, Belize & Yucatán: La Ruta Maya • Jamaica

EUROPE
Amsterdam • Austria • Baltics States phrasebook • Britain • Central Europe on a shoestring • Central Europe phrasebook • Czech & Slovak Republics • Denmark • Dublin • Eastern Europe on a shoestring • Eastern Europe phrasebook • Estonia, Latvia & Lithuania • Finland • France • French phrasebook • Germany • German phrasebook • Greece • Greek phrasebook • Hungary • Iceland, Greenland & the Faroe Islands • Ireland • Italian phrasebook • Italy • Lisbon • London • Mediterranean Europe on a shoestring • Mediterranean Europe phrasebook • Paris • Poland • Portugal • Portugal travel atlas • Prague • Russia, Ukraine & Belarus • Russian phrasebook • Scandinavian & Baltic Europe on a shoestring • Scandinavian Europe phrasebook • Slovenia • Spain • Spanish phrasebook • St Petersburg • Switzerland • Trekking in Spain • Ukrainian phrasebook • Vienna • Walking in Britain • Walking in Switzerland• Western Europe on a shoestring • Western Europe phrasebook

Travel Literature: The Olive Grove: Travels in Greece

INDIAN SUBCONTINENT
Bangladesh • Bengali phrasebook • Delhi • Goa • Hindi/Urdu phrasebook • India • India & Bangladesh travel atlas • Indian Himalaya • Karakoram Highway • Nepal • Nepali phrasebook • Pakistan • Rajasthan • Sri Lanka • Sri Lanka phrasebook • Trekking in the Indian Himalaya • Trekking in the Karakoram & Hindukush • Trekking in the Nepal Himalaya

Travel Literature: In Rajasthan • Shopping for Buddhas

COMPLETE LIST OF LONELY PLANET BOOKS

ISLANDS OF THE INDIAN OCEAN
Madagascar & Comoros • Maldives • Mauritius, Réunion & Seychelles

NORTH AMERICA
Alaska • Backpacking in Alaska • Baja California • California & Nevada • Canada • Deep South • Florida • Hawaii • Honolulu • Los Angeles • Mexico • Miami • New England • New Orleans • New York City • New York, New Jersey & Pennsylvania • Pacific Northwest USA • Rocky Mountain States • San Francisco • Southwest USA • USA phrasebook • Washington, DC & the Capital Region
Travel Literature: Drive thru America

NORTH-EAST ASIA
Beijing • Cantonese phrasebook • China • Hong Kong • Hong Kong, Macau & Guangzhou • Japan • Japanese phrasebook • Japanese audio pack • Korea • Korean phrasebook • Mandarin phrasebook • Mongolia • Mongolian phrasebook • North-East Asia on a shoestring • Seoul • Taiwan • Tibet • Tibet phrasebook • Tokyo
Travel Literature: Lost Japan

MIDDLE EAST & CENTRAL ASIA
Arab Gulf States • Arabic (Egyptian) phrasebook • Cairo • Central Asia • Central Asia phrasebook • Iran • Israel & the Palestinian Territories • Israel & the Palestinian Territories travel atlas • Istanbul • Jerusalem • Jordan & Syria • Jordan, Syria & Lebanon travel atlas • Lebanon • Middle East • Turkey • Turkish phrasebook • Turkey travel atlas • Yemen
Travel Literature: The Gates of Damascus • Kingdom of the Film Stars: Journey into Jordan

SOUTH AMERICA
Argentina, Uruguay & Paraguay • Bolivia • Brazil • Brazilian phrasebook • Buenos Aires • Chile & Easter Island • Chile & Easter Island travel atlas • Colombia • Ecuador & the Galápagos Islands • Latin American Spanish phrasebook • Peru • Quechua phrasebook • Rio de Janeiro • South America on a shoestring • Trekking in the Patagonian Andes • Venezuela
Travel Literature: Full Circle: A South American Journey

SOUTH-EAST ASIA
Bali & Lombok • Bangkok • Burmese phrasebook • Cambodia • Ho Chi Minh City • Indonesia • Indonesian phrasebook • Indonesian audio pack • Jakarta • Java • Laos • Laos travel atlas • Lao phrasebook • Malay phrasebook • Malaysia, Singapore & Brunei • Myanmar (Burma) • Philippines • Pilipino phrasebook • Singapore • South-East Asia on a shoestring • South-East Asia phrasebook • Thailand • Thailand's Islands & Beaches • Thailand travel atlas • Thai phrasebook • Thai Hill Tribes phrasebook • Thai audio pack • Vietnam • Vietnamese phrasebook • Vietnam travel atlas

For ordering information contact your nearest Lonely Planet office.

PLANET TALK

Lonely Planet's FREE quarterly newsletter

Every issue is packed with up-to-date travel news
and advice including:

- a letter from Lonely Planet co-founders Tony and
  Maureen Wheeler
- go behind the scenes on the road with a Lonely
  Planet author
- feature article on an important and topical travel
  issue
- a selection of recent letters from travellers
- details on forthcoming Lonely Planet promotions
- complete list of Lonely Planet products

To join our mailing list contact any Lonely Planet office.

LONELY PLANET PUBLICATIONS

AUSTRALIA
PO Box 617, Hawthorn 3122, Victoria
tel: (03) 9819 1877 fax: (03) 9819 6459
e-mail: talk2us@lonelyplanet.com.au

USA
Embarcadero West,
155 Filbert St, Suite 251,
Oakland, CA 94607
tel: (510) 893 8555
TOLL FREE: 800 275-8555
fax: (510) 893 8563
e-mail: info@lonelyplanet.com

UK
10a Spring Place,
London NW5 3BH
tel: (0171) 428 2800 fax: (0171) 428 4828
e-mail: go@lonelyplanet.co.uk

FRANCE:
71 bis rue du Cardinal Lemoine, 75005
Paris
tel: 1 44 32 06 20 fax: 1 46 34 72 55
e-mail: 100560.415@compuserve.com

**World Wide Web: http://www.lonelyplanet.com
or AOL keyword: lp**